ROBERT TOOMBS

STATESMAN, SPEAKER, SOLDIER,
SAGE

HIS CAREER IN CONGRESS AND ON THE HUSTINGS — HIS
WORK IN THE COURTS — HIS RECORD WITH
THE ARMY — HIS LIFE AT HOME

BY

PLEASANT A. STOVALL

"The blood which mingled at Cowpens and at Eutaw cannot be kept at
enmity forever."— *Toombs.*

NEW YORK
CASSELL PUBLISHING COMPANY
104 & 106 Fourth Avenue

THE MERSHON COMPANY PRESS,
RAHWAY, N. J.

ROBERT TOOMBS, AT THE AGE OF 75 YEARS.

For–

Miss Leola Townsend,
        Pine Level, Ala.
In Contest for Scholarship
and by State male Seminary
to secure Library–
    Donated by,
            Fred. P. Case
                Atlanta Ga,
        –"7-29-97"–

Dedication.

_____

*TO ROBERT TOOMBS DU BOSE, WHOSE INTEREST AND AID WERE
INVALUABLE, AND WITHOUT WHOSE COÖPERATION THE
BIOGRAPHY COULD NOT HAVE BEEN PREPARED,
THIS WORK IS DEDICATED BY
THE AUTHOR.*

"There are courageous and honest men enough in both sections to fight. There is no question of courage involved. The people of both sections of this Union have illustrated their courage on too many battlefields to be questioned. They have shown their fighting qualities shoulder to shoulder whenever their country has called upon them ; but that they may never come in contact with each other in fratricidal war, should be the ardent wish of every true man and honest patriot."—*Robert Toombs, Speech in U. S. Senate,* 1856.

CONTENTS.

vii

ROBERT TOOMBS.

CHAPTER I.

FAMILY, BOYHOOD, LIFE AT COLLEGE.

GABRIEL TOOMBS was one of General Braddock's soldiers who marched against Fort DuQuesne in 1755. He was a member of the sturdy Virginia line which protested against the dangerous tactics of the British martinet, and when the English regulars were ambushed and cut to pieces, Gabriel Toombs deployed with his men in the woods and picked off the savages with the steady aim and unerring skill of the frontiersman. Over one hundred years later Robert Toombs, his grandson, protested against the fruitless charge at Malvern Hill, and obliquing to the left with his brigade, protected his men and managed to cover the retreat of his division.

This was a family of soldiers. They were found in the old country fighting Cromwell's army of the rebellion.

Robert Toombs of Georgia was fond of tracing his lineage to the champions of the English king

who defended their sovereign at Boscobel. But
the American family was made up of lovers of
liberty rather than defenders of the King. It
was one of the anomalies in the life of the
Georgia Toombs, who resisted all restraint and
challenged authority in every form, that he should
have located his ancestry among the sworn royal-
ists of the seventeenth century.

William Toombs, the great-grandfather of
Robert, was the first of the English family to
come to America, about 1650. He settled in Virginia. Gabriel, who fought with Braddock, was
the son of William. Major Robert Toombs, the
father of the Georgia statesman, commanded a
Virginia regiment during the Revolution and rendered conspicuous service in Georgia against the
British. Major Toombs came to Georgia in 1783
and received a rich tract of 3000 acres of land in
Wilkes County. This was their share in the
award to distinguished soldiers of "the Virginia
line."

"They fought for their estates like feudal bar-
ons," General Toombs used to say, when speaking
of his ancestors, now sleeping in the red hills of
Georgia. When he was asked after the civil war
why he did not petition for relief of political disabilities, he declared that "no vote of Congress,
no amnesty proclamation, shall rob me of the glory
of outlawry. I shall not be the first of my name

for three centuries to accept the stigma of a pardon."

The elder Gabriel Toombs in 1795 made his last will and testament. He commended his soul to God who gave it, and blessed his Maker for the worldly goods that he was possessed of. Distributing his estate among his wife, Ann Toombs, and his six children, he expressly directed that his negroes and their increase must be appraised together; that they were not to be sold out of the family, and that they should be "used in a Christian-like manner." He divided up parcels of land in Greene and Wilkes counties among his sons, Robert Toombs and Dawson Gabriel Toombs, and his four daughters. Gabriel Toombs died in 1801.

When Major Robert Toombs, the Virginia veteran, and son of Gabriel, came to Georgia to claim his award of land, he settled on Beaverdam Creek, five miles from the town of Washington. It is probable that he stopped in Columbia County, for he married Miss Sanders, of that county. She died, leaving no children, and Major Toombs went back to Virginia and married Miss Catlett. One son was born, and this lady died. Miss Catharine Huling was the third wife. The Hulings were also Virginians, and by this marriage six children were reared. Sarah, who finally became Mrs. Pope; James, who was killed by accident while hunting; Augustus, Robert, and Gabriel.

Catharine Huling, the mother of Robert Toombs of Georgia, was a most excellent woman, of strong and exalted piety. She was of Welsh ancestry, a devout Methodist, and after accompanying her son to college, and seeing him married, prosperous, and distinguished, died in 1848, when he was a member of Congress. Mrs. Toombs gave generously of her own means, to family and friends. Robert Toombs proved to be a dutiful son. He visited his mother constantly, and carefully managed her property. Finally he induced her to move to Washington, so that he might be near her.

Robert Toombs was the fifth child of Robert and Catharine Toombs. He was born in Wilkes County, about five miles from Washington, July 2, 1810. His brother Gabriel, who still lives, was three years his junior, and was throughout his life his close and confidential adviser and friend.

Robert Toombs, in childhood, was a slender, active, mischievous lad, and it will be a surprise to those who remember his superb physical manhood, to hear that at school and college he bore the nickname of "Runt." He was marked for his energy and vivacity. He was not precocious. Nature gave no signs of her intentions in his youth. His development, physical and mental, was not rapid, but wholesome. He was fond of horseback riding, and the earliest glimpse we have of him is as a slender lad, with dark eyes and hair slightly touched with auburn, flying through the village, and sometimes carrying on his pony behind him his little brother to school.

He was always in good health. He boasted that he never took medicine until he was thirty-four years old. His mother said that he grew up almost without her knowledge, so little trouble had he given her. He was a fine horseman. Possibly this practice had much to do with his good spirits and physical strength.

In his younger days he rode sixty-five miles to Milledgeville, covering the distance in one day, and was fresh enough to attend a dance at night. He delighted in fox-hunting, although never a racer or in any sense a sporting man. During the earlier years of his career he practiced law in the saddle, as was the custom with the profession at that time, and never thought of riding to court on wheels until later in life. Throughout his active participation in the Civil War he rode his famous mare, " Gray Alice," and was a striking figure as, splendidly mounted and charged with enthusiasm, he plunged along the lines of the Army of Northern Virginia. In his long wandering from capture in 1865, he was in the saddle six months, riding to and from the wilds of northeast Georgia to the swamps of the Chattahoochee. There was something in his picturesque figure upon the horse which suggests John Randolph of Roanoke.

His first training was at what was known as an "old field school," taught by Welcome Fanning, a master of good attainments and a firm believer in the discipline of the rod. Afterward, Robert Toombs was drilled by a private tutor, Rev. Alexander Webster—an adjunct professor of the University of Georgia and a man of high repute as scholar and instructor. Mr. Webster was the friend and early preceptor of Alexander H. Stephens.

Young Toombs was christened Robert Augustus, and carried his middle name until 1840, when he seems to have dropped it as a useless piece of furniture. There is a report that some of his political foes, playing upon his initials, saddled him with the sobriquet of "Rat." Having out-grown one nickname he was prepared to shed another.

Young Toombs proved to be a great reader. Most of his learning developed in the Humanities; and a cultured visitor from Maryland who once stopped at his father's house declared that this boy of fourteen was better posted in history than anyone he had ever seen.

It was about this time that Robert Toombs was fitted out for Franklin College—now the State University—located in Athens, Ga., forty miles from Washington.

This institution, to which he was devotedly attached and of whose governing board he was a member at the time of his death, was chartered in 1785 by the State of Georgia. It was the early recipient of the deed of western lands, which the State subsequently purchased, assuming the perpetual endowment of the college. It has been to Georgia what Jefferson's school has proved to Virginia, the nursery of scholars and statesmen. Governor John Milledge had given the institution a home upon a beautiful hill overlooking the Oconee River, and this lovely spot they had named Athens. Here in 1824 young Robert Toombs repaired, animated with the feelings which move a college boy, except that his mother went with him and relieved him of the usual sense of loneliness which overtakes the student. Major Robert Toombs, his father, who was an indigo and tobacco planter, was reputed to be a wealthy man for those times, but it was the comfort of the early settler who had earned his demesne from the government rather than the wealth of the capitalist. He had enough to support his family in comfort. He died when Robert was five years old, and the latter selected as his guardian Thomas W. Cobb, of Greene County, a cousin of Governor Howell Cobb, a member of Congress himself and a man of high legal attainment.

When Robert Toombs entered college that

institution was under the Presidency of Moses
Waddell, a born educator and strict disciplinarian.
Three generations of this family have served the
State as preceptors in Franklin College.

It may well be imagined that the college had
not at that time reached the dignity of a university, for an entry in President Waddell's diary
was this: "Caught Jones chewing tobacco:
whipped him for it." Those were the old days
when boys were boys until they were twenty-one.
There is no record to show that Robert Toombs
in college was a close scholar. Later in life he became a hard student and laborious worker. But
if these industrious habits were born to him in
Athens there is no trace of them. That he was a
reader of Shakespeare and history he gave ample
evidence in his long career, but if the legends of his
college town are to be trusted, he was more noted
for outbreaks of mischief than for close application. Full of life and spirits, a healthy, impetuous boy, he was on good terms with his classmates, and took life easily. That was a time when
students were required to get up at sunrise and
attend prayers.

One night, the story goes, the vigilant proctor
actually found young Toombs playing cards with
some of his friends. Fearing a reprimand,
Toombs sought his guardian, who happened to be
in Athens on a visit from his home in Greenes-

boro. It is not certain that young Toombs com-
municated the enormity of his offense, but he
obtained leave to apply to Dr. Waddell for a
letter of discharge. The learned but severe
scholar had not received the proctor's report, and
gave the young student a certificate of honorable
dismissal.

Later in the day the President met Toombs
walking around the campus.

"Robert Toombs," said he, "you took advantage of me early this morning. I did not then
know that you had been caught at the card-table
last evening."

Toombs straightened up and informed the
doctor that he was no longer addressing a student
of his college, but a free-born American citizen.

The halls of Athens are fragrant with these
stories of Toombs. No man ever left so distinctive a stamp upon the place or gave such spicy
flavor to its traditions.

Among the college-mates of Robert Toombs at
Athens were Stephen Olin, Robert Dougherty,
and Daniel Chandler, the grandfather of the unfortunate Mrs. Maybrick of England, and the man
whose chaste and convincing appeal for female
education resulted in the establishment of Wes-
leyan Female College—the first seminary in the
world for the higher culture of women.

The closest of these companionships was that of

George F. Pierce, a young man like Toombs, full of brains and energy—even then a striking and sparkling figure. The path of these men commenced at the door of their *alma mater*, and although their ways were widely divergent, the friends never parted. Two of the finest orators in Georgia, one left his impress as strongly upon the Church as did the other upon the State. One became bishop of the Methodist Episcopal Church and the other a Whig senator. One day these men met, both in the zenith of power, when Toombs said : " Well, George, you are fighting the devil, and I am fighting the Democrats."

Closer in friendship their hands clasped as age swept over their raven locks and stalwart shoulders. Bishop Pierce never hesitated to go to Robert Toombs when his churches or his schools needed money. Toombs would give to the Methodist itinerant as quickly as he would to the local priest. Whether he was subscribing for a Catholic Orphans' Home or a Methodist College he would remark, as he gave liberally and freely, " I always try to honor God Almighty's drafts."

Pierce and Toombs had much in common—although the one was full of saintly fire and the other, at times, of defiant irreverence. It was Pierce whose visits Toombs most enjoyed at his own home, with whom he afterward talked of God and religion. The good bishop lived to bury the devoted Christian wife of the Georgia statesman, and finally, when the dross of worldliness was gone, to receive into the Methodist Church the bowed and weeping figure of the giant Toombs.

When Robert Toombs became prominent in Georgia, there is a story that his State university, in order to win back his friendship, conferred upon him an honorary degree. Toombs is represented as having spurned it with characteristic scorn. "No," said he, "when I was unknown and friendless, you sent me out disgraced, and refused me a diploma. Now that I would honor the degree I do not want it."

There is no record that the college ever conferred a degree upon Toombs at all. Later in life he was elected a trustee of this university, and each year his familiar figure was seen on the stage during commencement, or his wise counsel heard about the board. His attendance upon these duties was punctilious. He would leave the courthouse, the legislative halls, or Virginia Springs—wherever he happened to be—and repair to Athens the first week in August. Once or twice he delivered the annual address before the alumni; several times he secured appropriations for his *alma mater* from the State. His visits to Athens were always occasions of honor. Young men flocked wherever his voice was heard, fascinated by his racy conversation. No "Disinherited Knight" ever returned to more certain conquest or more princely homage.

There is a regular mythology about Toombs at his State university. The things he said would fill a volume of Sydney Smith, while the pranks he played would rival the record of Robin Hood. There is still standing in the college campus in Athens a noble tree, with the crown of a century upon it. Under its spreading branches the first college commencement was held one hundred years ago; under it the student Toombs once stood and addressed his classmates, and of all the men who have gone in and out beneath its shade, but one name has been found sturdy enough to link with this monument of a forgotten forest. The boys to this day call it "The Toombs Oak."

ROBERT TOOMBS, AGE 19, LAW STUDENT, UNIVERSITY OF VIRGINIA, 1829.

(From a miniature painting.)

CHAPTER II.

AFTER Robert Toombs left the University of
Georgia, he entered Union College at Schenectady,
N. Y., under the presidency of Dr. Eliphalet
Knott. Here he finished his classical course and
received his A. B. degree. This was in 1828, and
in 1829 he repaired to the University of Virginia,
where he studied law one year. In the Superior
Court of Elbert County, Ga., holden on the 18th
day of March, 1830, he was admitted to the bar.
The license to practice recites that "Robert A.
Toombs made his application for leave to practice
and plead in the several courts of law and equity
in this State, whereupon the said Robert A.
Toombs, having given satisfactory evidence of
good moral character, and having been examined
in open court, and being found well acquainted
and skilled in the laws, he was admitted by the
court to all the privileges of an attorney, solicitor,
and counsel in the several courts of law and equity
in this State."

The license is signed by William H. Crawford,
Judge, Superior Court, Northern Circuit. Judge

Crawford had served two terms in the United States Senate from Georgia. He had been Minister to Paris during the days of the first Napoleon. He had been Secretary of War and of the Treasury of the United States. In 1825 he received a flattering vote for President, when the Clay and Adams compact drove Jackson and Crawford to the rear. Bad health forced Mr. Crawford from the field of national politics, and in 1827, upon the death of Judge Dooly, Mr. Crawford was appointed Judge of the Northern Circuit. He held this position until his death in Elbert County, which occurred in 1834. Crawford was a friend and patron of young Toombs. The latter considered him the full peer of Webster and of Calhoun.

Robert Toombs was married eight months after his admission to the bar. His career in his profession was not immediately successful. A newspaper writer recently said of him that " while his contemporaries were fighting stubbornly, with varying luck, Toombs took his honors without a struggle, as if by divine right." This was no more true of Toombs than it is true of other men. He seems to have reached excellence in law by slow degrees of toil. Hon. Frank Hardeman, Solicitor-General of the Northern Circuit, was one of the lawyers who examined Toombs for admission to the bar. He afterward declared that Robert

Toombs, during the first four or five years of his practice, did not give high promise. His work in his office was spasmodic, and his style in court was too vehement and disconnected to make marked impression. But the exuberance or redundancy of youth soon passed, and he afterward reached a height in his profession never attained by a lawyer in Georgia.

His work during the first seven years of his practice did not vary in emolument or incident from the routine of a country lawyer. In those days the bulk of legal business lay in the country, and the most prominent men of the profession made the circuit with their saddle-bags, and put up during court week at the village taverns. Slaves and land furnished the basis of litigation. Cities had not reached their size and importance, corporations had not grown to present magnitude, and the wealth and brains of the land were found in the rural districts. "The young lawyers of to-day," says Judge Reese of Georgia, "are far in advance of those during the days of Toombs, owing to the fact that questions and principles then in doubt, and which the lawyers had to dig out, have been long ago decided, nor were there any Supreme Court reports to render stable the body of our jurisprudence."

The counties in which Robert Toombs practiced were Wilkes, Columbia, Oglethorpe, Elbert,

Franklin, and Greene. The bar of the Northern Circuit was full of eminent men. Crawford presided over the courts and a delegation of rare strength pleaded before him. There were Charles J. Jenkins, Andrew J. Miller, and George W. Crawford of Richmond County; from Oglethorpe were George R. Gilmer and Joseph Henry Lumpkin; from Elbert, Thomas W. Thomas and Robert McMillan; from Greene, William C. Dawson, Francis H. Cone; from Clarke, Howell Cobb; from Taliaferro, Alexander H. Stephens. Across the river in Carolina dwelt Calhoun and McDuffie. As a prominent actor in those days remarked: "Giants seem to grow in groups. There are seed plats which foster them like the big trees of California, and they nourish and develop one another, and seem to put men on their mettle." Such a seed plat we notice within a radius of fifty miles of Washington, Ga., where lived a galaxy of men, illustrious in State and national affairs.

In 1837 the great panic which swept over the country left a large amount of litigation in its path. Between that time and 1843, Lawyer Toombs did an immense practice. It is said that in one term of court in one county he returned two hundred cases and took judgment for $200,-000. The largest part of his business was in Wilkes and Elbert, and his fees during a single session of the latter court often reached $5000. During these six years he devoted himself diligently and systematically to the practice of his profession, broken only by his annual attendance upon the General Assembly at Milledgeville. It was during this period that he developed his rare powers for business and his surpassing eloquence as an advocate. He made his fortune during these years, for after 1843, and until the opening of the war between the States, he was uninterruptedly a member of Congress.

There was no important litigation in eastern or middle Georgia that did not enlist his services. He proved to be an ardent and tireless worker. He had grown into a manhood of splendid physique, and he spent the days and most of the nights in careful application. He never went into a case until after the most thorough preparation, where preparation was possible. But he had a wonderful memory and rare legal judgment. He was thoroughly grounded in the principles of law. He possessed, as well, some of that common sense which enabled him to see what the law ought to be, and above all else, he had the strongest intuitive perception of truth. He could strip a case of its toggery and go right to its vitals. He was bold, clean, fearless, and impetuous, and when convinced he had right on his side would fight through all the courts, with irresistible impulse.   He was susceptible to argument, but seemed absolutely blind to fear.

The brightest chapters of the life of Toombs are perhaps his courthouse appearances.   There is no written record of his masterly perform-ances, but the lawyers of his day attest that his jury speeches were even better than his political addresses.

A keen observer of those days will tell you that Mr. Stephens would begin his talk to the jury with calmness and build upon his opening until he warmed up into eloquence; but that Mr. Toombs would plunge immediately into his fierce and impassioned oratory, and pour his tor-rent of wit, eloquence, logic, and satire upon judge and jury.   He would seem to establish his case upon the right, and then defy them to disregard it.

In spite of this vehement and overpowering method he possessed great practical gifts.   He had the knack of unraveling accounts, and while not technically skilled in bookkeeping, had a gen-eral and accurate knowledge which gave him prestige, whether in intricate civil or criminal cases.   He was a rash talker, but the safest of counselors, and practiced his profession with the greatest scruple.   On one occasion he said to a client who had stated his case to him: " Yes, you can recover in this suit, but you ought not to do so. This is a case in which law and justice are on opposite sides."

The client told him he would push the case, anyhow.

"Then," replied Mr. Toombs, "you must hire someone else to assist you in your damned rascality."

On one occasion a lawyer went to him and asked him what he should charge a client, in a case to which Mr. Toombs had just listened in the court-house.

"Well," said Toombs, "I should have charged a thousand dollars; but you ought to have five thousand, for you did a great many things I could not have done."

Mr. Toombs was strict in all his engagements. His practice remained with him, even while he was in Congress, and his occasional return during the session of the Superior Court of the Northern Circuit gave rise at one time to some comment on the part of his opponents, the Democrats. The nominee of that party, on the stump, declared that the demands upon Mr. Toombs's legal talent in Georgia were too great to admit of his strict attendance to public business in Washington. When Mr. Toombs came to answer this point, he said : " You have heard what the gentleman says about my coming home to practice law. He promises, if elected to Congress, he will not leave his seat. I leave you to judge, fellow-citizens, whether your interest in Washington will be best protected by his continued presence or his occasional absence." This hit brought down the house. Mr. Toombs's addresses to the Supreme Court were models of solid argument. During the early days of the Supreme Court of Georgia, it was a migratory body; the law creating it tended to popularize it by providing that it should hold its sessions in the different towns in the State convenient to the lawyers. The court once met in the little schoolroom of the Lumpkin Law School in Athens. One of the earliest cases heard was a land claim from Hancock County, bristling with points and involving about $100,000 worth of property. A. H. Stephens, Benjamin H. Hill, Howell and Thomas Cobb were employed, but in this splendid fight of Titans, Justice Lumpkin declared that the finest legal arguments he ever heard were from the lips of Robert Toombs.

Hon. A. H. Stephens said the best speech Mr. Toombs ever made was in a case in which he represented a poor girl who was suing her stepfather for cruel treatment. The defendant was a preacher, and the jury brought in a verdict for $4000, the maximum sum allowed, and petitioned the Judge to allow them to find damages in a heavier amount.

One of the most celebrated causes Mr. Toombs was engaged in before the war was a railroad case heard in Marietta, Ga., in September, 1858. Howell Cobb and Robert Toombs were employed on one side, while Messrs. Pettigru and Memminger, of Charleston, giants of the Carolina bar, were ranged in opposition. The ordeal was a very trying one. The case occupied seven days. Mr. Toombs, always an early riser, generally commenced his preparation in this case at half-past five in the morning. The hearing of the facts continued in the courthouse until seven in the evening, and the nights were passed in consultation with counsel. Attendants upon this celebrated trial declared that Toombs's manner in the courtroom was indifferent. That, while other lawyers were busy taking notes, he seemed to sit a listless spectator, rolling his head from side to side, oblivious to evidence or proceeding. And yet, when his time came to conclude the argument, he arose with his kingly way, and so thorough was his mastery of the case, with its infinite detail, its broad principles, and intricate technicalities, that his argument was inspiring and profound. His memory seemed to have indelibly pictured the entire record of the seven days, and to have grouped in his mind the main argument of counsel. It was a wonderful display of retentiveness, acumen, learning, and power. On one occasion, while a member of the United States Senate, he came to Georgia to attend a session of the Supreme Court

in Milledgeville. He writes his wife : " I have had
a hard, close week's work. The lawyers very
kindly gave way and allowed my cases to come
on this week, which brought them very close together, and as I was but ill prepared for them,
not having given them any attention last winter,
and but little this spring, I have been pretty much
speaking all day and studying all night." In
March, 1856, Mr. Toombs wrote to his wife, whom
he had left in Washington City, that the spring
term of Wilkes court would be the most laborious and disagreeable he ever attended. Says he :
" For the first time in my life, I have business in
court of my own—that is, where I am a party.
The Bank of the State of Georgia has given me a
year's work on my own account. If I live I will
make the last named party repent of it."

At another time he wrote : " I had fine weather
for Elbert, and a delightful trip. Everything
went well in Elbert with my business." It usually
did. There was no county in which he was more
of an autocrat than in Elbert. He never failed to
carry the county in politics, even when Elbert had
a candidate of her own for Congress. His legal
advice was eagerly sought, and he was more consulted than any other man in Georgia about public
and private affairs. The reason of his phenomenal
success as counsel was that, united with his learning and forensic power, he had a genius for de-

tail. He was a natural financier. He used to tell President Davis, during the early days of the Confederacy, that four-fifths of war was business, and that he must " organize " victory.

During the sessions of Elbert court his arguments swept the jury, his word was law outside. His talk was inspiring to the people. His rare and racy conversation drew crowds to his room every night, and to an occasional client, who would drop in upon his symposium to confer with him, he would say, with a move of his head, "Don't worry about that now. I know more about your business than you do, as I will show you at the proper time." His fees at Elbert were larger than at any other court except his own home in Wilkes. It was during the adjournment of court for dinner that he would be called out by his constituents to make one of his matchless political speeches. He never failed to move the crowds to cheers of delight.

On one occasion he was at Roanoke, his plantation in Stewart County, Ga. He writes his wife: " I was sent for night before last to appear in Lumpkin to prosecute a case of murder: but as it appeared that the act was committed on account of a wrong to the slayer's marital rights, I declined to appear against him." Mr. Toombs was the embodiment of virtue, and the strictest defender of the sanctity of marriage on the part of man as

well as woman.   His whole life was a sermon of
purity and devotion.

Judge William M. Reese, who practiced law
with Mr. Toombs, and was his partner from 1840
to 1843, gives this picture of Toombs at the bar:
"A noble presence, a delivery which captivated
his hearers by its intense earnestness: a thorough
knowledge of his cases, a lightning-like perception
of the weak and strong points of controversy; a
power of expressing in original and striking language his strong convictions; a capacity and willingness to perform intellectual labor; a passion
for the contest of the courthouse; a perfect
fidelity and integrity in all business intrusted to
him, with charming conversational powers—all
contributed to an immense success in his profession.   Such gifts, with a knowledge of business
and the best uses of money, were soon rendered
valuable in accumulating wealth."

Although Mr. Toombs often appeared in courts
to attend to business already in his charge, he
gave out that he would not engage in any new
causes which might interfere with his Congressional duties.   The absorbing nature of public
business from 1850 to 1867 withdrew him from
the bar, and the records of the Supreme Court of
Georgia have only about twenty-five cases argued
by him in that time.   Some of these were of commanding importance, and the opinions of the

Justices handed down in that time bear impress of
the conclusiveness of his reasoning and the power
of his effort before that tribunal. Judge E. H.
Pottle, who presided over the courts of the Northern Circuit during the later years of Toombs's
practice, recalls a celebrated land case when
Robert Toombs was associated against Francis H.
Cone—himself a legal giant. Toombs's associate
expected to make the argument, but Cone put up
such a powerful speech that it was decided that
Toombs must answer him. Toombs protested,
declaring that he had been reading a newspaper,
and not expecting to speak, had not followed Judge
Cone. However, he laid down his paper and
listened to Cone's conclusion, then got up and
made an overmastering forensic effort which captured Court and crowd.

The last appearance Toombs ever made in a
criminal case was in the Eberhart case in Oglethorpe County, Ga., in 1877. He was then sixty-
seven years of age, and not only was his speech fine,
but his management of his case was superb. He
had not worked on that side of the court for many
years, but the presiding Judge, who watched him
closely, declared that he never made a mistake or
missed a point.

It was during a preliminary hearing of this case
that Toombs resorted to one of his brilliant and
audacious motions, characteristic of him. The

State wanted to divide the case and try the princi-
pals separately. Father and son were charged with
murder. The defense objected, but was overruled
by the Court. General Toombs then sprung the
point that Judge Pottle was not qualified to preside, on the ground of a rumor that he had selected
the men of the jury panel instead of drawing them.
Toombs further argued that the Court was not
competent to decide the question of fact. Judge
Pottle vacated the bench and the clerk of court
called Hon. Samuel H. Hardeman to preside.
Toombs and Benjamin H. Hill, his assistant, contended that the clerk had no right to appoint a
judge. Judge Hardeman sustained the point and
promptly came down, when Judge Pottle resumed
the bench and continued the case—just the result
that Toombs wanted. This case attracted immense
comment, and in the Constitution of 1877 a provision was made, growing out of this incident, providing for the appointment of judges *pro hac vice.*

He was a bitter enemy to anything that smacked
of monopoly, and during the anti-railroad agitation
of 1879–80, he said: "If I was forty-five years
old I would whip this fight." Still, he was an
exceedingly just man. Linton Stephens, noted
for his probity and honor, said he would rather
trust Robert Toombs to decide a case in which he
was interested than any man he ever saw.

During the last five years of General Toombs's

life he was seldom seen in the courtroom. He
was sometimes employed in important causes, but
his eyesight failed him, and his strength was visibly impaired. His addresses were rather disconnected. His old habit of covering his points in
great leaps, leaving the intervening spaces unex-
plained, rendered it difficult to follow him. His
mind still acted with power, and he seemed to presume that his hearers were as well up on his subject as he was. His manner was sometimes overbearing to the members of the bar, but no man was
more open to reason or more sobered by reflection,
and he was absolutely without malice. He was
always recognized as an upright man, and he maintained, in spite of his infirmities, the respect and
confidence of the bench and bar and of the people.

Chief Justice Jackson said : " In the practice of
law this lightning-like rapidity of thought distinguished Toombs. He saw through the case at a
glance, and grasped the controlling point. Yielding minor hillocks, he seized and held the height
that covered the field, and from that eminence
shot after shot swept all before it. Concentrated
fire was always his policy. A single sentence
would win his case. A big thought, compressed
into small compass, was fatal to his foe. It is the
clear insight of a great mind only that shaped out
truth in words few and simple. Brevity is power,
wherever thought is strong. From Gaul Cæsar

wrote '*Veni, vidi, vici.*' Rome was electrified, and the message immortalized. Toombs said to this Court, 'May it please your Honor—Seizin, Marriage, Death, Dower,' and sat down. His case was won, the widow's heart leaped with joy, and the lawyer's argument lives forever."

CHAPTER III.

WHEN Andrew Jackson and John C. Calhoun were waging their "irrepressible conflict," the county of Wilkes in the State of Georgia was nursing discordant factions. Just across the river in Carolina lived the great Nullifier. The Virginia settlers of Wilkes sided with him, while scores of North Carolinians, who had come to live in the county, swore by "Old Hickory." This political difference gave rise to numerous feuds. The two elements maintained their identity for generations, and the divisions became social as well as political. The Virginians nursed their State pride. The sons of North Carolina, overshadowed by the Old Dominion, clung to the Union and accepted Andrew Jackson, their friend and neighbor, as oracle and leader. The earliest political division in Georgia was between the Clarke and Crawford factions. General John Clarke, a sturdy soldier of the Revolution, came from North Carolina, while William H. Crawford, a Virginian by birth and a Georgian by residence, led the Virginia element. The feud between

29

Clarke and Crawford gave rise to numerous duels. Then came George M. Troup to reënforce the Crawford faction and defend States' Rights, even at the point of the sword. Troup and Clarke were rival candidates for Governor of Georgia in 1825, and the Toombs family ardently fought for Troup. Young Toombs was but fifteen years of age, but politics had been burnt into his ardent soul. Wilkes had remained a Union county until this campaign, when the Troup and Toombs influence was too strong for the North Carolina faction. Wilkes, in fact, seemed to be a watershed in early politics. It was in close touch with Jackson and Calhoun, with Clarke and Crawford, and then with Clarke and Troup. On the one side the current from the mountain streams melted into the peaceful Savannah and merged into the Atlantic; on the other they swept into the Tennessee and hurried off to the Father of Waters.

Robert Toombs cast his first vote for Andrew Jackson in 1832. He abandoned the Union Democratic-Republican party, however, after the proclamation and force bill of the Administration and joined the States' Rights Whigs. When young Toombs was elected to the General Assembly of Georgia in October, 1837, parties were sharply divided. The Democrats, sustained by the personal popularity of " Old Hickory," were still dominant in the State. The States' Rights

Whigs, however, had a large following, and although not indorsing the doctrines of Calhoun, the party was still animated by the spirit of George M. Troup. This statesman, just retired from public life, had been borne from a sick-bed to the United States Senate Chamber to vote against the extreme measures of President Jackson. The Troup men claimed to be loyal to the Constitution of their country in all its defined grants, and conceded the right of the Chief Magistrate to execute the office so delegated, but they resisted what they believed to be a dangerous latitude of construction looking to consolidated power. Robert Toombs was not a disciple of Calhoun. While admiring the generalities and theories of the great Carolinian, the young Georgian was a more practical statesman. The States' Rights Whigs advocated a protective tariff and a national bank. They believed that the depreciation of the currency had caused the distress of the people in the panic of 1837, and no man in this stormy era more vigorously upbraided the pet-bank and sub-treasury system than Robert Toombs. He introduced a resolution in the legislature declaring that President Van Buren had used the patronage of the government to strengthen his own party; that he had repudiated the practices and principles of his patriotic antecedents, and " had sought out antiquated

European systems for the collection, safe keeping,
and distribution of public moneys—foreign to our
habits, unsuited to our conditions, expensive and
unsafe in operation." Mr. Toombs contended,
with all the force that was in him, that a bank of
the United States, properly regulated, was "the
best, most proper and economical means for hand-
ling public moneys." Robert Toombs would not
have waited until he was twenty-seven years of
age before entering public life, had not the sentiment of his county been hostile to his party.
Wilkes had been a Union county, but in 1837 it
returned to the lower house two Democrats, and
Robert A. Toombs, the only Whig. Nothing but
his recognized ability induced the people to make
an exception in his favor. Besides his reputation
as an orator and advocate, Toombs had just returned from the Creek war, where he had commanded a company and served under General
Winfield Scott in putting down the insurrection
of Neahmatha, the Indian chief. He now brought
to public life the new prestige of a soldier. After
this, "Captain Toombs" was never defeated in his
county. He was returned at the annual elections
in 1839, 1840, 1842, and 1843—and succeeded in
preserving at home an average Whig majority of
100 votes. He did not care for the State Senate, preferring the more populous body, then
composed of 200 members. Parties in the

State were very evenly balanced, but Mr. Toombs preserved, in the varying scale of politics, a prominent place in the house. He was made chairman of the Judiciary Committee by his political opponents. . He served as a member of the Committee on Internal Improvements, as chairman of the all-important Committee on Banking, chairman of the Committee on State of the Republic, and in 1842 received the vote of the Whig minority in the house for Speaker. In 1840 the Whigs gained control of the government. The Harrison tidal wave swept their best men to the front in State and national councils. Charles J. Jenkins of Richmond was elected speaker of the house, and Mr. Toombs, as chairman of the Banking Committee, framed the bill which repealed the law authorizing the issue of bank bills to the amount of twice their capital stock. He went right to the marrow of honest banking and sound finance by providing for a fund to redeem the outstanding bills, and condemned the course of the State banks in flooding the State with irredeemable promises to pay.

It was at this session of the General Assembly that Mr. Toombs displayed the skill and sagacity of a statesman in fearlessly exposing a seductive scheme for popular relief. He was called upon to confront public clamor and to fight in the face of fearful odds, but he did not falter.

Just before the General Assembly of 1840 adjourned, Governor McDonald sent an urgent message to both houses calling upon them to frame some means for the speedy relief of the people. The situation in Georgia was very distressing. The rains and floods of that year had swept the crops from the fields, and there was much suffering among the planters. Coming upon the heel of the session, the Whig members of the legislature looked upon the message as a surprise, and rather regarded it as a shrewd political stroke. Mr. Toombs was equal to the emergency. He quickly put in a resolution asking the Governor himself to suggest some means of popular relief—throwing the burden of the problem back upon the executive. But Governor McDonald was armed. He drew his last weapon from his arsenal, and used it with formidable power. He sent in an elaborate message to the houses recommending that the State make a large loan and deposit the proceeds in bank, to be given out to the people on good security. The Senate committee, in evident sympathy with the scheme for relief, reported a bill authorizing the issue of two million six-year eight-per-cent. bonds to be loaned to private citizens, limiting each loan to one thousand dollars, and restricting the notes to three years, with eight per cent. interest.

The report of the House Committee was pre-

pared by Robert Toombs. It was the most
admirable and statesmanlike document of that
day. Mr. Toombs said that deliberation had
resulted in the conviction that the measure suggested by His Excellency should not be adopted.
While his committee was duly sensible of and
deeply regretted the pecuniary embarrassment of
many of their fellow-citizens, he felt constrained
by a sense of public duty to declare that he
deemed it unwise and impolitic to use the credit,
and pledge the property and labor of the whole
people, to supply the private wants of a portion
only of the people. The use of the public credit,
he went on to say, was one of the most important
and delicate powers which a free people could con-
fide in their representatives; it should be jealously
guarded, sacredly protected, and cautiously used,
even for the attainment of the noblest patriotic
ends, and never for the benefit of one class of the
community to the exclusion or injury of the rest,
whether the demand grew out of real or supposed
pecuniary difficulties. To relieve these difficulties by use of the public credit would be to
substitute a public calamity for private misfor-
tune, and would end in the certain necessity of
imposing grievous burdens in the way of taxes
upon the many for the benefit of the few. All
experience, Mr. Toombs went on to declare, ad-
monish us to expect such results from the pro-

posed relief measures, to adopt which would be to violate some of the most sacred principles of the social compact. All free governments, deriving their just powers from, and being established for the benefit of, the governed, must necessarily have power over the property, and consequently the credit, of the governed to the extent of public use, and no further. And whenever government assumed the right to use the property or credit of the people for any other purpose, it abused a power essential for the perfection of its legislative duties in a manner destructive of the rights and interests of the governed, and ought to be sternly resisted by the people. The proposed measures, he contended, violated these admitted truths, asserted the untenable principle that governments should protect a portion of the people, in violation of the rights of the remainder, from the calamities consequent on unpropitious seasons and private misfortunes.

He must have been an indifferent or careless spectator of similar financial schemes, Mr. Toombs declared, who could persuade himself that this plan of borrowing money, to lend again at the same rate of interest, could be performed without loss to the State. That loss must be supplied by taxation, and to that extent, at least, it will operate so as to legislate money from the pocket of one citizen to that of another. The committee declared that it knew of no mode of legislative relief except the interposition of unconstitutional, unwise, unjust, and oppressive legislation between debtor and creditor, which did not need their condemnation.

The argument was exhaustive and convincing. Never were the powers of the State or the soundness of public credit more strongly set forth. The whole scheme of relief was abandoned, and the General Assembly adjourned.

The relief measures, however, had a great effect upon the campaign. Rejected in the legislature under the rattling fire and withering sarcasm of Toombs, they were artfully used on the hustings. "McDonald and Relief" was the slogan. Men talked airily about "deliverance and liberty." Mr. Toombs declared that "humbuggery was reduced to an exact science and demonstrated by figures." The Act compelling the banks to make cash payments was represented as an unwise contraction of the currency and a great oppression to the people. Governor McDonald was consequently reëlected over William C. Dawson, the Whig nominee.

Robert Toombs was not a candidate for reëlection in 1841. He worked hard at the polls for the Whig ticket, and although his candidate for Governor received a majority of one in Wilkes County, the Whigs were defeated for the legislature. When he returned to the Assembly in 1842 he still found Governor McDonald and the Democrats supporting a central bank and the sub-treasury. They clamored to restore public finances to the old system. The Democrats held the legislature and elected to the United States Senate Walter T. Colquitt over Charles J. Jenkins. Although a member of the minority party, Mr. Toombs was appointed chairman of the Judiciary Committee. Here his high character and moral courage shone conspicuously. He proved a stone wall against the perfect flood of legislation designed for popular relief. To use his own words: "The calendar was strong with a heterogeneous collection of bills proposing stay-laws." He reported as "unwise, inexpedient, and injurious," proposed Acts "to protect unfortunate debtors"; "to redeem property in certain cases"; also a bill to "exempt from levy and sale certain classes of property." He held with Marshall the absolute inviolability of contracts; he believed in common honesty in public and private life; he was strict in all business obligations; he denounced the Homestead Act of 1868, and declared in his last days that there was "not a dirty shilling in his pocket." Mr. Toombs was nothing of the demagogue. He was highminded, fearless, and sincere, and it may be said of him what he afterward declared so often of Henry Clay, that " he would not flatter Neptune for his trident or Jove for his power to thunder." He was called upon at this session to fight the repeal of the law he had framed in 1840, to regulate the system of banking. He declared in eloquent terms that the State must restrict the issue of the banks and compel their payment in specie. The experiment of banking on public credit had failed, he said. It had brought loss to the government, distress to the people, and had sullied the good faith of Georgia.

It was at this session of the legislature that the Democrats proposed a vote of censure upon John McPherson Berrien, United States Senator from Georgia, for his advocacy of a national bank. Mr. Toombs ardently defended Senator Berrien. He said that the State legislature was not the custodian of a senator's conscience, and held that the people of Georgia sanctioned the expediency and utility of a national bank. When the resolution of censure came up in the house, the Whigs refused to vote, and raised the point of "no quorum." Speaker *pro tem.* Wellborn, who presided, counted a quorum and declared the resolutions adopted. Mr. Toombe fired up at this unusual decision. He threw himself before the Speaker with impetuous appeal and called for a reversal of the decision. But it was a Democratic house, and the Speaker was sustained by a vote of 96 to 40.

The craze for internal improvements now swept over the country. The Whigs were especially active, and we find resolutions adopted by the General Assembly, calling on the Federal Government to create ports of entry and to build government foundries and navy yards on the Southern seaboard. Mr. Toombs was chairman of the Committee of Internal Improvements, but his efforts were directed toward the completion of the Western and Atlantic Railroad. These enterprises had overshadowed the waterways, and the railway from Charleston, S. C., to Augusta, Ga., one of the very first in the country, had just been completed. Already a company had embarked upon the construction of the Georgia Railroad, and on May 21, 1837, the first locomotive ever put in motion on the soil of Georgia moved out from Augusta. A local paper described the event in sententious terms:

This locomotive started beautifully and majestically from the depository and, following the impetus given, flew with surprising velocity on the road which hereafter is to be her natural element.

The General Assembly decided that these rail lines should have an outlet to the West. This great road was finally built and operated from Atlanta to Chattanooga, and is still owned by the State, a monument to the sagacity and persistency of Toombs and his associates in 1840. The great possibilities of these iron highways opened the eyes of the statesmen of that day, Mr. Calhoun seemed to drop for a time his philosophical studies of States and slavery and to dream of railroads and commercial greatness. He proposed the connection of the Atlantic Ocean with the Mississippi River and the great West, through Cumberland Gap—a brilliant and feasible scheme. Governor Gilmer of Georgia declared in his message that these projected roads "would add new bonds to the Union." But King Cotton, with his millions in serfdom, issued his imperial decrees, and not even this great railroad development could keep down the tremendous tragedy of the century.

One of the measures to which Mr. Toombs devoted great attention during his legislative term was the establishment of a State Supreme Court. This bill was several times defeated, but finally in 1843 passed the house by a vote of 88 to 86. It was the scene of many of his forensic triumphs. He also introduced, during the sessions of 1842 and 1843, bills to abolish suretyship in Georgia. This system had been severely abused In the flush times men indorsed without stint, and then during the panic of 1837 "reaped the whirlwind." Fortunes were swept away, individual credit ruined, and families brought to beggary by this reckless system of surety. What a man seldom refused to do for another, Mr. Toombs

strove to reach by law. But the system had become too firmly intrenched in the financial habits
of the people. His bill, which he distinctly stated
was to apply alone to future and not past contracts, only commanded a small minority of votes.
It was looked upon as an abridgment of personal
liberty. Mr. Toombs exerted all of his efforts in
behalf of this bill, and it became quite an issue in
Georgia. It is not a little strange that when
Robert Toombs was dead, it was found that his
own estate was involved by a series of indorse-
ments which he had given in Atlanta to the
Kimball House Company. Had he maintained
the activity of his younger days, he would probably have turned this deal into a profitable invest-
ment. The complication was finally arranged,
but his large property came near being swept
away under the same system of surety he had
striven to abolish.

CHAPTER IV.

ENTERING public life about the same time, living a short distance apart, professing the same political principles, practicing in the same courts of law, were Alexander H. Stephens of Taliaferro and Robert Toombs of Wilkes. Entirely unlike in physical organism and mental make-up, differing entirely in origin and views of life, these two men were close personal friends, and throughout an eventful period of more than half a century, preserved an affectionate regard for each other.

Mr. Stephens was delicate, sensitive, conservative, and sagacious, while Toombs was impetuous, overpowering, defiant, and masterful. Stephens was small, swarthy, fragile, while Toombs was leonine, full-blooded, and majestic. And yet in peace and war these two men walked hand in hand, and the last public appearance of Robert Toombs was when, bent and weeping, he bowed his gray head at the coffin and pronounced the funeral oration over Alexander Stephens.

In the General Assembly of 1843, Robert Toombs was a member of the house, but his

43

ability and power had marked him as a candidate
for Congress, and Mr. Stephens had already been
promoted from the State Senate to a seat in the
national legislature at Washington. The law re-
quiring the State to choose congressmen on the
district plan had been passed, and the General
Assembly was then engaged in laying off the
counties into congressional districts. The bill, as
first reported, included the counties of Wilkes and
Taliaferro in the second district of Georgia. Here
was a problem. Toombs and Stephens had been
named as Whig candidates for the Clay campaign
of 1844. To have them clash would have been to
deprive the State of their talents in the national
councils. It would be interesting to speculate as
to what would have been the result had these
two men been opposed. Stephens was naturally
a Union man, and was no very ardent advocate of
slavery. Toombs inherited the traditions of the
Virginia landowners. It is not improbable that
the firmness of the one would have been a foil for
the fire of the other. History might have been
written differently had not the conference committee in the Georgia Legislature in 1843 altered
the schedule of districts, placing Taliaferro in the
seventh and Wilkes in the eighth Congressional
district. Both were safely Whig, and the future
Vice-President and premier of the Southern Confederacy now prepared for the canvass which was

to plunge them into their duties as members of the national Congress.

Robert Toombs had already made his appearance in national politics in 1840. Although still a member of the Georgia Legislature, he took a deep interest in the success of the Whig ticket for President. His power as a stump speaker was felt in eastern Georgia, where the people gathered at the "log cabin and hard cider" campaigns. The most daring feat of young Toombs, just thirty years old, was in crossing the Savannah River and meeting George McDuffie, the great Democrat of South Carolina, then in the zenith of his fame. An eye-witness of this contest between the champions of Van Buren and Harrison declared that McDuffie was "harnessed lightning" himself. He was a nervous, impassioned speaker. When the rash young Georgian crossed over to Willington, S. C., to meet the lion in his den, Toombs rode horseback, and it was noticed that his shirt front was stained with tobacco juice, and yet Toombs was a remarkably handsome man. "Genius sat upon his brow, and his eyes were as black as death and bigger than an ox's." His presence captivated even the idolators of McDuffie. His argument and invective, his overpowering eloquence, linger in the memory of old men now. McDuffie said of him: "I have heard John Randolph of Roanoke, and met Burgess of

Rhode Island, but this wild Georgian is a Mirabeau."

In 1844 Robert Toombs was a delegate to the
Baltimore convention which nominated Henry
Clay, and during this visit he made a speech in
New York which attracted wide attention. It
threatened to raise a storm about his head in
Georgia. In his speech he arraigned Mr. Calhoun
for writing his "sugar letter" to Louisiana, and
for saying that he would protect sugar because it
was the production of slave labor. Mr. Toombs
declared: "If any discrimination is made between
free and slave labor it ought to be in favor of free
labor." "But," said he, "the Whigs of Georgia
want no such partial protection as Mr. Calhoun offers; they want protection for all classes of labor
and home industry. The Whigs protest against
these efforts to prejudice the South against the
North, or the North against the South. They have
a common interest as well as a common history.
The blood that was mingled at Yorktown and at
Eutaw cannot be kept at enmity forever. The
Whigs of Bunker Hill are the same as the Whigs
of Georgia." Mr. Toombs was actually charged
in this campaign with being an Abolitionist. He
was accused of saying in a speech at Mallorysville,
Ga., during the Harrison campaign, that slavery
was "a moral and political evil." This was now
brought up against him. Mr. Toombs admitted

saying that slavery was a political evil. He wrote
a ringing letter to his constituents, in which he declared that "the affected fear and pretended sus-
picion of a part of the Democratic press in relation
to my views are well understood by the people.
I have no language to express my scorn and contempt for the whole crew. I have no other reply
to make to these common sewers of filth and false-
hood. If I had as many arms as Briareus they
would be too few to correct the misrepresentations
of speeches I have made in the past six months."

It was on the 3d of October, 1844, that Robert
Toombs spoke at a memorable political meeting in
Augusta, Ga. Augusta was in the heart of the
district which he was contesting for Congress, and
the Democrats, to strengthen their cause, brought
over McDuffie from South Carolina. Large crowds
were present in the shady yard surrounding the
City Hall ; seats had been constructed there, while
back in the distance long trenches were dug, and
savory meats were undergoing the famous process
of barbecue. Speaking commenced at ten o'clock
in the morning, and, with a short rest for dinner,
there were seven hours of oratory. People seldom
tired in those days of forensic meetings. Toombs
was on his mettle. He denounced the Democrats
for dragging the slavery question before the people
to operate upon their fears. It was a bugbear
everlastingly used to cover up the true question at

issue. It was kept up to operate on the fears of
the timid and the passions and prejudices of the
unsuspecting.

The young Whig then launched into a glowing
defense of the National Bank. The Democrats
had asked where was the authority to charter a
bank? He would reply, "Where was the authority, in so many words, to build lighthouses? Democrats were very strict constructionists when it was
necessary to accomplish their political purposes,
but always found a way to get around these doubts
when occasion required." He taunted McDuffie
with having admitted that Congress had power to
charter a bank.

Mr. Toombs contended that a tariff, with the
features of protection to American industry, had
existed since the foundation of the government.
This great system of "plunder" had been supported by Jefferson. Eloquently warming up under
the Democratic charge that the tariff was a system
of robbery, Mr. Toombs appealed to every Whig
and Democrat as an American who boasted of this
government as " a model to all nations of the earth;
as the consummation of political wisdom; who asks
the oppressed of all nations to come and place himself under its protection, because it upholds the
weak against the strong and protects the poor
against the rich, whether it has been going on in a
system of plunder ever since it sprang into power."
"It is not true," he said, " it is not true!"

Turning with prophetic ken to his Augusta friends, he asked what would be the effect were the Savannah River turned through the beautiful plains of Augusta, and manufactures built up where the industrious could find employment. Hundreds of persons, he said, would be brought together to spin the raw cotton grown in the State, to consume the provisions which the farmers raised, thus diversifying their employment and increasing their profits. " Would any man tell me," shouted the orator, his eyes blazing, and his arms uplifted, " that this would impoverish the country—would make paupers of the people ? To increase the places where the laborer may sell his labor would never make him a pauper. Be controlled," said he, " in the administration of government and in all other things, by the improvement of the age. Do not tie the living to the dead. Others may despise the lights of science or experience; they have a right, if they choose, to be governed by the dreams of economists who have rejected practical evidence. But no such consistency is mine. I will have none of it."

McDuffie in his speech declared that all the plundering which England had been subjected to from the days of Hengist and Horsa could not equal the plundering which the people of the exporting States had sustained.

Toombs answered that if a man must pay tax to sustain the government it was better he should

pay it in such a way as to benefit his own countrymen than for the benefit of foreign manufacturers
and foreign capitalists.

Mr. Toombs alluded to a letter of James K.
Polk to a Pennsylvania manufacturer, as leaning
toward protection.

McDuffie said that Polk's letter was "composed
for that meridian."

"Henry Clay does not need an interpreter,"
cried Toombs. "He is the same in the North as in
the South. He would rather be right than President."

"Dallas, the Democratic nominee for vice
president, is a high-tariff man," said Toombs.
"He voted for the tariff of 1832 and against the
compromise measures. Although the sword was
drawn to drink the blood of McDuffie's friends in
Carolina, Dallas would still adhere to his pound of
flesh."

Toombs concluded his great reply to McDuffie:
"We have lived under the present order of things
for fifty years, and can continue to live under it
for one thousand years to come, if the people of
the South are but content to stand upon their
rights as guaranteed in the Constitution, and not
work confusion by listening to ambitious politicians: by taking as much pains to preserve a good
understanding with our Northern brethren, the
vast majority of whom are inclined to respect the
limitations of the Constitution."

This was perhaps the greatest political meeting Georgia ever held. Politics were at white heat. Toombs and McDuffie each spoke two hours· The campaign cry was for the Whigs: "Clay, Frelinghuysen, Toombs, and our glorious Union," and by the Democrats: "Polk, Dallas, Texas, and Oregon." It was Whig *vs.* Loco-foco. The Whig leaders of the South were Pettigru, Thompson, and Yeadon of South Carolina, Merriweather, Toombs, and Stephens, of Georgia, while the Democratic lights were McDuffie, Rhett, and Pickens of South Carolina, and Charlton, Cobb, Colquitt, and Herschel V. Johnson of Georgia.

The campaign of 1844 was bitter in Georgia. The Whigs carried the burden of a protective tariff, while the memories of nullification and the Force bill were awakened by a ringing letter from George M. Troup, condemning the tariff in his vigorous style. This forced Mr. Toombs, in his letter accepting the congressional nomination, to review the subject in its relation to the States' Rights party in Georgia. "The tariff of 1824," said he, "which was voted for by Andrew Jackson, carried the principle of protection further than any preceding one. Jackson was the avowed friend of the protective policy, yet he received the vote of Georgia, regardless of party. In 1828 the Harrisburg convention demanded additional protection, and this measure was carried through Congress by the leading men of the Democratic party. It created discontent in the South, and the Act of 1832 professed to modify the tariff—but this measure not proving satisfactory was 'nullified' by South Carolina. General Jackson then issued his proclamation which pronounced principles and issues utterly at war with the rights of the States, and subversive of the character of the government. The opponents of consolidating principles went into opposition. Delegates met in Milledgeville in 1833, adopted the Virginia and Kentucky resolutions, denounced the sentiments of Jackson's proclamation, and affirmed the doctrine of States' Rights."

"The Democratic party was then," said Toombs, "cheek by jowl with the whole tariff party in the United States, sustaining General Jackson, and stoutly maintaining that the leaders of that spirited little band in our sister State, whose talent shed a glory over their opposition, deserved a halter. They sustained John C. Forsythe in voting against the Compromise bill—that peace offering of the illustrious Henry Clay."

Mr. Toombs declared in this campaign that the effect of a tariff on the productive industries of a country has been a disputed question among the wisest statesmen for centuries, and that these influences are subject to so many disturbing causes, both foreign and domestic, that they are incapable of being reduced to fixed principles.

Mr. Toombs did not hesitate, however, to condemn "the theories of the South Carolina school of politics."

Mr. Toombs opposed the acquisition of Texas. He did not believe the North would consent. "It matters not," he said, "that Mexico is weak, that the acquisition is easy. The question is just the same: Is it right, is it just, is it the policy of this country to enlarge its territory by conquest? The principle is condemned by the spirit of the age, by reason, and by revelation. A people who love justice and hate wrong and oppression cannot approve it. War in a just cause is a great calamity to any people, and can only be justified by the highest necessity. A people who go to war without just and sufficient cause, with no other motive than pride and love of glory, are enemies to the human race and deserve the execration of all mankind. What, then, must be the judgment of a war for plunder?" He denounced the whole thing as a land job, and declared that he would rather have "the Union without Texas than Texas without the Union."

The Democratic opponent of Mr. Toombs in this canvass was Hon. Edward J. Black of Screven, who had been in Congress since 1838. The new district was safely Whig, but the young candidate had to fight the prestige of McDuffie and Troup and opposition from numberless

sources. It was charged that he always voted in
the Georgia Legislature to raise taxes. He retorted, "It is right to resort to taxation to pay the
honest debt of a State. I did vote to raise taxes,
and I glory in it. It was a duty I owed the
State, and I would go to the last dollar to preserve
her good name and honor."

While Mr. Toombs was making a speech in
this canvass a man in the audience charged him
with having voted for the free banking law and
against the poor-school fund. "The gentleman,"
said Mr. Toombs, "seems to find pleasure in
reveling in my cast-off errors. I shall not disturb him."

"How is this, Mr. Toombs," shouted a Democrat at another time, "here is a vote of yours
in the house journal I do not like."

"Well, my friend, there are several there that I
do not like: now what are you going to do about
it?"

Especially was opposition bitter to Henry
Clay. Cartoons were published from Northern
papers, of Clay whipping a negro slave, with this
inscription: "The Mill Boy of the *Slashes*."
Pictures appeared in the Democratic papers of a
human figure surmounted by a pistol, a bottle, and
a deck of cards. To this a *résumé* of Clay's mis-
deeds was appended:

"In 1805 quarreled with Colonel Davis of Kentucky, which led to his first duel. In 1808 challenged Humphrey Marshall, and fired three times at his breast. In 1825 challenged the great John Randolph, and fired once at his breast. In 1838 he planned the Cilley duel, by which a murder was committed and a wife made a mourner. In 1841, when sixty-five years old, and gray-headed, is under a five thousand dollar bond to keep the peace. At twenty-nine he perjured himself to secure a seat in the United States Senate. In 1824, made the infamous bargain with Adams by which he sold out for a six thousand dollar office. He is well known as a gambler and Sabbath-breaker."

But the eloquent Harry of the West had a large and devoted following. He visited Georgia in March of this year, and charmed the people by his eloquence and magnetism. Robert Toombs had met him at the social board and had been won by his superb mentality and fine manners. Women paid him the tribute of their presence wherever he spoke, and little children scattered flowers along his path. But the November election in Georgia, as elsewhere, was adverse to the party of Henry Clay. Toombs and Stephens were sent to Congress, but the electoral vote of Georgia was cast for Polk and Dallas, and the Whigs, who loved Clay as a father, regarded his defeat as a personal affliction as well as a public calamity.

CHAPTER V.

ROBERT TOOMBS took his seat in the twenty-ninth Congress in December, 1845. The Democrats organized the House by the election of John W. Davis of Indiana, Speaker. The House was made up of unusually strong men, who afterward became noted in national affairs. Hannibal Hamlin was with the Maine delegation; ex-President John Quincy Adams had been elected from Massachusetts with Robert C. Winthrop; Stephen A. Douglas was there from Illinois; David Wilmot from Pennsylvania; R. Barnwell Rhett and Armistead Burt from South Carolina; Geo. C. Droomgoole and Robert M. T. Hunter of Virginia, Andrew Johnson of Tennessee, were members, as were Henry W. Hilliard and W. L. Yancey of Alabama, Jefferson Davis and Jacob Thompson of Mississippi, and John Slidell of Louisiana. Toombs, Stephens, and Cobb were the most prominent figures in the Georgia delegation.

The topics uppermost in the public mind of that day were the Oregon question, Texas, and the ubiquitous tariff. It looked at one time as if war with Great Britain were unavoidable. Presi-

56

dent Polk occupied an extreme position, and declared in his message to Congress that our title to the whole of Oregon was clear. The boundary of the ceded territory was unsettled. The Democrats demanded the occupation of Oregon, with the campaign cry of "fifty-four forty or fight."

Mr. Toombs did not accept President Polk's position. His first speech in the House was made January 12, 1846, and at once placed him in the front rank of orators and statesmen. He said that it was not clear to him that our title was exceptional up to 54° 40'. Our claim to the territory north of the Columbia River was the Spanish title only, and this had been an inchoate right.

Mr. Toombs wanted the question settled by reason. He impetuously declared that "neither the clamors within nor without this hall, nor the ten thousand British cannon, floating on every ship, or mounted on every island, shall influence my decision in a question like this." He was for peace—for honorable peace. "It is the mother of all the virtues and hopes of mankind," No man would go further than he to obtain honorable peace; but dishonorable peace was worse than war—it was the worst of all evil.

War was the greatest and the most horrible of calamities. Even a war for liberty itself was rarely compensated by the consequences. "Yet the common judgment of mankind consigned to lasting infamy the people who would surrender their rights and freedom for the sake of a dishonest peace."

"Let us," cried the speaker, turning to his Southern colleagues, "let us repress any unworthy sectional feeling which looks only to the attainment of sectional power."

His conclusion was an apotheosis of Georgia as a Union State. He said: "Mr. Speaker, Georgia wants peace, but she would not for the sake of peace yield any of her own or the nation's rights. A new career of prosperity is now before her; new prospects, bright and fair, open to her vision and lie ready for her grasp, and she fully appreciates her position. She has at length begun to avail herself of her advantages by forming a great commercial line between the Atlantic and the West. She is embarking in enterprises of intense importance, and is beginning to provide manufactures for her unpaid laborers. She sees nothing but prosperity ahead, and peace is necessary in order to reveal it; but still, if war must come, if it has been decreed that Oregon must be consecrated to liberty in the blood of the brave and the sufferings of the free, Georgia will be found ready with her share of the offering, and, whatever may be her sacrifice, she will display a magnanimity as great as the occasion and as prolonged as the conflict."

Mr. Toombs indorsed the conservative action of the Senate, which forced President Polk from his extreme position and established the parallel of 49° as the northern boundary.

The tariff bill of 1846 was framed, as President Polk expressed it, in the interest of lower duties, and it changed the basis of assessment from specific, or minimum duties, to duties *ad valorem*.

Mr. Toombs made a most elaborate speech against this bill in July, 1846. If his Oregon speech had shown thorough familiarity with the force and effect of treaties and the laws of nations, his tariff speech proved him a student of fiscal matters and a master of finance. His genius, as Jefferson Davis afterward remarked, lay decidedly in this direction. Mr. Toombs announced in his tariff speech that the best of laws, especially tax laws, were but approximations of human justice. He entered into an elaborate argument to controvert the idea that low tariff meant increased revenue. The history of such legislation, he contended, had been that the highest tariff had raised the most money. Mr. Toombs combated the *ad valorem* principle of levying duty upon imports.

Mr. Toombs declared to his constituents in September, 1846, that the President had marched his army into Mexico without authority of law. "The conquest and dismemberment of Mexico, however brilliant may be the success of our

arms," said he, " will not redound to the glory
of our republic."

The Whigs approached the Presidential campaign of 1848 with every chance of success.
They still hoped that the Sage of Ashland
might be the nominee. George W. Crawford,
ex-Governor of Georgia, and afterward member of the Taylor Cabinet, perceiving that the
drift in the West was against Mr. Clay, offered a resolution in the Whig convention that
"whatever may have been our personal prefer-
ences, we feel that in yielding them at the present time, we are only pursuing Mr Clay's own illustrious example." Mr. Toombs stated to his constituents that Clay could not be nominated because Ohio had declared that no man who had opposed the Wilmot Proviso could get the vote of
that State. The Whigs, who had opposed the
Mexican war, now reaped its benefits by nominating one of its heroes to the Presidency, and Zachary Taylor of Louisiana became at once a popular candidate. Millard Fillmore of New York
was named for vice president, and " Rough and
Ready " clubs were soon organized in every part
of Georgia. The venerable William H. Crawford
headed the Whig electoral ticket in Georgia, while
Toombs, Stephens, and Thomas W. Thomas led
the campaign.

The issue of the campaign in Georgia was the

Clayton compromise which the Georgia senators had sustained, but which Stephens and Toombs had defeated in the House. This compromise proposed that all questions concerning slavery in the governments of the ceded territory be referred to the Supreme Court of the United States. Mr. Toombs declared that the Mexican law prohibiting slavery was still valid and would so remain; that Congress and not the courts must change this law.

The Clayton compromise, Mr. Toombs said, was only intended as " the Euthanasia of States' Rights. When our rights are clear, security for them should be free from all ambiguity. We ought never to surrender territory, until it shall be wrested from us as we have wrested it from Mexico. Such a surrender would degrade and demoralize our section and disable us for effective resistance against future aggression. It is far better that this new acquisition should be the grave of the republic than of the rights and honor of the South—and, from present indications, to this complexion it must come at last."

Mr. Toombs demanded that what was recognized by law as property in the slaveholding States should be recognized in the Mexican territory. "This boon," he pleaded, "may be worthless, but its surrender involves our honor. We can permit no discrimination against our section

or our institutions in dividing out the common
property of the republic. Their rights are not to
be abandoned, or bartered away in presidential
elections."

So Toombs and Stephens were central figures
in this national campaign. It was during this
canvass that Mr. Stephens became embroiled with
Judge Francis H. Cone, a prominent lawyer of
Georgia and a near neighbor. Mr. Stephens
heard that Judge Cone had denounced him as a
traitor for moving to table the Clayton compromise. Stephens had retorted sharply that if
Cone had said this he would slap his face. After
some correspondence the two men met in Atlanta,
September 4, 1848. The trouble was renewed:
Judge Cone denounced Mr. Stephens, who rapped
him over the shoulders with a whalebone cane.
Mr. Stephens was a fragile man, and Judge Cone,
with strong physique, closed in and forced him to
the floor. During the scuffle Mr. Stephens was
cut in six places. His life for a while was de-
spaired of. Upon his recovery he was received
with wild enthusiasm by the Whigs, who cheered
his pluck and regarded his return to the canvass
as an omen of victory.

Shortly afterward he wrote to Mrs. Toombs,
thanking her for her interest and solicitude during
his illness. He managed to write with his left

hand, as he could not use his right. "I hope," he says, "I will be able to take the stump again next week for old Zach. I think Mr. Toombs has had the weight of the canvass long enough, and though he has done gallant service, this but inspires me with the wish to lend all aid in my power. I think we shall yet be able to save the State. My faith is as strong as Mr. Preston's which, you know, was enough to move mountains. I got a letter the other day from Mr. C——, who gives it as his opinion that Ohio would go for General Taylor. If so, he will be elected. And you know how I shall hail such a result."

During Mr. Stephens' illness Mr. Toombs canvassed many of the counties in the Stephens district. Both men were reëlected to Congress, and Zachary Taylor received the electoral vote of Georgia over Lewis Cass of Michigan, and was elected President of the United States.

The Democrats, who put out a candidate this year against Mr. Toombs, issued an address which was evidently not inspired by the able and deserving gentleman who bore their standard, but was intended as a sharp rebuke to Mr. Toombs. It is interesting as showing how he was regarded by his friends, the enemy.

"Of an age when life's illusions have vanished," they said of the Democratic candidate, "he has no selfish aspirations, no vaulting ambition to carry him astray: no vanity to lead where it is glory enough to follow." They accorded to Mr. Toombs "a very showy cast of talent—better suited to the displays of the stump than the grave discussions of the legislative hall. His eloquence has that sort of splendor mixed with the false and true which is calculated to dazzle the multitude. He would rather win the applause of groundlings by some silly tale than gain the intelligent by the most triumphant course of reasoning." Mr. Toombs carried every county in the district and was returned to Congress by 1681 majority.

When Mr. Toombs returned to Washington he had commanded national prominence. He had not only carried his State for Zachary Taylor, but his speech in New York, during a critical period of the canvass, had turned the tide for the Whig candidate in the country. Toombs and Stephens naturally stood very near the administration. They soon had reason to see, however, that the Taylor Cabinet was not attentive to Southern counsels.

During the fight over the compromise measure in Congress the Northern papers printed sensational accounts of a rupture between President Taylor and Messrs. Toombs and Stephens. According to this account the Georgia congressmen

called on the President and expressed strong dis-
approbation of his stand upon the bill to organize
the Territory of New Mexico. It was said that
they even threatened to side with his opponents
to censure him upon his action in the case of
Secretary Crawford and the Golphin claim. The
President, the article recited, was very much
troubled over this interview and remained despond-
ent for several days. He took his bed and never
rallied, dying on the 9th of July, 1850. Mr.
Stephens published a card, promptly denying this
sensation. He said that neither he nor his colleague Mr. Toombs had visited the President at
all during or previous to his last illness, and that
no such scene had occurred.

Toombs and Stephens, in fact, were warm personal friends of George W. Crawford, who was
Secretary of War in Taylor's Cabinet. He had
served with them in the General Assembly of
Georgia and had twice been Governor of their
State. The Golphin claim, of which Governor
Crawford had been agent, had been collected from
the Secretary of the Treasury while Governor
Crawford was in the Cabinet, but President Taylor
had decided that as Governor Crawford was at the
head of an entirely different department of the
government, he had been guilty of no impropriety.
After the death of President Taylor, Governor

Crawford returned to Augusta and was tendered a public dinner by his fellow-citizens, irrespective of party. He delivered an eloquent and feeling address. He made an extensive tour abroad, then lived in retirement in Richmond County, enjoying the respect and confidence of his neighbors.

CHAPTER VI.

No legislative body ever assembled with more momentous measures before it than the thirty-first Congress of the United States. An immense area of unsettled public domain had been wrested from Mexico. The Territories of California, Utah, and New Mexico, amounting to several hundred thousand square miles, remained undisposed of. They comprised what Mr. Calhoun had termed the "Forbidden Fruit," and the trouble which beclouded their annexation threatened to surpass the storms of conquest.

Congress felt that it was absolutely without light to guide it. It had declined to extend the Missouri Compromise line to the Pacific Ocean. Henry Clay had pronounced such division of public domain between the sections a "Utopian dream," and Zachary Taylor had condemned the principle in the only message he ever delivered to Congress. What Mr. Lincoln afterward embodied in his famous expression that the Union could never exist "half slave, half free," had been actually anticipated. The whole territorial ques-

67

tion came up as a new problem. But if the crisis was now momentous the body of statesmen which considered it was a great one. The men and the hour seemed to meet in that supreme moment. The Senate consisted of sixty members, and for the last time that great trio of Clay, Calhoun, and Webster met upon its floor. Commencing their careers a generation before, with eventful lives and illustrious performance, they lingered one moment in this arena before passing forever from the scenes of their earthly efforts. All three had given up ambition for the Presidency, none of them had commenced to break in mental power, and each one was animated by patriotism to serve and save his country. William H. Seward had entered the Senate from New York; James M. Mason and Robert M. T. Hunter represented Virginia; Wm. C. Dawson had joined Mr. Berrien from Georgia; Salmon P. Chase appeared from Ohio; Jefferson Davis and Henry S. Foote illustrated Mississippi; Stephen A. Douglas had been promoted from the House in Illinois, and Samuel Houston was there from Texas. The House was unusually strong and divided with the Senate the stormy scenes and surpassing struggles over the compromise measures of 1850. It was the time of breaking up of party lines, and many believed that the hour of disunion had arrived.

The Whig caucus, which assembled to nominate a candidate for Speaker of the House, sustained a serious split. Robert Toombs offered a resolution that Congress should place no restriction upon slavery in the Territories. The Northern Whigs scouted the idea and Toombs led the Southern members out of the meeting. The organization of the House was delayed three weeks, and finally, under a plurality resolution, the Democrats elected Howell Cobb of Georgia Speaker over Robert C. Winthrop of Massachusetts. In the midst of these stormy scenes Mr. Toombs forced the fighting. He declared with impetuous manner that he believed the interests of his people were in danger and he was unwilling to surrender the great power of the Speaker's chair without security for the future.

" It seems," he said, " that we are to be intimidated by eulogies of the Union and denunciations of those who are not ready to sacrifice national honor, essential interests, and constitutional rights upon its altar. Sir, I have as much attachment to the Union of these States, under the Constitution of our fathers, as any freeman ought to have. I am ready to concede and sacrifice for it whatever a just and honorable man ought to sacrifice. I will do no more. I have not heeded the expression of those who did not understand or desired to misrepresent my conduct or opinions in relation to these questions, which, in my judgment, so vitally

affect it. The time has come when I shall not
only utter them, but make them the basis of my
political actions here. I do not then hesitate to
avow before this House and the country, and in the
presence of the living God, that if by your legislation you seek to drive us from the Territories purchased by the common blood and treasure of the
people, and to abolish slavery in the District, there-
by attempting to fix a national degradation upon
half the States of this confederacy, I am for disunion, and if my physical courage be equal to the
maintenance of my convictions of right and duty
I will devote all I am and all I have on earth to
its consummation.

" Give me securities that the power of organization which you seek will not be used to the injury
of my constituents; then you can have my coöperation, but not till then. Grant them, and you
prevent the disgraceful scenes of the last twenty-
four hours and restore tranquillity to the country.
Refuse them, and, as far as I am concerned, let
discord reign forever."

This speech fell like a clap of thunder. The
Wilmot Proviso waved like a black flag over the
heads of Southern men. No one had spoken
outright until Mr. Toombs in his bold, dashing,
Mirabeau style accepted the issue in the words
just given. The House was filled with storms of

applause and jeers, and, as can be imagined, Mr. Toombs' speech did not soothe the bitterness or alter the determination of either side.

On the 22d of December a conference was held by Whigs and Democrats, the Southern Whigs excepted, and a resolution reported that the person receiving the largest number of votes for Speaker, on a certain ballot, should be declared elected, provided this number should be the majority of a quorum, but not a majority of the House. Mr. Stanton of Tennessee offered this "plurality resolution."

Mr. Toombs sprang to his feet and declared that the House, until it organized, could not pass this or any other rule.

Members stood up and called Mr. Toombs to order, claiming that there was already a question pending. Mr. Stanton contended that he had the floor.

Toombs called out: "You may cry 'order,' gentlemen, until the heavens fall; you cannot take this place from me. I have the right to protest against this transaction. It is not with you to say whether this right shall be yielded or when it shall be yielded."

Mr. Stevens of Pennsylvania: "I call the gentleman to order."

Mr. Toombs: "I say that by the law of 1789

this House, until a Speaker is elected and gentlemen have taken the oath of office, has no right to
adopt any rules whatever."

(Loud cries of " order.")

Mr. Toombs: "Gentlemen may amuse themselves crying ' order.' "

(Calls of "order.")

Mr. Toombs: " But I have the right and I intend to maintain the right to——"

Mr. Vandyke called upon the clerk to put the preceding question. "Let us see," he said, "whether
the gentleman will disregard the order of this
House."

Mr. Toombs: "I have the floor, and the clerk
cannot put the question."

"The House," he said, "has no right. Gentlemen may cry 'order' and interrupt me. It is
mere brute force, attempting by the power of
lungs to put me down."

Confusion increased. Members called out to encourage Mr. Toombs, and others to put him down.
In the midst of this babel he continued to speak,
his black hair thrown back, his face flushed, and
his eyes blazing like suns. His deep voice could
be heard above the shouts like a lion's roar. Members shouted to the clerk to call the roll for the
yeas and nays.

Toombs continued : " If you seek by violating the
common law of parliament, the laws of the land,

and the Constitution of the United States, to put me down ["order, order, call the roll"], you will find it a vain and futile attempt. ["Order."] I am sure I am indebted to the ignorance of my character on the part of those who are thus disgracing themselves ["order, order"], if they suppose any such efforts as they are now making will succeed in driving me from the position which I have assumed. I stand upon the Constitution of my country, upon the liberty of speech which you have treacherously violated, and upon the rights of my constituents, and your fiendish yells may be well raised to drown an argument which you tremble to hear. You claim and have exercised the power to prevent all debate upon any and every subject, yet you have not as yet shown your right to sit here at all.   I will not presume that you have any such right ["order, order"]. I will not suppose that the American people have elected such agents to represent them.   I therefore demand that they shall comply with the Act of 1789 before I shall be bound to submit to their authority." (Loud cries of "order.")

The Act to which Mr. Toombs referred recited that the oath must be administered by the Speaker to all the members present, and to the clerk, previous to entering on any other business.   This he tried to read, but cries of "order" drowned his voice.

Throwing aside his manual Mr. Toombs walked further out into the aisle and assumed a yet more defiant position.

"You refuse," he said, "to hear either the Constitution or the law. Perhaps you do well to listen to neither; they all speak a voice of condemnation to your reckless proceedings. But if you will not hear them the country will. Every freeman from the Atlantic to the Pacific shore shall hear them, and every honest man shall consider them. You cannot stifle the voice that shall reach their ears. The electric spark shall proclaim to the freemen of this republic that an American Congress, having conceived the purpose to violate the Constitution and the laws to conceal their enormities, have disgraced the record of their proceedings by placing upon it a resolution that their representatives shall not be heard in their defense, and finding this illegal resolution inadequate to secure so vile an end, have resorted to brutish yells and cries to stifle the words of those they cannot intimidate."

The clerk continued to call the roll, and Mr. Toombs with splendid audacity turned upon him. Pointing his finger at the *locum tenens*, he cried with scorn: "I ask by what authority that man stands there and calls these names. By what authority does HE interfere with the rights of a member of this House. [The clerk continued to call.] He is an intruder, and how dares he to interrupt

members in the exercise of their constitutional
rights. Gentlemen, has the sense of shame departed with your sense of right, that you permit a
creature, an interloper, in no wise connected with
you, to stand at that desk and interrupt your
order ? "

Mr. Toombs continued, amid these boisterous
scenes, his alternate rôle of argument, of appeal,
of denunciation. He contended that a power delegated to the House must be used by a majority of
the House. He concluded :

" I therefore demand of you before the country,
in the name of the Constitution and the people, to
repeal your illegal rule, reject the one on your
table, and proceed to the discharge of your high
duties, which the people have confided to you, according to the unvarying precedents of your people
and the law of the land."

This performance was denounced by Northern
restrictionists as menacing and insolent. Mr. Stephens, in his " War Between the States," contended that it should rather be considered in the
light of a wonderful exhibition of physical as well
as intellectual prowess—in this, that a single man
should have been able, thus successfully, to speak
to a tumultuous crowd and, by declamatory denunciations combined with solid argument, to silence
an infuriated assembly.

The noise during the delivery of this speech

gradually ceased. The clerk stopped calling the roll, all interruptions were suspended and "every eye," says Mr. Stephens, "was fixed upon the speaker." It was a picture worthy of ranking with Lamartine's great speech to the revolutionists in France.

On the 29th of February Mr. Toombs addressed the House upon the general territorial question. He said:

"We had our institutions when you sought our allegiance. We were content with them then, and we are content with them now. We have not sought to thrust them upon you, nor to inter-fere with yours. If you believe what you say, that yours are so much the best to promote the happiness and good government of society, why do you fear our equal competition with you in the Territories? We only ask that our common government shall protect us both, equally, until the Territories shall be admitted as States into the Union, then to leave their citizens free to adopt any domestic policy in reference to this subject which in their judgment may best promote their interest and their happiness. The demand is just. Grant it, and you place your prosperity and ours upon a solid foundation; you perpetuate the Union so necessary to your prosperity; you solve the problem of republican government. If it be demonstrated that the Constitution is powerless for our protection, it will then be not only the right but the duty of the slaveholding States to resume the powers which they have conferred upon this government and to seek new safeguards for their future protection. . . . We took the Constitution and the Union together. We will have both or we will have neither. This cry of Union is the masked battery behind which the rights of the South are to be assaulted. Let the South mark the man who is for the Union at every hazard and to the last extremity ; when the day of her peril comes he will be the imitator of that character, the base Judas, who for thirty pieces of silver threw away a pearl richer than all his tribe."

On the 15th of June, 1850, while the compromise measures were shifting from House to House, the question was put to some of the advocates of the admission of California, whether they would under any circumstances admit a slave State into the Union. They declined to say.

Mr. Toombs arose and declared that the South did not deny the right of a people framing a State constitution to admit or exclude slavery. The South had uniformly maintained this right.

"The evidence is complete," he said. "The North repudiated this principle."

"I intend to drag off the mask before the consummation of the act. We do not oppose California on account of the antislavery clause in her constitution. It was her right, and I am not even prepared to say she acted unwisely in its exercise—that is her business: but I stand upon the great principle that the South has the right to an equal participation in the Territories of the United States. I claim the right for her to enter them with all her property and security to enjoy it. She will divide with you if you wish it: but the right to enter all, or divide, I will never surrender. In my judgment this right, involving, as it does, political equality, is worth a dozen such Unions as we have, even if each were a thousand times more valuable than this. I speak not for others, but for myself. Deprive us of this right, and appropriate this common property to yourselves; it is then your government, not mine. Then I am its enemy, and I will then, if I can, bring my children and my constituents to the altar of liberty, and like Hamilcar, I will swear them to eternal hostility to your foul domination. Give us our just rights, and we are ready, as ever heretofore, to stand by the Union, every part of it, and its every interest. Refuse it, and, for one, I will strike for independence."

Mr. Stephens declared that this speech produced the greatest sensation he had ever seen in the House. "It created a perfect commotion."

These heated arguments of Mr. Toombs were

delivered under the menace of the Wilmot Proviso, or slavery restriction. When this principle was abandoned and the compromise measures passed, Mr. Toombs uttered, as we shall see, far different sentiments.

In the Senate Mr. Clay, the Great Pacificator, had introduced his compromise resolutions to admit California under the government already formed, prohibiting slavery; to organize territorial governments for Utah and New Mexico without slavery restrictions; to pass a fugitive-slave law, and to abolish the slave trade in the District of Columbia. On the 7th of March, 1850, Mr. Webster delivered his great Union speech, in which for the first time he took strong grounds against congressional restriction in the Territories. It created a profound sensation. It was on the 4th of March that Senator Mason read for Mr. Calhoun the last speech that the latter ever prepared. It was a memorable moment when the great Carolinian, with the stamp of death already upon him, reiterated his love for the Union under the Constitution, but declared, with the prescience of a seer, that the only danger threatening the government arose from its centralizing tendency. It was "the sunset of life which gave him mystical lore."

Debate continued through the spring and summer with increasing bitterness. On the 31st of

July Mr. Clay's "Omnibus Bill," as it was
called, "went to pieces," but the Senate took up
the separate propositions, passed them, and trans-
mitted them to the House.

Here the great sectional contest was renewed.
Mr. Toombs offered an amendment that the
Constitution of the United States, and such
statutes thereof as may not be locally inapplica-
ble, and the common law, as it existed in the
British colonies of America until July 4, 1776,
shall be the exclusive laws of said Territory upon
the subject of African slavery, until altered by
the proper authority. This was rejected by the
House. On September 6 the Texas and New
Mexico bill, with the Boyd amendment, passed
by a vote of 108 to 97—and the anti-restriction-
ists, as Mr. Stephens said, won the day at last.
This was the great compromise of that year, and
the point established was that, since the principle
of division of territory between the North and
South had been abandoned, the principle of congressional restriction should also be abandoned,
and that all new States, whether north or south
of 36° 30', should be admitted into the Union
"either with or without slavery as their constitution might prescribe at the time of their
admission."

During this memorable contest Mr. Toombs
was in active consultation with Northern states-

men, trying to effect the compromise. He insisted that there should be no congressional exclusion of slavery from the public domain, but that in organizing territorial governments the people should be allowed to authorize or restrict, as they pleased. Until these principles were settled, however, he would fight the admission of California. Into this conference Mr. Stephens and Howell Cobb were admitted, and at a meeting at the house of the latter an agreement was reached between the three Georgians and the representatives from Kentucky, Ohio, and Illinois, that California should be admitted: that the Territories should be organized without restriction, and that their joint efforts should be used to bring this about as well as to defeat any attempt to abolish slavery in the District of Columbia. Here was the essence of the compromise, built upon the great measures of Henry Clay, and finally ripening into the legislation of that session. Here was the agreement of that compact which formed the great "Constitutional Union Party" in Georgia, and which erected a bulwark against disunion, not only in Georgia, but on the whole Southern seaboard. The disunion movement failed in 1850. "At the head of the States which had the merit of stopping it," said Thomas H. Benton, "was Georgia, the greatest of the South Atlantic States." And that Georgia stood

steadfast in her place, and declined every over-
ture for secession, was because of the united
prestige and splendid abilities of Howell Cobb,
Alexander H. Stephens, and Robert Toombs.

During this stormy session Mr. Toombs' heart
continually yearned for home. He was a model
husband and a remarkable domestic character.
The fiery scenes of the forum did not ween him
from his family. On the 29th of August, 1850,
he wrote to his wife :

We have before us the whole of the territorial questions,
and shall probably pass or reject them in a few days or at
most in a week. I am greatly in hopes that we will not
pass over them without final action of some sort, and if we
can get rid of them I shall have nothing to prevent my
coming home at the time appointed. I begin to be more
anxious to see you than to save the republic. Such is a
sweet woman's fascination for men's hearts. The old
Roman Antony threw away an empire rather than abandon his lovely Cleopatra, and the world has called him a
fool for it. I begin to think that he was the wiser man,
and that the world was well lost for love.

CHAPTER VII.

WHEN Mr. Toombs came home in the fall of 1850 he found the State in upheaval. Disunion sentiment was rife. He was confronted by garbled extracts of his speeches in Congress, and made to pose as the champion of immediate secession. He had aided in perfecting the great compromise and was resolved that Georgia should take her stand firmly and unequivocally for the Union and the Constitution. Governor Towns had issued a call for a State convention; Mr. Toombs took prompt issue with the spirit and purpose of the call. He declared that the legislature had endangered the honor of the State and that the Governor had put the people in a defile. "We must either repudiate this policy, or arm," he said. "I favor the former measure."

Mr. Toombs issued a ringing address to the people. It bore date of October 9, 1850. He proclaimed that "the first act of legislative hostility was the first act of Southern resistance." He urged the South to stand by the Constitution and the laws in good faith, until wrong was consummated or the act of exclusion placed upon the statute books.

Mr. Toombs said that the South had not secured its full rights. " But the fugitive-slave law which I demanded was granted. The abolition of slavery in the District of Columbia and proscription in the Territories were defeated, crushed, and abandoned. We have firmly established great and important principles. The South has compromised no right, surrendered no principle, and lost not an inch of ground in this great contest. I did not hesitate to accept these acts, but gave them my ready support."

Addressing himself to the disunionists he said : " They have abandoned their errors, but not their object. Being bent upon the ruin of the republic they use truth or error for its accomplishment, as best suits the exigencies of the hour. If these people are honest in their convictions, they may find abundant consolation in the fact that the principle is neither conceded, compromised, nor endangered by these bills. It is strengthened, not weakened by them, and will survive their present zeal and future apostasy."

Mr. Toombs called on all men of integrity, intellect, and courage to come into the service of the State and prove their devotion to the Constitution and the Union. " With no memory of past differences," he said, " careless of the future, I am ready to unite with any portion or all my countrymen in defense of the integrity of the republic."

Mr. Toombs took the stump, and his words rang out like an alarm bell. Men speak to-day of his activity and earnestness in that great campaign, as with "rapid and prompt perception, clear, close reasoning, cutting eloquence, and unsparing hand he rasped the follies of disunion and secession." A prominent journal of that day, speaking of his speech in Burke County, Ga., declared that "his manly eloquence has shaken and shivered to the base the pedestal upon which the monument of American ruin was to be erected."

In November of that year a convention of delegates from Southern States was held at Nashville. Ex-Governor Charles J. McDonald represented Georgia. That meeting protested against the admission of California with slavery restriction; charged that the policy of Congress had been to exclude the Southern States from the Territories, and plainly asserted that the powers of the sovereign States could be resumed by the States separately. On November 3 the election of delegates to the Georgia convention was held. Toombs had already turned the tide. A great majority of Union men were chosen. Whigs and Democrats united to save the State. Toombs stood convicted before many of his old followers of " unsoundness on the slavery question "—but he was performing his greatest public work.

Among the delegates elected by the people to the Georgia convention, which met at Milledge-ville, December 10, 1850, were Toombs and Ste-phens and many of the best men in the State.

The work of the distinguished body was mem-orable. They adopted the celebrated "Georgia Platform," whose utterances were talismanic. Charles J. Jenkins reported the resolutions. They recited, first, that Georgia held the American Union secondary in importance to the rights and principles it was bound to perpetuate. That as the thirteen original colonies found union impossi-ble without compromise, the thirty-one of this day will yield somewhat in the conflict of opinion and policy, to preserve the Union. That Georgia had maturely considered the action of Congress (em-bracing the compromise measures) and—while she does not wholly approve it—will abide by it as a permanent adjustment of this sectional controversy. That the State would in future resist, even to the disruption of the Union, any act prohibiting slav-ery in the Territories, or a refusal to admit a slave State. The fifth plank declared for a faithful ex-ecution of the Fugitive-slave bill.

Upon this platform the Union men selected Howell Cobb as their candidate for Governor. The Southern Rights men selected Charles J. Mc-

Donald. This party claimed that the South was degraded by the compromise measures. Their platform was based upon the Virginia and Kentucky resolution. It asserted the right of secession and maintained the constitutionality and necessity of intervention by Congress in favor of admitting slavery into the Territories. The distinct doctrine of the compromise measures was non-intervention.

Howell Cobb was a born leader of men. Personally he was the most popular man in the State. Entering public life at an early age he had been a congressman at twenty-eight. He had been leader of the Southern party, and was chosen Speaker, as we have seen, in 1849, when only thirty-four years old. He had been known as a strong friend of the Union, and some of the extreme States' Rights men called him a "consolidationist."

In his letter accepting the nomination for Governor, he alluded to the long-cherished doctrine of non-intervention. The Wilmot Proviso had been withdrawn and the Union saved. The people had been awarded the right to determine for themselves in the Territories whether or not slavery was to be a part of their social system.

No man was so tireless or conspicuous in this campaign as Mr. Toombs. Although expressing a desire that someone else should go to Congress from his district, he accepted a renomination to assert his principles. He did not, however, con-

fine his work to his district. He traveled from
one end of the State to the other. He recognized
that party organization in Georgia had been over-
thrown and party lines shattered in every State in
the Union. He boldly declared that a continuance of the Union was not incompatible with the
rights of every State. He asserted that the ani-
mating spirit of his opponents, the States' Rights
party, was hostility to the Union. Some of the
members still submitted to the humiliation of rais-
ing the cry of "the Union," he said, but it was a
"masked battery," from which the very Union was
to be assailed. Mr. Toombs announced on the
stump that "the good sense, the firmness, the patriotism of the people, would shield the Union from
assault of our own people. They will maintain
it as long as it deserves to be maintained."

Mr. Toombs admitted that the antislavery sentiment of the North had become more violent from
its defeat on the compromise measures.

"What did this party demand, and what did it
get?" he asked on the stump. "It was driven
from every position it assumed. It demanded the
express prohibition of slavery, the Wilmot Proviso,
in the Territories. It lost it. It demanded the
abolition of slavery in the District of Columbia,
and the slave trade between the States. It lost
both. It demanded the affirmance of the oft-re-
peated declaration that there should be no more

slave States admitted into the Union. Congress enacted that States hereafter coming into the Union should be admitted with or without slavery, as such States might determine for themselves. It demanded a trial by jury for fugitives at the place of arrest. It lost this also. Its acknowledged exponent is the Free-Soil party. The Whig party has succumbed to it. It is thoroughly denationalized and desectionalized, and will never make another national contest. We are indebted to the defeat of the policy of these men for the existence of the government to-day. The Democratic party of the North, though prostrated, is not yet destroyed. Our true policy is to compel both parties to purge themselves of this dangerous element. If either will, to sustain it. If neither will, then we expect to preserve the Union. We must overthrow both parties and rally the sound men to a common standard. This is the only policy which can preserve both our rights and the Union."

On the 1st of August, 1851, Mr. Toombs spoke in Elberton. He was in the full tide of his manhood, an orator without equal; a statesman without fear or reproach. Personally, he was a splendid picture, full of health and vitality. He had been prosperous in his affairs. He was prominent in public life and overbore all opposition. His powers were in their prime. In his speech to his constituents he mentioned the fact that his oppo-

nents had criticised the manner in which he traveled (alluding to his fine horses and servants). He
wanted the people to know that the money was
his, and that he made $5000 a year in Elbert
alone. " Who would say that he had not earned
his money? He had a right to spend it as he
chose. Perish such demagogy—such senseless
stuff." The people cheered him to the echo
for his candor and audacity.

" What presumption," he said, " for the States'
Rights men to nominate McDonald for Governor
—a man who supported Jackson's Force bill—a
man who had grown gray in federalism? He
was the man brought to teach the people of
Elbert States' Rights. It would be a curious
subject of inquiry to find out when this neo-
phyte had changed, and by what process the
change had been wrought."

Toombs was alluded to by the correspondents
as " Richard, the Lion-hearted," with strong arm
and ponderous battle-ax, as he went about winning
victories. Stephens, no less effective and influen-
tial, seemed to be the great Saladin with well-
tempered Damascus blade—so skillful as to sever
the finest down. The people were in continued
uproar as Toombs moved from place to place.

In Jefferson County, Mr. Toombs denied that
the South had yielded any demand she ever made,
or had sacrificed any principle she ever held. He

cried that "opposition to Toombs and Stephens seemed to be the principle of political faith on the other side." Toombs declared that Stephens "carried more brains and more soul for the least flesh of any man God Almighty ever made."

Mr. Toombs repeated that if the slaveholders had lost the right to carry slavery into California, they had lost it upon sound principle. The right of each State to prescribe its own institutions is a right above slavery. Slavery is only an incident to this right. This principle lies at the foundation of all good government. He had always held it and would always hold it:

Till wrapped in flames the realms of ether glow,
And Heaven's last thunder shakes the world below.

He deeply sympathized with those Southern Rights men who denounced the Union they professed to love.

Speaking of the sudden change of some of his opponents in political principles, Toombs declared they "would profess any opinion to gain votes. It had been the belief of Crawford that if a man changed politics after thirty he was a rascal."

In Marietta Mr. Toombs addressed an enthusiastic crowd. A journalist said of him: "He is my *beau idéal* of a statesman. Frank, honest, bold, and eloquent, he never fails to make a deep impression. Many of the fire-eaters (for they *will* go to hear him) looked as if they would make their escape from his withering and scathing rebuke." Toombs derided the States' Rights men for declaring that they were friends of the Union under which they declared they were "degraded and oppressed." The greatest stumbling-block to Toombs' triumphant tour was to be presented with bits of his own speeches delivered during the excitement of the last Congress.

He had said in one of these impassioned outbursts: "He who counts the danger of defending his own home is already degraded. The people who count the cost of maintaining their political rights are ready for slavery."

In Lexington he was accused of having said that if the people understood this slavery question as well as he did "they would not remain in the Union five minutes." This provoked a bitter controversy. Mr. Toombs denied the remark, and declared he was willing to respond personally and publicly to the author.

As the campaign became more heated, Toombs, Stephens, and Cobb redoubled their efforts and drew their lines more closely. This combination was invincible. It was evident that they would carry the State, but some of the prominent men in Georgia were ruled out under what was thought to be the bitter spirit of the canvass. One of these was Charles J. Jenkins, and the

other, John McPherson Berrien. The former had
drawn the celebrated Georgia Platform, and was
devoted to the Union. The latter was United
States Senator from Georgia, and, as his successor
was to be chosen by the legislature soon to be
elected, there was much curiosity to find out his
real position in this canvass. Mr. Jenkins declared that he considered Mr. Berrien "as good a
Union man and as safe a representative of the
party as any within its ranks." Berrien acquiesced
in but did not eulogize the compromise measures.
He did not oppose or favor the State convention
of 1850. When he submitted to the Senate the
Georgia Platform, he declared that he did not
surrender the privileges of a free choice. He
supported McDonald for Governor against Cobb,
and it was soon evident that he was not in full
sympathy with the winning party.

The Constitutional Union men won a signal
victory. Howell Cobb was elected Governor by
a large majority over Charles J. McDonald, who
had been twice Governor and who was one of the
strongest men in Georgia. Robert Toombs was
reëlected to Congress over Robert McMillen of
Elbert, and Mr. Stephens defeated D. W. Lewis
of Hancock.

The legislature convened in November, 1851.
It was largely made up of Union men. Judge
Berrien was not a candidate for reëlection to the

United States Senate. He wrote a letter ⸯa which he reviewed his course during the campaign. He said:

"I asserted in terms which even cavilers could not misunderstand nor any honest man doubt, my devotion to the Union, my unfaltering determination to maintain by all constitutional means, and with undiminished zeal, the equal rights of the South, and my acquiescence in the compromise measures. Satisfied that such declarations, in the excited state of feeling, would not meet the exactions of either party in a contest peculiarly bitter, and unable to sacrifice for the purpose of victory the dictates of conscience or the convictions of judgment, I expressed a willingness to retire."

On the 10th of November Robert Toombs was elected United States Senator. In the caucus he secured 73 votes, and in the open Assembly next day he received 120 votes, scattering, 50.

Never was reward more swift or signal to the master-mind of a campaign. If he had been the leader of the extreme Southern wing in Congress, he had shown his willingness to accept a compromise and go before the people in defense of the Union.

He was charged with having aroused the Secession storm. If he had unwittingly done so in Congress in order to carry his point, he proved himself powerful in stopping it at home. What some of his critics had said of him was true:

"The rashest of talkers, he was the safest of counselors." Certain it is that at a moment of national peril he repelled the charge of being an "irreconcilable," and proved to be one of the stanchest supporters of the Union.

In Milledgeville, during the turmoil attending the election of United States Senator in November, 1851 Mr. Toombs wrote to his wife as follows :

Since I wrote you last I have been in the midst of an exciting political contest with constantly varying aspects. The friends of Judge Berrien are moving every possible spring to compass my defeat, but as yet I have constantly held the advantage over them. They started Mr. Jenkins and kept him up, under considerable excitement, until he came to town yesterday and instantly withdrew his name. To-day they have started a new batch of candidates : Judge Hill, Hines Holt, Warren, Charlton, and others, all of whom they seek to combine. I think I can beat the whole combination, though it is too close to be comfortable. It is impossible to give an idea of every varying scene, but as I have staked my political fortunes on success, if I am defeated in this conflict my political race is over, and perhaps I feel too little interest in the result for success.

Dawson is at home sick ; Stephens is not here ; so I am standing very much on my own hand, breasting the conflict alone. So I shall have the consolation of knowing that, if I succeed, the victory will be all my own. The contest will be decided by Monday next, and perhaps sooner. . . . . As soon as it is over I shall leave here and shall be at home at furthest to-day week. If I were not complicated in this business, nothing would induce me to

go into it. There are so many unpleasant things connected
with it, which will at least serve as lessons for the future,
whatever may be the result. You can see from this letter
how deeply I am immersed in this contest, yet I am getting
so impatient to come home that even defeat would be better than this eternal annoyance.

Toombs.

CHAPTER VIII.

In this first struggle between Secession and the
Union Georgia had taken the lead, but Georgia
had not been the only State involved. The fight
was waged just as fiercely in Mississippi, when
Henry S. Foote, the Union candidate, was elected
Governor over Jefferson Davis. But the Georgia
Platform was the corner-stone of the Southern
victory. Her action gave peace and quiet to the
whole Union, and the success of the triumvirate
that year offered assurance of strength and security
to the country. The national parties were quick
to align themselves on this platform. The Democratic convention, which assembled in Baltimore
June 1, declared that "the party would abide by
and adhere to a faithful execution of the Acts
known as the Compromise Measures, settled by the
last Congress." The Whig convention, which met
also at Baltimore, June 16, proclaimed that "the
series of Acts of the thirty-first Congress, known as
the Compromise Measures of 1850, the Act known
as the Fugitive-slave law included, are received and
acquiesced in by the Whig party of the United
States as a settlement in principle and substance

97

of the dangerous and exciting questions which they embrace."

"The truth is," said Mr. Stephens in his " War Between the States," " an overwhelming majority of the people, North as well as South, was in favor of maintaining these principles."

Under these conditions the presidential campaign of 1852 was opened. The Southern Whigs did not, as a body, accept the Baltimore nominee, General Winfield Scott. They claimed that he had refused to express any direct approval of the platform relating to the compromise. Mr. Toombs demanded that his candidate plant himself unequivocally upon this platform. He noticed that the opponents of the Fugitive-slave law were strong for Scott. Feeling in the South was still running high. Some extremists held that no Northern man was fit to be trusted. Mr. Toombs declared that there were good and true men at the North and that he would " hold party associations with no others."

In a speech to his own townspeople in Washington, Ga., during this presidential campaign, Mr. Toombs declared that he had not changed one iota, but was ready now to support the men who would plant themselves on the broad principles of the Constitution and the country. He said General Scott had no claims whatever upon the people. He spoke of him as a great general, and alluded in glowing terms to his achievements in arms against the Mexicans and Indians. But General Scott, he believed, was a Free-Soil candidate. He would be in favor of annexing Canada, but no more slave territory. Mr. Toombs alluded to the Democratic candidate for President, General Franklin Pierce, as a very consistent man in all his senatorial career, and believed he was the safest man on the slavery question north of Mason and Dixon's line. He preferred Pierce to Scott, but said he would not vote for either. The contest was "between a big general and a little general."

Mr. Toombs launched into a magnificent tribute to Daniel Webster as a statesman and friend of the Constitution. It was Webster who had stayed the flood of abolition and killed the Wilmot Proviso; who had dared, in the face of the North, and in defiance of his constituents, to boldly defend the rights of the South and exclaim, "O God, I will be just!"

This allusion of Mr. Toombs rang throughout the State. Its significance lay in the fact that the Whigs of Georgia, in convention assembled, had nominated Daniel Webster for President and Charles J. Jenkins for vice-president of the United States. Without chance of national success, this ticket was received with strong expression of indorsement. Since his celebrated "4th of March"

speech, in the Senate, Mr. Webster had been a
favorite in the South. He had abandoned the
Wilmot Proviso and accepted the Fugitive-slave
law to conciliate the sections, and the addition of
his great name to seal the Compromise of 1850
was regarded in the South as an act of patriotism
reached by few men in the country's history. His
speech had made a profound impression. "The
friends of the Union under the Constitution were
strengthened in their hopes, and inspired with renewed energies by its high and lofty sentiments."
Commanding always the respect and admiration of
the Southern people Mr. Webster now took the
place in their affections just made vacant by the
death of Henry Clay. Mr. Webster must have
put aside all political ambition when he made
this peaceful concession. His new-found strength
in the South did not add to his popularity in
the North. When the Whig convention of 1852
met in Baltimore, Mr. Webster was Secretary of
State under President Fillmore. He had added
fresh luster to his name by his latest services to
the nation. But the prestige of his life and labors
did not override the passions of the hour, and Winfield Scott was nominated for the Presidency.
This broke the last tie which held the Southern
Whigs in national allegiance. Circumstances were
forcing them into the Democratic party, but they

made a final stand under the name of Daniel Webster.

To Mr. Toombs, the regard of the Whigs of Georgia for Mr. Webster was especially gratifying. He had lived next door to the great Massachusetts statesman during his residence in Washington, and had seen him often in the privacy of his home. He had consulted closely with him during the exciting days of the compromise measures, and was advised by Mr. Webster about the Whig platform at Baltimore. He recognized the surpassing greatness of the man, and when he sounded the praises of Webster it came straight from an honest heart.

Charles J. Jenkins, a native of Beaufort, S. C., had studied law with Senator Berrien and practiced in Augusta. His nomination to second place on the Webster ticket was a pledge of the high favor of the Whigs. Mr. Jenkins was five years the senior of Mr. Toombs; had served with him in the State Legislature and, like Toombs, had been allied with the Troup party in Georgia. Mr. Jenkins had been three times Speaker of the lower branch of the General Assembly, and in 1842 had received the entire Whig vote for United States Senator. Upon the resignation of McKennon of Pennsylvania, President Fillmore had, through Mr. Toombs, offered the Interior Department to Mr. Jenkins. This position, however, was declined because of pressing duties in the courts.

In the senatorial election of 1851 Mr. Jenkins would have been a formidable candidate for United States Senator again, had not his strong friendship both for Senator Berrien and Mr. Toombs dictated his declining the use of his name. He was a man of high ability and pure character.

Georgia became a national battle-ground during this campaign. Besides the regular Whig and Democratic and the Webster tickets, there was an extreme faction of States' Rights men, who would not accept any of these candidates. They called on George M. Troup, then living in retirement in Montgomery County. He wrote a ringing letter accepting the nomination of the " Southern Rights " party for President. He was seventy-two years old, but his cherished principles, which he had proclaimed in the face of Adams and Jackson, were now repeated for the people of another generation,

The gallant body of Union Whigs were destined to deep affliction. On the 24th of October, 1852, ten days before the national election, Daniel Webster died. The land was filled with lamentation, for there was no North, no South, in this sorrow.

The State of Georgia, which in 1848 had voted for Taylor, now turned about and voted for Pierce and King. On November 2d the South Carolina Legislature also cast 135 votes for the Pierce electors. General Scott carried but four States in the Union, caused, as Mr. Stephens and Mr. Toombs thought, by his refusal to indorse the Compromise of 1850.

On July 3, 1852, Mr. Toombs, then a member of the House, submitted an elaborate statement of his political position. He made the point that presidents, as then put forward, were not real representatives of the country or even of a party. From the beginning of the government up to 1836 the presidency had been filled by ripe statesmen and tried patriots. *All* were excluded from competition except those who had great experience in public affairs, and who had commended themselves to the people by wisdom, virtue, and high services. Such men had no need of hired biographers and venal letter-writers to inform the people who they were. They needed no interpreters of letters to the public, cunningly devised to mystify what they pretended to elucidate. National conventions, Mr. Toombs contended, were contrivances to secure popular support to those who were not entitled to public confidence.

Mr. Toombs was an enemy to mere convention. All party machinery, all irregular organizations, which are unknown to the Constitution, he re-

garded as dangerous to public liberty. He had
noticed that this machinery had been deadly to
the great men of the nation and productive only
of mediocrity. Obedience to them, he contended,
was infidelity to popular rights. " This system,"
said he, " has produced none of those illustrious
men who have become so distinguished in their
country's history; none of those political lights
which have shone so brilliantly on this Western
continent for half a century. Nearly all of them
have departed from us. Who is to take the
place of the distinguished Carolinian ? " he asked.
" He was the handiwork of God himself and of
the people—not party machinery. Who is to
fill the place of the great Kentuckian ? When
worthily filled, it will not be by these nurseries
of faction.

" The friends of the Compromise," said Mr.
Toombs, " demand no sectional candidate. They
were willing to accept the great New England
statesman, notwithstanding they may point to
disagreements with him in the past. He has
thrown the weight of his mighty intellect into the
scales of concord, in the darkest and most perilous hour of the conflict. And Southern Whigs
would have struggled with pride and energy to
have seen the greatest intellect of the age preside
over the greatest republic of the world. He was
defeated in convention by the enemies of the

compromise measure, because he was its friend. And this was the true reason of his exclusion. It is a sufficient reason for the friends of the measure, North and South, to oppose and defeat General Scott's nomination. My action shall respond to my convictions."

Mr. Toombs had seen Calhoun, Clay, and Webster, one by one, retired before Van Buren, Harrison, and Scott. Was it any wonder that, in breaking away from the old Whig party, he should denounce the system which had blighted its brightest men and which, in his opinion, had retired the greatest statesman in the world before an issue of sectional prejudice ? Mr. Toombs never again gave allegiance to conventions or obeyed the dictates of party caucuses. From 1854 to 1860 he was a Democrat. After the war he acted mainly with the party which sympathized with the South. But his great power made him independent. He did not hesitate to criticise Pierce or Buchanan, or to upbraid Jefferson Davis, the head of the Southern Confederacy. He repudiated the nomination. of Horace Greeley by his party. He called a meeting in his own room in an Atlanta hotel in 1872, and put A. H. Stephens before the people for Congress. In 1878, when the organized Democracy of Georgia antagonized Dr. William H. Felton for Congress in the seventh Georgia district, Mr Toombs wrote a letter to the press, in which he declared that party conventions were merely advisory. " When their action becomes authoritative, they are usurpers. They deprive the people of free elections. Let their actions be approved or disapproved by the elections of the people." He supported Mr. Stephens, who did not hesitate to " tote his own skillet," when occasion required. Toombs' independence was lordly. He believed in the utmost freedom in public affairs. Machinery was as hateful to him as to Thomas Jefferson. He was " the prince of innovation ; the foe to all convention." No less than of Burke, it was said of him that " born for the universe, he did not surrender to party," but General Longstreet declared of Robert Toombs that he needed only discipline to make him a great military genius. This was the radical flaw in his make-up. How near he came to the ideal of a statesman posterity must judge.

CHAPTER IX.

TOOMBS IN THE SENATE.

WHEN Robert Toombs entered the Senate of the United States, in 1853, the *personnel* of that body had changed since the great debates on the compromise measures. Calhoun had died before the compromise was effected, and only a short time after his last address had been read to the Senate by Mr. Mason of Virginia. Clay survived his last greatest work but two years, and on the 29th of June, 1852, was no more. Daniel Webster lived only four months longer than Mr. Clay. Among the new leaders in that body were Stephen A. Douglas of Illinois, William M. Seward of New York, Salmon P. Chase of Ohio, and Charles Sumner of Massachusetts. To this list may be added the familiar names of Thompson of Mississippi, Bayard of Delaware, Toucey of Connecticut, Slidell of Louisiana, Achison of Missouri, Bell of Tennessee, and Cass of Michigan.

The third great sectional fight on the Territories came up on the report to organize a government for that tract of public domain lying in the

107

Louisiana cession, known as Kansas and Nebraska. In doing this, Mr. Douglas, as chairman of the Committee on Territories, adopted the same principle on the slavery question as had been settled in the Utah and New Mexico bills of 1850.

The words of the Nebraska bill were that " said Territory, or any portion of the same, shall be received into the Union with or without slavery as their constitutions may prescribe at the time of their admission." Mr. Douglas claimed that the question of congressional interference was an " exploded doctrine "; that the Missouri Compromise bill had been ignored by North and South ; that the Wilmot Proviso had been rejected altogether ; and that the principles of 1850 had superseded the principles of 1820. The committee sought to avoid the perils of slavery agitation for all time, they claimed, by withdrawing the question of slavery from the halls of Congress and from national politics. " Let the new States and Territories," they said, " settle this matter for themselves." Mr. Sumner of Massachusetts took the lead in opposing the Kansas-Nebraska bill. He declared that the bill violated the principles of the Missouri Compromise, which prohibited slavery in all that territory ceded by France and lying north of 36° 30'. He and his friends held that this was a "sacred compact," and this territory could not be controlled by the same principles as the land secured from Mexico.

The second bill drawn by Mr. Douglas, which provided for the establishment of two territorial governments in Kansas and Nebraska, instead of one, expressly repealed the Missouri Compromise as being inconsistent with the principles of non-intervention by Congress. Here, then, the contest waged anew.

One of the first speeches made by Senator Toombs was on the 23d of February, 1854, on the Kansas-Nebraska bill.

Douglas was in charge of the Territorial bills, and his readiness in debate, his sinewy intellect, his tact and shrewdness, had gained for him the name of "Little Giant." Seward, Chase, and Sumner had been elected from their States as "independent Democrats" by the Abolitionists, who held the balance of power in New York, Ohio, and Massachusetts. Mr. Toombs was more than willing to measure swords with the champions of free soil. He declared that he would address himself to the consideration of the Kansas-Nebraska bill "with a heart filled with gratitude to the Disposer of human events, that after the conflicts of more than a third of a century this great question has found its solution, not in temporary expedients for allaying sectional discord, but in the true principles of the Constitution and upon the broad foundation of justice and right, which forms the only true basis of fraternity and of national concord."

Mr. Toombs repudiated the libel cast by Mr. Sumner upon Northern men who "dared to exercise the rights of freemen" and differ from the Abolitionists upon this question. "It appears," said he, "from the speeches of the senator from Massachusetts, that all such are white slaves, whose manhood has been debased and enervated by the irresistible attractions of slave power." He declared that the men who talked about "solemn compact" in this connection were men whom "no oaths can bind and no covenants restrain." They called the Missouri Compromise a compact, yet showed their willingness to violate it.

"In all governments," said Mr. Toombs, "the acquisitions of the state belong rightfully to the people. Much more strongly does this principle apply to a purely popular government. Therefore, any exercise of power to injure or destroy those who have equal rights of enjoyment is arbitrary, unauthorized by the contract, and despotic."

"You have no power to strike from the meanest Indian trapper, the basest trader or camp-follower, as the senator from New York styled these people, their equal privileges, this sovereignty of right, which is the birthright of every American citizen. This sovereignty may—nay, it must—remain in abeyance until society becomes sufficiently strong and stable to be entitled to its full exercise, as sovereignty does not belong to the general government, and its exercise is a marked usurpation."

"The power and duty, then, of this government over the inchoate society of the Territories, is simply to protect this equality of right of persons and property of all the members of society until the period shall arrive when this dormant sovereignty shall spring into active existence and exercise all the powers of a free, sovereign, and independent State. Then it can mold, according to its own sovereign will and pleasure, its own institutions, with the single restriction that they must be republican."

"Justice," said Mr. Toombs, "is the highest expediency, the supremest wisdom. Applying that test to the principles of this measure, I say that no fair man in any portion of the country can come to any other conclusion than that it establishes between the people of this Union, who are bound together under a common Constitution, a firm, a permanent, a lasting bond of harmony.

" What is it that we of the South ask? Do we make any unjust or unequal demands on the

North? None. Do we ask what we are not willing on our side to grant to them? Not at all. We say to them 'Gentlemen, here is our common territory. Whether it be ceded by old States, whether it be acquired by the common treasure, or was the fruits of successful war to which we rallied, and in which we all fought, we ask you to recognize this great principle of the revolution: let such as desire, go there, enjoy their property, take with them their flocks and herds, their men-servants and maid-servants, if they desire to take them there; and when the appropriate time comes for the exercise of the dormant sovereignty of the people, let them fix the character of their institutions for themselves.'"

Senator Toombs ridiculed the idea of the "thunder of popular indignation." "If even this were true, it should in no wise control the actions of American senators. But it is not real but melodramatic thunder—nothing but phosphorus and sheet-iron."

Senator Toombs admitted that the North had the power to reject the principles of the Kansas-Nebraska bill. They had a majority in the House and Senate. Aristides had said, "True, you can do it; you have got the power; but, Athenians, it is unjust."

Senator Toombs was a bold man. When he adopted a line of argument, he was willing to fol-

low wherever its conclusions led. He did not
hesitate, in this speech, to admit that "if you
yield to the people the right to mold their institutions, the establishment of polygamy may result
legitimately therefrom." This point had been
made in debate to fight the principle of the
Kansas-Nebraska bill. Said Senator Toombs:
"It is just what they have a right to do. When
the people of Utah make their organic law for admission to the Union, they have a right to ap-
proximate, as nearly as they please, the domestic
manners of the Patriarchs. Connecticut may establish polygamy to-morrow. The people of
Massachusetts may do the same. How did they
become possessed of greater rights, in this or any
other respect, than the people of Utah? The
right in both cases has the same foundation—the
sovereignty of the people."

Senator Toombs adverted to the fact that Henry
Clay had denied that he framed the Missouri
Compromise; that it did not originate in the
House, of which he was a member; that he did
not even know if he voted for it. Senator Toombs
held the Act of 1820 to be no compact—binding
upon no man of honor; but, on the contrary, a
plain and palpable violation of the Constitution
and the common rights of the citizens, and ought to
be immediately abrogated and repealed. He declared that it had been rejected by the North

when passed, and rejected when Arkansas was admitted, when Oregon was formed, when California was received as a State. If the Kansas bill was settled upon sound and honest principles, he maintained that it should be applied to territory ceded from France just as elsewhere. He contended that the Missouri Compromise of 1820 was not a compromise in any sense of the term, but an unconstitutional usurpation of power. "When we look into the Constitution, we find no anti-slavery power planted in that instrument. On the contrary, we find that it amply provides for the perpetuity and not for the extinction of slavery."

Senator Toombs closed his first speech in the Senate with these words: "The senator from New York asks where and when the application of these principles will stop. He wishes not to be deceived in the future, and asks us whether, when we bring the Chinese and other distant nations under our flag, we are to apply these principles to them? For one, I answer yes; that wherever the flag of the Union shall float, this republican principle will follow it, even if it should gather under its ample folds the freemen of every portion of the universe."

The Kansas-Nebraska bill reopened the whole question of slavery. In the North, it was a firebrand. Mr. Buchanan, in his book, written after his retirement from the presidency, said that the South was for the first time the aggressor in this legislation. Mr. Fillmore declared that the repeal of the Missouri Compromise was "the Pandora Box of Evil." Mr. Douglas was reviled by his opponents and burned in effigy at the North. His leadership in this fight was ascribed to his overweening ambition to reach the presidency. The clergymen of New England and of Chicago flooded the Senate with petitions crying against this "intrigue." On May 26, 1854, at one o'clock in the morning, the bill passed the Senate by a vote of 31 to 13. The "nays" were Messrs. Allen, Bell, Chase, Clayton, Fish, Foote, Gillet, Hamlin, James, Seward, Sumner, Wade, and Walker.

The enactment of this measure into a law did not settle the question. It resulted in a strife in the Territories themselves. For two years Kansas was in a state of civil war. The Emigrant Aid Societies of New England raised large sums of money to send to the Territories Free-Soil settlers and other agitators. A counter-stream of agitators set in from Missouri, in sympathy with the slavery men, and the result was a long series of bloody disorders. In February, 1856, Mr. Toombs made a speech upon the message of the President in regard to the lawless condition of Kansas. The Governor informed President Pierce that the laws were obstructed and openly resisted by bodies of armed men; that prisoners were rescued from the sheriffs, peaceable inhabitants murdered, and houses burned. Another authority informed the President that an overwhelming force was crossing the border for the avowed purpose of invading Kansas and butchering the unoffending Free-State citizens. One side claimed protection from insurrection within, the other from invasion without.

As to the Emigrant Aid Societies, Mr. Toombs said, " Whatever be their policy, whatever their tendency to produce strife, if they simply aid emigrants from Massachusetts to go to Kansas to become citizens of that Territory, I am prepared to say that they violate no law; they have a right to do it, and every attempt to prevent their doing so violates the law and ought not to be sustained. But if they send persons there furnished with arms, with the intent to offer forcible resistance to the constituted authorities, they are guilty of the highest crime known to civil society, and are amenable to its penalties. I shall not undertake to decide upon their conduct. The facts are not before me, and I therefore pass it by."

Mr. Toombs thought it would be difficult to imagine a case calling more loudly for the intervention of Federal power. Mr. Toombs favored the supremacy of the law in the Territories at any cost. " If traitors seek to disturb the peace of the country, I desire that it shall be no sectional contest. I do not see the end of that. I prefer that the conflict shall be between the Federal Government and the lawless. I can see the end of that. The law will triumph and the evil stop."

" We who pass this Kansas-Nebraska bill, both at the North and South, intend to maintain its principles. We do not intend to be driven from them by clamor nor by assault. We intend that the actual *bona fide* settlers of Kansas shall be protected in the full exercise of all the rights of freemen ; that, unawed and uncontrolled, they shall freely and of their own will legislate for themselves, to every extent allowed by the Constitution, while they have a territorial government ; and when they shall be in a condition to come into the Union and may desire it, that they shall come into the Union with whatever republican constitution they may prefer and adopt for themselves ; that in the exercise of their rights they shall be protected from insurrection from within and invasion from without."

In answer to Senator Hale of New Hampshire, Senator Toombs agreed that the Territory of Kansas would certainly be a free State. Such, he thought would be its future destiny. "The sen-

ator from New Hampshire," he said, " was unable
to comprehend the principles of the bill. The
friends of the Kansas bill, North and South, supported the bill because it was right, and left the
future to those who were affected by it. The
policy of the Kansas bill wrongs no man, no section of our common country. We have never
asked the government to carry by force, or in any
way, slavery anywhere. We only demand that
the inhabitants of the Territories shall decide the
question for themselves without the interference
of the government or the intermeddling of those
who have no right to decide."

Mr. Toombs and Senator Hale of New Hampshire seem to have been pitted squarely against
each other in this great debate.

In 1854, during the progress of the Kansas debate, Mr. Toombs occupied Mr. Hale's desk, and
alluded to the taunts which Mr. Hale had heaped
upon the heads of senators who had sustained
the compromise measures of 1850. He had predicted that they would be driven from their seats ;
that the mighty North would drive them from
their benches. The distinguished senator from
Michigan, Mr. Cass, was the especial object of
these assaults. " But the result," said Mr. Toombs,
looking about him, " is that the gentleman who made
these declarations is not here."

In 1856, however, Mr. Hale was returned to the

Senate and met Mr. Toombs in the Kansas debate, and the discussion was continued with the same acrimony.

"Let there be no legislative aggression on either side," continued Mr. Toombs. "If the senator from New Hampshire is sincere, he will stand there. The common property is open to the common enjoyment of all. Let it remain so."

Mr. Toombs charged Senator Hale with saying that the North had always been practically in a minority in the Senate, because the South bought up as many Northern men as it wanted. "Sir, I stand here to-day in behalf of the North to repel the accusation."

Mr. Hale : "Who made it ? "

Mr. Toombs : "You said it. I have it before me in your printed speech. I heard it delivered, and you are correctly reported."

In a letter to Mr. B. F. Hallet of Boston, in 1856, Mr. Toombs denied saying that he would "call the roll of his slaves at the base of Bunker Hill Monument." He charged Senator Hale with misrepresenting him to this extent.

No man was oftener misquoted by word of mouth or in public print. As bold as he was in speech and as free to speak out what was in his mind, he once remarked to an intimate friend, Dr. Steiner of Augusta, that he rarely ever saw his name in print that it was not attached to a lie.

We are not left to tradition or the dictum of political opponents to know how seriously Mr. Toombs regarded the question of war between the North and South. In this same debate with Senator Hale, Mr. Toombs said : " He told us the North would fight. I believe that nobody ever doubted that any portion of the United States would fight on a proper occasion. Sir, if there shall ever be civil war in this country, when honest men shall set about cutting each other's throats, those who are least to be depended upon in a fight will be the people who set them at it. There are courageous and honest men enough in both sections to fight. . . . . No, sir, there is no question of courage involved. The people of both sections of the Union have illustrated their courage on too many battlefields to be questioned. They have shown their fighting qualities, shoulder to shoulder, whenever their country has called upon them; but that they may never come in contact with each other in fratricidal war, should be the ardent wish and earnest desire of every true man and honest patriot."

CHAPTER X.

In the fall of 1854 the elections were generally adverse to the Democrats. The slavery agitation at the North, intensified by the passage of the Kansas-Nebraska bill, resulted in a large number of Free-Soil candidates and "anti-Nebraska" Whigs being elected to the House. In the West and South, the "Know-nothing" movement had arisen as in a single night, and with secrecy and strength had asserted itself on election day. The consequence was that the Democratic majority in the House which had been elected with Franklin Pierce now disappeared. The years of 1854-55 were full of uncertainty in Georgia. The old-line Whigs, who had broken away from their party associates upon the nomination of General Scott for President, had not yet gone into full affiliation with the Democrats. Many of these men joined the "American party," which had arisen out of antagonism to the large foreign population flowing into the States and Territories. This party put out candidates for Congress and the State offices in Georgia.

To Alexander H. Stephens, more than to any
other man, was due the honor of breaking up the
Know-nothing movement in Georgia. Amazed at
the rapidity with which this party organized and
the completeness with which it worked; repudiating the principles which it held and the pro-
scriptions which it enforced, Alexander Stephens
announced, early in the day, that he would not be
a candidate for reëlection to Congress. He declared, in a letter, that, from the secrecy of the
order, he was unable to know what they were
doing, and, as political principles should come out
in the open sunlight for inspection, he could not
submit his candidacy to any such concern. He
did not hesitate to condemn the practices and
creed of the American party in public. Prominent leaders in his district who recognized his
ability made it known that they were willing to
support him, if he would not be so severe in his
denunciations. Mr. Stephens promptly replied
that the crisis required the knife, not the poultice.
However, he did run for Congress and scored the
secret order on every stump in the district. He
declared, in a speech in Augusta, that he " was
not afraid of anything on the earth, above the
earth, or below the earth, except to do wrong."
Mr. Stephens was elected. Religious fanaticism
and race prejudice received a death blow in

Georgia. "It writhed in pain, and died among its worshipers."

Mr. Toombs had already made himself felt in this campaign. He was in the shadow of a domestic affliction. His youngest daughter died in February of that year. This occurrence brought him to decide upon a trip abroad, which he had long anticipated, but which his busy and eventful life had not allowed him to enjoy.

In April, 1855, he wrote his wife:

I feel more and more anxious to get abroad and out of this country; to be relieved of the thousand harassments of business, and look for a great deal of pleasure in our quiet and uninterrupted strolling over the hills and plains of Europe, where nobody knows us and nobody can harass me with business or their troubles. I wish I could, like our darling child, thank God there was rest in Heaven.

Just before he left the State, he attended the Supreme Court of Georgia, at Milledgeville. At that time he wrote his wife:

I have had a hard, close week's work. The lawyers very kindly gave way and allowed my cases to come this week, which brought them very close together, and, as I am but ill prepared for them, not having given them any attention last winter, and but little this spring, I have been pretty much speaking all day and studying all night—and that without the benefit of "specks," which I am beginning to need.

All the old Whigs here have joined the Know-nothings, and keep very shy of me, as I have spoken not softly of the miserable wretches who expect to govern a great country like this with imbecility, if they can only cover it with secrecy. I have been greatly beset not to go to Europe this summer, as the political campaign is likely to be hot. I shall go, and the rather that I may avoid such an event, and take that leisure and repose with my family in foreign countries which I seem to be totally incapable of getting at home.

Mr. Toombs left no doubt as to how he regarded the American party. In a speech on the Kansas-Nebraska bill, he had declared that the country could assimilate the foreigners from Europe and the Chinamen from Asia, and gather under the ample folds of the American flag every nation on earth.

It is related that in the early part of Mr. Toombs' political career he was accused of having subscribed to build a Catholic church in Georgia. The charge was repeated secretly from ear to ear until it came to his friends. It was on the eve of an election in Wilkes County, and a delegation, in spite of the lateness of the hour, went to Mr. Toombs' residence, awoke him, and asked for an authoritative denial of what they considered a damaging charge. Mr. Toombs listened to the delegation, and then declared with emphasis, not free from profanity, that it was so. "I have responded to their calls just as I have those of other denominations. You can tell the

people that the distribution of my money is none
of their business."

This bold and prompt reply did not prevent his
reëlection to the legislature the next day.

No man was more liberal in matters of religion
and conscience than Mr. Toombs. In 1851 he
wrote his wife in reply to a letter informing him
that his daughter wanted to join the Methodist
Church :

I am content if she desires, and you wish it. My opinions about revivals, to which you refer, have been long
formed and much strengthened by my experience in the
world, but I am not at all desirous that they should be the
rule of anybody's conduct but my own. I have therefore
endeavored to stand upon the Protestant principle in matters of conscience, of judging for myself and allowing others to do the same. The Judge of the Earth will do right
at the final hearing.

On June 6, 1855, Mr. Toombs set sail from
New York, in company with his wife and daughter, and Mr. W. F. Alexander, his son-at-law. In
ten days, after a smooth trip, he landed in Liverpool, with just enough roughness off the coast of
Ireland to show old Neptune in his element. Mr.
Toombs was in the very prime of a vigorous life.
He had accumulated a competency at the law, was
in fine physical condition, and had a mind broad,
sensitive, and retentive. He could stand any
amount of travel—this man who rode his circuits on his horse, and who endured the wear-

ing trips from Georgia to the national capital. He remarked at the outset of his European trip that he had more money than time, so he secured special conveyances at every available place, and pushed his journey to all points of interest. From London he went to Paris, Lyons, Marseilles, thence to the Mediterranean, where he passed the Fourth of July plowing his way to Naples, sleeping on deck to escape the stuffy stateroom of the little steamer, and catching all the cinders from the smokestack. Embarking at Naples, he went to Rome, where he was entranced to see the historic spots of the Eternal City. Rome had for him more charms than Paris. Crossing the Alps, he went to Geneva, and striking the Rhine, he proceeded by boat to Amsterdam, thence to Brussels, where he walked over the field of Waterloo. Leaving his family in Paris, he crossed to England and made a tour alone through Ireland and Scotland.

As an American senator, Robert Toombs bore letters of introduction to prominent people in Europe. His reputation was international, his acquaintance with the diplomatists of the Old World was extensive, and his knowledge of the history and government of the different countries was complete. But he did not seek notoriety in his trip abroad. He presented none of his letters. He preferred to travel among the people, and at night, like Jean Valjean, he loved to see the *bour-*

geois in their gardens and at their ease, in order to study their habits and condition. He took great interest in the laborers. On one occasion he got down from his *diligence* to ask a man, who was drawing water from a well to irrigate the land, how much he was paid for this slow and cumbersome process. He was astonished to hear that it was but twelve cents a day.

Mr. Toombs spoke the French language; he studied the people, and no man was a better judge of human nature. He said when he returned that the Southern slave was better treated and was a better laborer than most of the peasants whom he had seen.

His conversation during his European trip was bright and racy. He never fagged in body or mind. He never became a trifler or a tease. He was not a man who cared for his personal comforts or appetites. Occasionally he would abuse the hotels as being far behind the American hostelry. Now and then he would jest with his guide or indulge in bright raillery over the Italian peddler with the inevitable cigarette. He made it a rule to smoke a cigar in every country, to test the tobacco, and also to sample the wine of every nation. He drank but little at that time, never touching ardent spirits in any way. Good-humor, good health, and happiness followed him as he made the circuit of the Continent.

Just three months were passed by him in the Old World. He arrived in New York in September, 1855, where telegrams awaited him, summoning him to a desperate campaign in Georgia.

The contest in Georgia that year was sharp. The American party elected several members of Congress, but their candidate for Governor, Judge Andrews, was defeated by Herschel V. Johnson. The latter was one of the strongest Democrats in Georgia. He had, in 1853, been elected Governor over so able a man as Charles J. Jenkins.

Mr. Toombs plunged at once into the canvass and proceeded, in his own vigorous way, to fight the Know-nothings.

CHAPTER XI.

In 1856, Mr. Toombs visited Boston, and delivered a lecture upon slavery. It was a bold
move, and many of his friends advised against it.
They did not see what good would come from the
appearance of an extreme Southern man in the
heart of abolitionism, carrying his doctrines to the
very citadel of antislavery. But Toombs, with
dramatic determination, decided to accept. Several Southern statesmen had been invited to appear before Boston audiences, but prudence had
kept them from complying.

On the evening of the 24th of January, Mr.
Toombs ascended the stage at Tremont Temple.
A large audience greeted him. There was great
curiosity to see the Southern leader. They ad-
mired the splendid audacity of this man in coming
to the place where Garrison had inveighed against
slavery and had denounced the Constitution as a
"league with Hell and a covenant with the Devil";
where Wendell Phillips had exerted his matchless
oratory, and where Charles Sumner had built up
his reputation as an unflagging enemy of South-

ern propagandism.   Mr. Toombs was in good trim
for this supreme effort.   Inspired by the significance of his mission, he seemed possessed of unusual strength.   His fine eye lighted with his
theme, and his brow seemed stamped with confidence rather than defiance.   His long, black hair
was brushed from his forehead, and his deep
voice filled the historic hall.   He was indeed a
fine specimen of a man—a Saul among his fellows.
Possibly he was moved by the thought that he
stood where Webster had pleaded for the Union,
for concession, and for harmony six years before,
when the people for the first time had turned
from him and when Fanueil Hall had been closed
against him.

Senator Toombs was attended upon the stage
by William and Nathan Appleton, whose guest
he was.   Their presence was a guarantee that the
speaker should receive a respectful hearing.   It
was noticed at the outset that he had abandoned
his fervid style of speaking.   He delivered his
address from notes in a calm and deliberate manner.   He never prepared a speech with so much
care.   His discourse was so logical and profound,
his bearing so dignified and impressive, that his
hearers were reminded of Webster.

It was evident early in the evening that his
lecture would produce a powerful effect.   To
many of his hearers his views were novel and

fresh, as they had never heard the Southern side of this great question. " With the exception of Sam Houston," said a New York paper, " Mr. Toombs is the only Southern man who has had the pluck to go into the antislavery camp and talk aloud of the Constitution. Other Southern men, not afraid to face Boston, have been afraid to face opinion at home."

In referring to the clause of the Constitution providing for the return of fugitive slaves, Mr. Toombs was greeted by a hiss. The speaker turned in the direction of the noise and said, " I did not put that clause there. I am only giving the history of the action of your own John Adams; of your fathers and mine. You may hiss them if you choose." The effect was electrical. The hiss was drowned in a storm of applause. The readiness and good-nature of the retort swept Boston off her feet, and for one moment prejudice was forgotten.

The New York *Express* declared that the speaker was earnest and deliberate, presenting his argument with great power, and his lecture of an hour and a half was, for the most part, listened to with respect and attention. There was some conduct in the audience at the close which the Boston *Journal* was forced to denounce as " ungentlemanly." Three cheers, not unmixed with dissent, were given to the distinguished speaker. Some-

one called out, " When will Charles Sumner be
allowed to speak in the South ? "

The New York *Express* declared that " if
Toombs and other hotheads would lecture in
Syracuse, Oswego, Ashtabula, and other points of
'Africa,' they would do a good deal of good in
educating the innocents and becoming themselves
educated and freed from fire, froth, fury, and
folly."

This lecture of Mr. Toombs at Boston will live
as the most lucid defense of slavery in law and
in practice ever delivered. Slavery has fallen and
mankind has made up its verdict; but this address
will still be read with interest.

He did not hesitate to say that Congress had no
right to limit, restrain, or impair slavery ; but, on
the contrary, was bound to protect it. At the time
of the Declaration of Independence, slavery was a
fact. The Declaration did not emancipate a single
slave; neither did the Articles of Confederation.
The Constitution recognized slavery. Every clause
relative to slavery was intended to strengthen and
protect it. Congress had no power to prohibit
slavery in the Territories. The clause giving Congress power to make regulations for the Territories
did not confer general jurisdiction. It was not
proper nor just to prohibit slavery in the Territories. Penning the negro up in the old States
would only make him wretched and miserable, and

would not strike a single fetter from his limbs. Mr. Toombs simply asked that the common terri- tory be left open to the common enjoyment of all the people of the United States; that they should be protected in their persons and property by the general government, until its authority be super- seded by a State constitution, when the character of their democratic institutions was to be deter- mined by the freemen thereof. "This," he said, "is justice. This is constitutional equity." Mr. Toombs contended that the compromise measures of 1850 and the Kansas-Nebraska Act of 1854 were made to conform to this policy. "I trust—I believe," he continued, "that when the transient passions of the day shall have subsided, and reason shall have resumed her dominion, it will be ap- proved, even applauded, by the collective body of the people."

Upon the second branch of his theme, Mr. Toombs contended that so long as the African and Caucasian races co-exist in the same society, the subordination of the African is the normal and proper condition, the one which promotes the highest interests and greatest happiness of both races. The superiority of the white man over the black, he argued, was not transient or artificial. The Crown had introduced slavery among the American colonists. The question was not whether it was just to tear the African away from bondage

in his own country and place him here. England
had settled that for us. When the colonies became free they found seven hundred thousand
slaves among them. Our fathers had to accept
the conditions and frame governments to cover it.
They incorporated no Utopian theories in their
system. They did not so much concern themselves
about what rights man might possibly have in a
state of nature, as what rights he ought to have in
a state of society. The lecturer maintained that
under this system, the African in the slaveholding
States is found in a better position than he has
ever attained in any other age or country, whether
in bondage or freedom. The great body of this
race had been slaves in foreign lands and slaves in
their native land. In the Eastern Hemisphere the
African had always been in a servile condition.
In Hayti and Jamaica experiments had been tried
of freeing them, under the auspices of France and
England. Miseries had resulted and ruin over-
whelmed the islands. "Fanaticism may palliate,
but could not conceal the utter prostration of the
race." The best specimens of the race were to be
found in the Southern States, in closest contact
with slavery. The North does not want the negro,
does not encourage his immigration. The great
fact of the inferiority of the race is admitted
everywhere in our country.

"Our political system gives the slave great and

valuable rights. His life is protected; his person secured from assault against all others except his master, and his master's power in this respect is placed under salutary legal restriction." He gets a home, ample clothing and food, and is exempted from excessive labor. When no longer capable of labor, from age or disease, he is a legal charge upon his master. The Southern slave, he said, is a larger consumer of animal food than any population in Europe, and larger than any laboring population in the United States, and their natural increase is equal to that of any other people. Interest and humanity coöperate in harmony for the well-being of slave labor. Labor is not deprived of its wages. Free labor is paid in money, the representative of products; slave labor in the products themselves. The agricultural and unskilled laborers of England fail to earn the comforts of the Southern slave. The compensation of labor in the Old World has been reduced to a point scarcely adequate to the continuation of the race.

"One-half the lands of the cotton States is annually planted in food crops. This half is consumed by the laborers and animals. The tenant in the North does not realize so much."

Mr. Toombs believed that the Southern men were awakening to the conviction that the slave should be taught to read and write, as being of more use to himself, his master, and society. He realized that the laws should protect marriage and other domestic ties, forbidding the separation of families, and stated that some of the slaveholding States had already adopted partial legislation for the removal of these evils. But the necessities of life and the roving spirit of the white people produced an infinitely greater amount of separation in families than ever happened to the colored race. "The injustice and despotism of England toward Ireland has produced more separation of Irish families and sundered more domestic ties within the last ten years than African slavery has effected since its introduction into the United States." England keeps 100,000 soldiers, a large navy, and innumerable police to secure obedience to her social institutions, and physical force is the only guarantee of her social order, the only cement of her gigantic empire. The laws restrain the abuses and punish the crimes of the slave system. Slavery is impossible in England and Europe, because wages have gone down to a point where they are barely sufficient to support the laborer and his family. Capital could not afford to own labor. Slavery ceased in England in obedience to this law, and not from any regard to liberty and humanity.

Senator Toombs declared that the condition of the African might not be permanent among us. He might find his exodus in the unvarying law of population. Increase of population may supply to slavery its euthanasia in the general prostration of all labor. The emancipation of the negro in the West Indies had not made him a more useful or productive member of society. The slave States, with one-half the white population, and between 3,000,000 and 4,000,000 slaves, furnish three-fifths of the annual product of the republic. In this relation, the labor of the country is united with and protected by its capital, directed by the educated and intelligent.

Senator Toombs combated the idea that slavery debased and enervated the white man. To the Hebrew race were committed the orders of the Most High. Slaveholding priests ministered at their altars. Greece and Rome afforded the highest forms of civilization. Domestic slavery neither enfeebles nor deteriorates a race. Burke had declared that the people of the Southern colonies of America were much more strongly, and with a higher and more stubborn spirit, attached to liberty that those to the Northward. Such were our Gothic ancestors; such were the Poles; such will be all masters of slaves who are not slaves themselves. In such a people the haughtiness of domination combines itself with the spirit of freedom, fortifies it, and renders it invincible.

Senator Toombs declared that, in the great agitation which for thirty years had shaken the national government to its foundation and burst the bonds of Christian unity among the churches, the slaveholding States have scarcely felt the shock. Stability, progress, order, peace, content, prosperity reign through our borders. Not a single soldier is to be found in our domain to overawe or protect society. Mr. Toombs pictured the progress of the Southern churches, schools and colleges multiplying. None of these improvements had been aided by the Federal Government. "We have neither sought from it protection for our private interests nor appropriations for our public improvements. They have been effected by the unaided individual efforts of an enlightened, moral, and energetic people. Such is our social system and such our condition under it. We submit it to the judgment of mankind, with the firm conviction that the adoption of no other, under such circumstances, would have exhibited the individual man, bond or free, in a higher development or society in a happier civilization."

Mr. Toombs carried his principles into practice. He owned and operated several large plantations in Georgia, and managed others as agent or executor. He had the care of, possibly, a thousand slaves. His old family servants idolized him. Freedom did not alter the tender bond of affection. They clung to him, and many of them remained with him and ministered to his family to the day of his death. The old plantation negroes never failed to receive his bounty or good will. During the sale of a plantation of an insolvent estate Mr. Toombs, who was executor, wrote to his wife, "The slaves sold well. There were few instances of the separation of families." He looked after the welfare of all his dependents. While he was in the army, his faithful servants took care of his wife and little grandchildren, and during his long exile from his native land they looked after his interests and watched for his return.

CHAPTER XII.

BUCHANAN'S ADMINISTRATION.

THE great contest of 1856 was coming on. A President was to be chosen. The relations of the sections were more strained every day. The elections of 1854 had emboldened the antislavery men to form the Republican party, and to put out, as their candidate, John C. Frémont, "pioneer and pathfinder," who had saved California to the Union. Frémont was not a statesman, but a hero of the kind who dazzled men, and was thought to be especially available as a presidential candidate. "Free soil, Free men, Frémont" was the cry, and it was evident that the Abolitionists had swept all the wavering Whigs into their lines and would make a determined fight. The American party nominated Millard Fillmore, and the Democracy, with a wealth of material and a non-sectional following, wheeled into line. President Pierce was willing to succeed himself. Stephen A. Douglas, who had rushed into the convention of 1852 with such reckless dash to put aside "the old fogies" of the party, was an avowed candidate. His championship of the Kansas-Ne-

140

braska bill had made him a favorite in the South, although it injured his chances at the North. It is not a little remarkable that Douglas, whose candidacy had the effect of setting aside Buchanan for Pierce in 1852, should afterward have been the means of turning down Pierce for Buchanan.

James Buchanan of Pennsylvania had just returned from London, where he had served with dignity as American Minister. Free from recent animosities, he entered the field, fresh and full of prestige. He was nominated for President on the fifth day of the Democratic Convention, Georgia casting her vote for him. The Cincinnati platform adopted this plank:

"*Resolved:* That we recognize the right of the people of the Territories, including Kansas and Nebraska, acting through the legally and fairly expressed will of a majority of the actual residents, and whenever the number of their inhabitants justifies it, to form a Constitution, either with or without domestic slavery, and to be admitted into the Union upon terms of perfect equality with all the other States."

Among the causes contributing to the current bitterness was the assault made upon Charles Sumner, senator from Massachusetts, by Preston S. Brooks, a representative from South Carolina. This happened in May, 1856, while Mr. Sumner was sitting at his desk, after the Senate had ad-

journed. Mr. Brooks took exception to some
remarks printed in Mr. Sumner's speech, entitled
"The Crime against Kansas." In this speech, the
senator had referred, in rather caustic terms, to
Senator Butler of South Carolina. The latter
was a kinsman of Mr. Brooks. The weapon used
by Mr. Brooks was a gutta-percha cane, and Senator Sumner, who was a large, powerful man, in his
effort to rise from his seat, forced his desk from its
hinges and fell heavily to the floor. The assault
created an immense sensation. It was associated
in the heated minds at the North with the "slavery aggressions of the South." At the South, it
was generally excused as the resentment of an
impetuous young man to an insult offered an
elderly kinsman. Northern men denounced the
assault in unmeasured terms on the floor of the
House and Senate. The affair led to several chal-
lenges between the representatives of both sections. Congressman Brooks resigned his seat, but
was immediately reëlected.

When Senator Sumner made his statement of
the attack, he said that, after he was taken from
the floor, he saw his assailant standing between
Senator Douglas and Senator Toombs. This led
to the assertion by some parties that the attack
was premeditated, and that the senator from
Illinois and the senator from Georgia, who were
strong political antagonists of Mr. Sumner, were

aiding and abetting it. Both senators denied this from their places.

The political activity was not confined to the North. There was a large element in Georgia which disapproved of the Kansas-Nebraska bill as an unwise concession on the part of the South. This class, combined with the American party, presented an active front against the party led by Senator Toombs. No contest was ever waged more vigorously in Georgia. New blood and new issues were infused into the fight. Mr. Toombs was at the maximum of his greatness. He took redoubled interest in the campaign in that the legislature to be chosen in 1857 was to elect his successor to the Senate, and because the principles in this national contest were taking shape for a State campaign the following year.

CHAPTER XIII.

AMONG the young men on the stump that year was Benjamin H. Hill. He had come up from the plow-handles in Jasper County. Working his way to an education, he had graduated at the State University in 1845, with the first honors of his class. He was at this time barely more than thirty years of age, but he had won distinction at the bar and served his county in the State Senate. He was known for his aggressive, ringing eloquence, and a clear, searching style which had made him something more than local reputation. It was understood that he was the choice of the American party for Governor, and it was assumed that he would win his spurs in the national campaign. He did not hesitate to go into the thickest of the fight. He challenged Toombs and Stephens in their strongholds; on the 22d of October meeting Mr. Stephens at his stamping-ground in Lexington, Oglethorpe County, and the next day confronting Mr. Toombs at his home in Washington, Ga. There was a charm in the very audacity of this young Georgian. The man who

144

would beard "the Douglas in his hall" was a curiosity to the people, for since the leadership of Toombs was established in 1844, no one, probably, had assumed to cross swords with him before his home people. The fact that young Hill had rather frustrated Mr. Stephens, in their first meeting, gave him fresh impetus for his clash with Toombs. People flocked to Washington by thousands. A large part of the audience which had cheered Ben Hill in Oglethorpe followed him to Wilkes.

The speaking took place in Andrews' Grove, a noble cluster of oaks near the town, and by breakfast-time the place was filled with carriages and wagons. The red hills leading to Washington were alive with farmers and their wives and children, wheeling into the grove to hear the noble veteran and the brilliant young stranger debate upon current topics. Old and young men were there, and babies in arms. It was before the days of a universal press. People took their politics from the stump. They were trained in the great object-lessons of public life. The humble farmer knew all about the Missouri Compromise and the Nebraska bill. What they had learned was thorough. Every man was a politician.

Ben Hill opened the discussion. He had the advantage of being a new and untried man, while Toombs and Stephens had spread their records upon the pages of hundreds of speeches. In those days of compromises and new departures, it was easy for a quick, bright fellow to make capital out of the apparent inconsistencies of public men. Hill was a master of repartee. He pictured Toombs' change from Whig to Democrat. He made a daring onslaught upon Toombs. Hill's bump of reverence was not large, and the way he handled this great statesman was a surprise. He did not hesitate to call him "Bobuel," and to try to convict him out of his own mouth of error.

Toombs sat back with his fine features lit with scorn. His facial expression was a rare part of his strength. He seemed to repel with his look the impudence of this fearless young statesman. Hill saw the effect of his own audacity, and "plied his blows like wintry rain." A keen observer of this dramatic by-play declares that the pose of these two men reminded him of Landseer's picture of "Dignity and Impudence."

Hill declared that Toombs had been in Congress, "sleeping over our rights." Toombs retorted, "I have been protecting your rights and your children's rights in spite of yourselves."

Hill charged that Toombs had tried to dodge the issues of this campaign. Toombs, when he answered this part, cried out to the people impetuously: "Did I dodge the question, when in the presence of two thousand people, in the City of Augusta, and as I was about to travel in foreign lands, I denounced the secret midnight organization which was being fastened upon the freemen of the South? An organization whose chief measure was to prescribe a religious test in this land of liberty, and raise up a barrier to the entrance of the sons of the Old World, whose gallant sires aided us in achieving our independence?

"Did I dodge, when, just before putting my foot on shipboard, I wrote a letter to my beloved South, warning them against this insidious organization creeping into their midst, piloted by dark lanterns to midnight lodges? Did I dodge, when, hearing, as I traveled, that this deadly order had taken hold and fastened its fangs in my State, I suspended my travels and took the first ship that bore me back to my native shores, and, raised my cry against these revolutionary measures?

"Did I dodge, when, as soon as landing in Georgia, I traveled all night and spoke all next day against these blighting measures? If this be called dodging, I admit that I dodged, and the gentleman can make the most of it."

Mr. Hill declared that the Kansas-Nebraska bill embodied the principles of "squatter sovereignty" and alien suffrage. The bill was not identical with the Utah and New Mexico bill, as Toombs and Stephens had alleged. The restrictive provisions of the Utah bill would prohibit this Territorial

Legislature from excluding slavery. It could not do that until it became a State, while the Kansas bill allowed a majority of the actual residents to determine whether slavery should or should not exist, even prior to its admission as a State. He denounced the Kansas bill as a cheat, a swindle, and a surrender of our dearest rights. As to the National Convention, Mr. Hill declared that the South may have framed the platform, but the North secured the candidate. Mr. Hill, relative to territorial questions, recognized the right of native born and naturalized citizens of the United States, permanently residing in any Territory, to frame a constitution and laws and to regulate their social and domestic affairs in their own way. The American party proposed to extend the term required for naturalization and to bar the foreigners from holding office. Mr. Hill had strong sympathizers in the extreme Southern Rights' men, who were on hand in abundance.

Mr. Toombs replied with great dignity and warmth. He said that the Nebraska bill was a reiteration of the true intent of the compromise measures of 1850 ; that whoever opposed the Kansas bill was opposed to the South. It was a touchstone for fixing party affiliations. It only carried out the Georgia platform protesting against Congressional prohibition of slavery in the Territories. He paid high tribute to Douglas as a patriot

and friend to the South. "Whoever condemned
Douglas needed watching himself." Mr. Toombs
charged that the representatives of the Know-nothing party had voted for the Kansas-Nebraska bill,
and now claimed ignorance of its provisions. He
denied that either he or Mr. Stephens had declared
that the Kansas bill was identical with the Utah
bill. Mr. Hill insisted that they had said so. Affirmance and denial became heated, and talk of
holding each other "personally responsible" was
indulged in, but pretty soon the debate went back
into the political grooves. Mr. Toombs denied
that the bill was a "Pandora's box of evil," or that
its passage was violative of the good faith of the
South. This part of his argument, of course, was
directed to meet Northern criticism. "The North,"
Mr. Toombs said, "had tried, by the Wilmot Proviso, to legislate the South out of the right of equal
enjoyment of the Territories. The South had endeavored to take the question of these rights out
of Congress, to establish the doctrine of non-intervention." This doctrine triumphed in 1850 and,
despite the assertion of his opponent, was reaffirmed
in the Kansas-Nebraska Act. This Act of 1854
was the great measure of justice and equality to the
South.

Mr. Toombs ridiculed the assertion of Millard
Fillmore that the repeal of the Missouri Compromise was a violation of a sacred compact. "Fill-

more," said Mr. Toombs, "is an amiable, clever sort of fellow, not to be trusted upon the great questions now before the country. He had withheld action upon the compromise measures of 1850 until his attorney-general told him that he must sign them."

Someone reminded Toombs that he had supported Fillmore for vice president in 1848. He replied, "Yes, and I said then, that if Fillmore was at the head of the ticket, I would not support it." Several persons in the audience declared that they had heard him say it. "I am glad to know," said he, "that, since my opponents address you people as if you had no sense, you, at least, have shown that you have memories."

Turning to the crowd who had cheered the opposition speaker, Mr. Toombs said: "For those of you who have yelled so long and lustily, when your dearest rights were assailed, I can but feel the profoundest commiseration. Should you continue in your wild strife against the experience of the past, I look to a kind Providence and to wise men to protect you from yourselves."

In regard to aliens in America, Mr. Toombs said: "I go for giving them all—the oppressed of all nations—a place of refuge, and say even to the paupers and criminals; 'We will forgive you for the past and try you for the future.' You may start in your railroad and go to Memphis, and then,

follow the setting sun day by day, and week by
week, until you find him setting in the Pacific
Ocean, and all the time you are passing over fertile
lands where industry and thrift may meet appropriate rewards, and the blessings of liberty and
peace find a resting-place in the bosom of freedom."

Mr. Hill said that Toombs was a turncoat. He
had been a Whig, and now he abused the Whigs.
Mr. Toombs told the people that he came not to
abuse the Democrats or Whigs, but with the
weapon of truth and the shield of the Constitution
to aid in preserving the Union and maintaining the
rights of the South. He did not appear before
the people to carry majorities, but to promote their
constitutional rights.

Mr. Toombs was charged with being a disunionist. He said he stood upon the Georgia platform
of 1850, and leaning upon that faithful support,
"I will say, that should Frémont be elected, I will
not stand and wait for fire, but will call upon my
countrymen to take to that to which they will be
driven—the sword. If that be disunion, I am a
disunionist. If that be treason, make the most of
it. You see the traitor before you."

Opinion as to the result of the debate at Washington was divided. Good judges thought that
Mr. Hill relied too much on the *ad captandum*
argument, and did not meet the points of Mr.

Toombs; but there are men living in Washington who heard the great contest and who delight to tell how the young warrior from Troup charged right into the enemy's camp, and rode away with the laurels of the day.

Buchanan was elected President in November. He carried nineteen States, Georgia among them. Buchanan and Breckenridge received 174 electoral votes and 1,838,169 popular votes.

Frémont carried eleven States and 114 electoral votes, receiving 1,341,264 popular votes. Fillmore carried Maryland with 8 electoral votes. His vote through the country amounted to 874,534.

Mr. Toombs, while a member of Congress, became possessed of a large tract of land in Texas. It was known as the Peter's Colony Grant, which had never been settled. The lands, he was informed by a competent surveyor, were valuable, and free to settlers. They comprised about 90,000 acres in Northern Texas, on the clear fork of the Trinity, in the neighborhood of Dallas and Fort Worth. Mr. Toombs had a clear head and keen perception for business. His temperament was restless and fiery. His life had been spent at the bar and in the forum. His gifts of oratory were remarkable. It was a strange combination which added shrewd business sense, but he had it in an eminent degree. He was a princely liver, but a careful financier. He saw that this part of Texas must some day bloom into an empire, and fifty years ago he gave $30,000 for this tract of land. As Texas commenced to fill up the squatters occupied some of the most valuable parts of the country and refused to be removed. These desperate fellows declared that they did not believe there was any such man as Toombs, the reputed owner of the land ; they had never seen him, and certainly they would not consent to be dispossessed of their holdings.

It was in 1857 that Senator Toombs, accompanied by a few of his friends, decided to make a trip to Texas and view his large landed possessions. For hundreds of miles he traveled on horseback over the plains of Texas, sleeping at night in a buffalo robe. He was warned by his agents that he had a very desperate set of men to deal with. But Toombs was pretty determined himself. He summoned the squatters to a parley at Fort Worth, then a mere spot in the wilderness. The men came in squads, mounted on their mustangs, and bearing over their saddles long squirrel rifles. They were ready for a shrewd bargain or a sharp vendetta. Senator Toombs and his small coterie were armed ; and standing against a tree, the landlord confronted his tenants or trespassers, he hardly knew which. He spoke firmly and pointedly, and pretty soon convinced the settlers that they were dealing with no ordinary man. He said he was willing to allow each squatter a certain sum for betterments, if they would move off his land, or, if they preferred to stay, he would sell the tract to each man at wild-land prices; but, failing in this, they must move away, as he had the power to put them out, and would certainly use it. There was a good deal of murmuring and caucussing among the men, but they concluded that there was a man named Toombs, and that he meant what he said. The matter was settled in a business way, and Senator Toombs rode back over the prairies, richer by a hundred thousand dollars. These lands were immensely valuable during the latter part of his life. They formed the bulk of his fortune when the war closed; and during his stay in Paris, an exile from his country, in 1866, he used to say that he consumed, in his personal expenses, an acre of dirt a day. The land was then worth about five dollars an acre.

It was while he was returning home from his Texas trip that the postman met him on the plains and delivered a letter from Georgia. This was in July, 1857. The letter announced that the Democratic State Convention in Georgia had adjourned, after nominating for Governor Joseph E. Brown. Senator Toombs read the letter and, looking up in a dazed way, asked, "And who in the devil is Joe Brown?"

CHAPTER XIV.

THE CAMPAIGN OF 1856.

THERE was a good deal of significance in the inquiry. There was a hot campaign ahead. The opposition party, made up of Know-nothings and old-line Whigs, had nominated Benjamin H. Hill for Governor. Senator Toombs knew that it would require a strong man to beat him. Besides the Governor, a legislature was to be chosen which was to elect a successor to Senator Toombs in the Senate. He was personally interested in seeing that the Democratic party, with which he had been in full accord since the passage of the Kansas-Nebraska bill, had a strong leader in the State. All the way home he was puzzling in his brain about "Joe Brown."

About the time that he returned, he was informed that Hill and Brown had met at Glen Spring, near Athens. A large crowd had attended the opening discussion. Howell Cobb wrote to Senator Toombs that he had better take charge of the campaign himself, as he doubted the ability of Judge Brown to handle "Hill of Troup."

155

Joseph E. Brown had come up from the people. He was a native of Pickens, S. C., of old Scotch-Irish stock that had produced Calhoun and Andrew Jackson. The late Henry W. Grady, in a bright fancy sketch, once declared that the ancestors of Joseph E. Brown lived in Ireland, and that "For seven generations, the ancestors of Joe Brown have been restless, aggressive rebels—for a longer time the Toombses have been daunt-less and intolerant followers of the King. At the siege of Londonderry, Margaret and James Brown were within the walls, starving and fighting for William and Mary; and I have no doubt there were hard-riding Toombses outside the walls, charging in the name of the peevish and unhappy James. Certain it is that forty years before, the direct ancestors of Robert Toombs, in their estate, were hiding the good King Charles in the oak at Boscobel, where, I have no doubt, the father and uncle of the Londonderry Brown, with cropped hair and severe mien, were proguing about the place with their pikes, searching every bush in the name of Cromwell and the psalm-singers. From these initial points sprang the two strains of blood—the one affluent, impetuous, prodigal, the other slow, resolute, forceful. From these ancestors came the two men—the one superb, ruddy, fashioned with incomparable grace and fullness—the other pale, thoughtful, angular, stripped down

to brain and sinew.   From these opposing theories
came the two types: the one patrician, imperious,
swift in action, and brooking no stay; the other
democratic, sagacious, jealous of rights, and sub-
mitting to no opposition.   The one for the king,
the other for the people."

Young Joe Brown had taught school, studied
law, finally completing his course at Yale College.
He was admitted to the bar in 1845.   In 1849 he
was elected as a Democrat to the State Senate by
Cherokee County.   In 1851 he had been a Southern Rights' man, voting for McDonald against
Cobb, the Union candidate for Governor.   In
1852 he was Democratic elector for Pierce.   In
1855 he was elected by the people judge of the
Blue Ridge Circuit.   He was very strong in
North Georgia.   The convention which selected
him as the candidate for Governor met in Milledgeville, June 24, 1857.   The Democrats had
no lack of eminent men.   There were candidates
enough.   James Gardner, the brilliant and in-
cisive editor of the Augusta *Constitutionalist*, led
the ballot, but Brown was finally brought in as a
compromise man.   His nomination was a surprise.

When Senator Toombs met the young nominee,
by appointment, to talk over the campaign, he
found that he was full of good sense and sagacity.
He joined him in his canvass, lending his own
name and prestige to the Democratic meetings.

But he found much shrewdness and homely wisdom about Joseph E. Brown, and he became convinced that he was able to make his way to the favor of the people without outside aid. The Democratic nominee proved his ability to stand before the luminous oratory of Ben Hill himself. Brown had courage, clearness, and tact, with growing ability and confidence. He soon developed the full strength of the Democratic party, which, in Georgia, was overwhelming. Joseph E. Brown was elected Governor, and the last vestige of the American party went down in 1857. The legislature was overwhelmingly Democratic.

On the 6th of November, 1857, Mr. Toombs wrote from Milledgeville to his wife, pending the election of United States Senator:

I got here Wednesday and found the usual turmoil and excitement. Governor McDonald is here and has been trying hard to beat me, but I find very unexpected and gratifying unanimity in my favor. The party met this evening and nominated me by acclamation, with but two or three dissenting votes, and they speak of bringing on the election to-morrow. I am very anxious to see you, and am tired of wandering about in excited crowds ; but I suppose after to-morrow I will have peace, so far as I am concerned, for the next six years. I think I shall be entitled to exemption from the actual duties of future campaigns to stay at home with you.

He was reëlected to the United States Senate for the term beginning March 4, 1857.

When President Buchanan was inaugurated, he announced that a case was pending in the Supreme Court upon the occupation of the Territories. By this decision he would abide. The day after the inauguration the decision was announced. It was the celebrated Dred Scott case. It fell like a bomb into the antislavery camp. The great question involved was whether it was competent for Congress, directly or indirectly, to exclude slavery from the Territories of the United States. The Supreme Court decided that it was not. Six judges out of eight made this decision. The opinion was delivered by Chief Justice Roger B. Taney.

This decision added to the fury of the storm. It was announced that the Chief Justice had announced the doctrine that "negroes had no rights that a white man was bound to respect"; a sentiment so atrocious that this official repelled it with indignation. Efforts were made to bury the Chief Justice in obloquy.

The struggle over the admission of Kansas into the Union was prolonged in Congress. But the situation in Kansas became warmer every year. The Eastern immigrant societies were met by inroads of Missouri and Southern settlers. A state of civil war virtually obtained in 1856–57, and throughout Buchanan's administration there was a sharp skirmish of new settlers and a sharp

maneuver of parties for position. The Georgia
State Democratic Convention of 1857 demanded
the removal of Robert J. Walker, who had been
appointed Governor of Kansas. He was a Southern
man, but was regarded as favoring the antislavery
party in its efforts to organize the Territory. The
truth was, as Senator Toombs had clearly foreseen
and expressed in his speech in the Senate in 1856,
Kansas was destined to be a free State, and amid
the violence of the agitation, confined to no one
side, was marching steadily toward this destiny.
The administration favored the admission of Kansas
with the Lecompton Constitution, which was
decidedly favorable to the proslavery men. Senator Douglas opposed this plan. He had become
committed to the policy of squatter sovereignty
during the debate on the Kansas-Nebraska bill in
1854. He contended that the settlers of a Territory could determine the character of their institutions, a position which the Buchanan party denounced as inconsistent with Democratic principles.
Mr. Douglas indorsed the Dred Scott decision,
but maintained his position on popular sovereignty.
He became at once unpopular with the rank and
file of the Southern Democracy, with whom he
had long been a favorite. He was also estranged
from the administration, and it was evident that
he would have no easy matter to be reëlected
United States Senator. This election came off in

the fall of 1858. It was clear to him that, to maintain his prominence in politics, he must carry Illinois. Unless he could save his own State his chance for President was gone. So he went into this memorable canvass with his own party divided and a determined opponent in the person of Abraham Lincoln. The young Republican party in Illinois had been gathering strength with each new phase of the slavery question.

The joint debate between Douglas and Lincoln was memorable. As a dexterous debater, Douglas had no equal in the Union. He was strong on the stump and incomparable in a popular assembly. Without grace or imagination, he was yet a plausible, versatile man, quick and ingenious, resolute and ready, with a rare faculty for convincing men. He was small and sinewy, with smooth face, bright eye, and broad brow, and his neighbors called him the "Little Giant." He could be specious, even fallacious; he employed an *ad captandum* kind of oratory, which was taking with a crowd and confusing to an adversary. The man who met him in these debates was a tall, impressive personage, rough, original, but direct and thoroughly sincere. In many points he was the opposite of Douglas.

He was rather an ill-ordered growth of the early West, a man who had toiled and suffered from his youth up. He was full of sharp corners and rough edges, and his nature was a strange mixture of patience and melancholy.   As Mr. Stephens said, he regarded slavery "in the light of a religious mysticism," and believed that his mission to beat it down was God-ordained.   And yet he was a statesman, a public man of breadth and prominence, a speaker of force and persuasion.   He had the robust courage of a pioneer and the high purpose of a reformer.   It was in this debate that Mr. Lincoln, at Freeport, Ill., asked Mr. Douglas that memorable question, on the stump: "Can the people of a Territory, in any lawful way, exclude slavery from their limits, prior to the formation of a State constitution?"   Mr. Douglas promptly answered, "Yes."   This was his doctrine of popular sovereignty.   But the answer cost him the Democratic nomination to the Presidency.   The theory that a mass of settlers, squatting in a Territory, could fix and determine the character of the Territory's domestic institutions, was repugnant to a large portion of the Southern people.   They claimed that under the Dred Scott decision, slavery already existed in the Territories, and must be protected by the Constitution; and that it was not competent for the people to determine for themselves the question of slavery or no slavery, until they formed a constitution for admission into the Union as a State.

The election in Illinois, in the fall of 1858, gave Stephen A. Douglas a majority of eight in the

General Assembly over Abraham Lincoln, and Douglas was reëlected for the new term. In this contest he had been opposed by the Buchanan Democrats, who cast over 8000 votes in Illinois.

In the Senate, the debate on popular sovereignty was renewed. This time Jefferson Davis, a senator from Mississippi, attacked this position as incompatible with the Constitution and the laws. Mr. Davis was a skillful debater. His mind was singularly graceful and refined. He was eloquent, logical, and courageous. His career as soldier and statesman, as War Minister under Pierce, and as senator for Mississippi, made him a prominent figure. He was cultured, classical, and well rounded, equipped by leisure and long study for the career before him. He had vanquished Sergeant S. Prentiss in public discussion over the national bank, and contested, inch by inch, the domination of Henry S. Foote in Mississippi. His career in the Mexican war had been a notable one. Allied to Zachary Taylor by marriage, a West Pointer by training, a Southern planter by occupation, he was a typical defender of slavery as it existed. Davis was as slender and frail as Douglas was compact and sinewy. Like Lincoln, his mind grasped great principles, while Douglas was fighting for points and expedients.

Douglas declared that the territorial settler could determine whether slavery should exist, by his influence in providing or withholding police power; although he denied the constitutional right to legislate slavery out of the Territories, yet he believed the "popular sovereign" could, by means of "unfriendly legislation," bar out the Southern settler with his slaves. It was not difficult for Mr. Davis to impale him upon this plea.

Senator Douglas had saved his seat in the Senate, but his position in the Democratic party was weakened. The Lecompton Constitution passed the Senate in spite of Douglas's steady opposition.

Senator Toombs took no part in the subtleties of the Douglas-Davis debate. He listened to the refinements of that discussion with decided convictions of his own, but with clear appreciation of the fact that every point scored against Douglas was cleaving the Democratic party in twain. Mr. Toombs favored the adoption of the Lecompton Constitution, but when it was rejected by the House, he promptly accepted the English compromise, to refer the matter back to the people. Mr. Toombs had always been partial to Douglas. In the campaign of 1856 he declared, in Georgia, that "the man who condemned Senator Douglas needed watching himself." He viewed with some pain the Douglas departure over popular sovereignty; indeed he once declared that had he not been called away from the Senate for quite a time in 1856, Mr. Douglas would never have gone off on this tangent. When asked if Douglas were really a great man, Senator Toombs, in 1860, answered with characteristic heartiness and exaggeration, "There has been but one greater, and he, the Apostle Paul."

It was very evident that the people of the South would demand new guarantees for the protection of slavery against the dogma of popular sovereignty. The platform of the Cincinnati convention, upon which Buchanan had been elected, must be recast. The platform had declared that immigrants to any part of the public domain were to settle the question of slavery for themselves. The new plank, which President Buchanan framed, was that the government of a Territory was provisional and temporary, and during its existence, all citizens of the United States had an equal right to settle with their property in the Territory, without their rights, either of person or property, being destroyed or impaired by Congressional or Territorial legislation. The two last words contained the gist of the resolution, which was aimed at Senator Douglas. However right as an abstract principle, Mr. Stephens declared that this was a departure from the doctrine of non-intervention.

It was at this time that Senator Toombs made one of the most important speeches of his life. This was delivered in Augusta, Ga., September 8, 1859, during an exciting campaign. Governor

Brown was a candidate for reëlection, and a strong opposition party had developed in Georgia, representing the extreme Southern sentiment.

Senator Toombs said that the opposition to the Kansas bill had continued because it was said to recognize the right of the people of a Territory, through the Territorial legislature, to establish or prohibit slavery. "When we condemned and abrogated Congressional intervention against us," said he, "that was a great point gained. Congress had actually excluded us from the Territories for thirty years. The people of a Territory had in no instance attempted such an iniquity. I considered it wise, prudent, and politic to settle the question against our common enemy, Congress, even if I left it unsettled as to our known friends, the people of the Territories. We could not settle the question of the power of the people over slavery while in a territorial condition, because Democrats differed on that point. We, therefore, declared in the Kansas bill that we left the people of the Territories perfectly free to form and regulate their domestic institutions in their own way, subject only to the Constitution of the United States. We decided to refer the question to the Supreme Court. It has gone there and been decided in our favor. The Southern friends of the measure repudiate the principle of squatter sovereignty. I stand its steady and uncompromising adversary. The doctrine of Douglas has not a leg to stand upon. Yet I do not belong to those who denounce him. The organization of the Democratic party leaves this an open question, and Mr. Douglas is at full liberty to take either side he may choose, and if he maintains his ground of neither making nor accepting new tests of political soundness, I shall consider him a political friend, and will accept him as the representative of the party, whatever it may tender him. I do not hesitate to tell you that, with his errors, I prefer him and would support him to-morrow against any opposition leader in America.

" We are told," said Mr. Toombs, " that we must put a new plank in the platform of the Democratic party, and demand the affirmance of the duty of Congress to prohibit slavery in a Territory, where such Territory may fail to discharge this duty. I reply, I do not think it is wise to do the thing proposed, and the inducement would not help the proposition. While I have already asserted full and complete power of Congress to do this, I think, with Mr. Madison, that it should be prudently and carefully exercised, and it ought not to be exercised until the occasion is imperative. There has been no occasion, from 1789 to this hour, calling for it, and I am more than willing that the Territorial settlers shall continue to govern themselves in their own way, so long as they respect the rights of all the people. I will not insult them by supposing them capable of disregarding the Constitution of the United States, or by assuming that they are incapable of honest self-government.

"No; I shall prescribe no new test of party fealty to Northern Democrats, those men who have hitherto stood with honor and fidelity upon their engagements. They have maintained the truth to their own hurt. They have displayed a patriotism, a magnanimity rarely equaled in the world's history, and I shall endeavor, in sunshine and in storm, with your approbation if I can get it, without it if I must, to stand by them with fidelity equal to their great deserts. If you will stand with me, we shall conquer faction in the North and South, and shall save the country from the curse of being ruled by the combination now calling itself the opposition. We shall leave this country to our children as we found it—united, strong, prosperous and happy."

This was a memorable speech, strong, sincere, and conservative, and had a marked effect. It was intended, not only to influence the canvass then pending, but to have an effect in controlling the National convention to be held six months later. It was copied far and wide, and the success of the State candidates whom Mr. Toombs supported showed that its statesmanlike utterances were adopted overwhelmingly in Georgia.

CHAPTER XV.

But events were moving fast and furiously. The times needed no new Mirabeau. The people were slowly welding a revolution, which must sweep statesmen from their feet and bear upon its fierce current the strong and weak alike. It has been asserted, and with truth, that disunion was precipitated by the people, not by the politicians— by the North as well as by the South.

The raid of John Brown of Kansas into Virginia was not an event which would have stirred the people in ordinary times. It was the wild foray of a fanatic, who tried to stir up a slave insurrection. He was captured, tried, convicted, and hanged. There were demoralized followers and duped negroes with him, when he was overcome by Colonel Robert E. Lee, with a detachment of marines, at Harper's Ferry. This affair created a feverish excitement. The South did not know how far this movement extended, nor by what authority it had been started. The criminal was execrated at the South and intemperately defended at the North. The man, who under normal con-

169

ditions of society would have been sent to the
insane asylum, was sentenced speedily to the gal-
lows and mourned as a martyr by many at the
North. Bells were tolled in his honor. Following
this remarkable episode, several free States passed
strong laws against the detention of fugitive slaves,
and the Northern press and pulpit teemed with
new lessons and fresh morals. John Brown's body,
in the language of the sentimental dirge, "lay
moldering in his grave"; but the spirit of the
Kansas boomer actually pervaded the land.

What the Dred Scott decision had wrought at
the North, the Ossawatomie raid awoke at the
South. The main features of Buchanan's administration to hasten the "irrepressible conflict" were
the well-weighed words of the Chief Justice and
the wild invasion of a border ruffian. Strange
paradox, but such were the influences at work
in those disordered times. Men lost their moor-
ings, and political parties abandoned settled policies. Events crowded with remorseless impact
upon certain civil strife.

Under this new condition of things Mr. Toombs
made his great "door-sill" speech in the United
States Senate, on the 24th of January, 1860. It
was upon the resolution offered by Senator Douglas calling for a measure of protection of each
State and Territory against invasion by the authorities and inhabitants of every other State and

Territory. Senator Toombs declared that the resolution opened up a new page in the history of our country. It was a step in the right direction. He feared that the disease lay too deep for the remedy. Heretofore the people of the United States could grapple and surmount all difficulties, foreign and domestic. A spirit of nationality, a common interest, a common danger, carried the country through revolutions. Now all this has changed. The feeling of loyalty and common destiny is rapidly passing away. Hostility to the compact of the Union, to the tie which binds us together, finds utterance in the tongues of millions of our countrymen, animates their bosoms, and leads to the habitual disregard of the plainest duties and obligations. Large bodies of men now feel and know that party success involves danger; that the result may bring us face to face with revolution.

"The fundamental principles of our Union are assailed, invaded, and threatened with destruction: our ancient rights and liberties are in danger; the peace and tranquillity of our homes have been invaded by lawless violence, and their further invasion is imminent; the instinct of self-preservation arms society to their defense."

Mr. Toombs contended that this was no new principle introduced into our Constitution. It was inserted in the ordinance of 1787. The New

England Confederation adopted it in 1643. The Supreme Judicial tribunal of Prussia affirmed it as the public law of Europe as late as 1855. It was acknowledged to be a sound principle of public law in the days of Pericles, and its violation by one of the States of Greece was the chief cause of the Peloponnesian War, which devastated Greece for twenty-one years. The Megareans had given refuge to the revolted slaves of Athens."

"I say," he continued, "the bargain is broken— broken by the States whose policy I have reviewed; broken by the Republican party, which did the work in their legislatures and elsewhere. Their hands are soiled with the blood of the compact. They cannot be permitted to minister at its altar. Their representatives on this floor mock at constitutional obligations; jeer at oaths. They have lost their shame with their virtue. . . . . In the name of the people, I repeat, I demand the bond. In the name of every true and honest man at the North as well as the South, I demand the resumption of your plighted faith. Upon these terms I have ever been willing to let the Union stand, but upon no other.

"Who is responsible for the murder, treason, and arson of John Brown? I have never known of his acts being approved or palliated by any other person than a Republican. Thousands of them have done it and are now doing it. In charging this dark catalogue of crime against this organization, I would not be unjust. I have no doubt that thousands of persons belonging to that organization throughout the North, loathe and despise John Brown's raid; but it is equally true that there are other thousands in the same organization who do approve it. They tell us that they condemn his acts, but admire his heroism. I think the Republican party must be pressed for a hero. The 'Newgate Calendar' can furnish them with a dozen such saints. To 'die game' and not to 'peach' are sometimes useful, if not heroic, virtues in an accomplice. The thousands of blind Republicans who do openly approve the treason, murder, and arson of John Brown, get no condemnation from their party for such acts. They are its main defenders and propagandists all over the North, and, therefore, the party is in moral complicity with the criminal himself. No society can long exist in peace under these injuries, because we are in virtual civil war; hence, I denounce their authors, the Republican party, as enemies of the Constitution and enemies of my country.

"It is vain, in face of these injuries, to talk of peace, fraternity, and common country. There is no peace; there is no fraternity; there is no common country; all of us know it.

"Sir, I have but little more to add—nothing for myself. I feel that I have no need to pledge my poor services to this great cause, to my country. My State has spoken for herself. Nine years ago a convention of her people met and declared that her connection with this government depended upon the faithful execution of the Fugitive-slave law. I was a member of that convention, and I stood then and stand now pledged to its action. I have faithfully labored to arrest these calamities; I will yet labor until this last contingency happens, faithfully, honestly, and to the best of my ability. When that time comes, freemen of Georgia, redeem your pledges! I am ready to redeem mine. Your honor is involved, your faith is plighted. I know you feel a stain as a wound. Your peace, your social system, your friends are involved. Never permit this Federal Government to pass into the traitors' hands of the black Republican party. It has already declared war against you and your institutions. It every day commits acts of war against you; it has already compelled you to arm for your defense. Listen to no vain babbling; to no treacherous jargon about 'overt acts'; they have already been committed. Defend yourselves! The enemy is at your door; wait not to meet him at your hearthstone; meet him at the door-sill, and drive him from the Temple of Liberty, or pull down its pillars and involve him in a common ruin."

CHAPTER XVI.

It was an unfortunate time for the meeting of the Democratic National Convention. The hope that the party which had so often brought harmony from discord could unite upon the soil of an extreme Southern State was destined to be broken. The body met in Charleston on April 23, 1860. The place was worthy of the assemblage. For the first time in the party history, its convention had met south of Cincinnati or Baltimore. Redolent with the beauties of spring and the tint of historic interest, Charleston, with its memories of Moultrie, inspired feelings of patriotic pride. If it suggested the obstruction of Calhoun, it recalled the Revolutionary glory of Marion and Rutledge, and the bold challenge of Hayne to Webster, that if there be one State in the Union which could challenge comparison with any other for a uniform, ardent, and zealous devotion to the Union, that State was South Carolina.

It was a memorable meeting. The convention was presided over by Caleb Cushing of Massachusetts, the devoted friend of Daniel Webster, and

Attorney-General under Franklin Pierce. In its
ranks were Henry B. Payne of Ohio, Benjamin F.
Butler of Massachusetts, and James A. Bayard of
Delaware. These men were towers of strength in
the North. They were the men to whom Robert
Toombs had appealed in the Senate, when he
turned from his fiery imprecation and, lowering his
great voice, declared, with tenderness and pride,
" I have no word of invocation to those who stand
to-day in the ranks of Northern Democracy, but to
remember and emulate their past history. From
the beginning of this controversy they have stood
firmly by the Constitution. No body of men in
the world's history ever exhibited higher or nobler
devotion to principle under such adverse circumstances. . . . . Amid the opprobrious epithets, the
gibes and jeers of the enemies of the Constitution;
worse than this, amid words of distrust and reproach even from men of the South, these great-
hearted patriots have marched steadily in the path
of duty. . . . . The union of all these elements
may yet secure to our country peace and safety.
But if this cannot be done, safety and peace are
incompatible in the Union. Amid treachery and
desertion at home, and injustice from without,
amid disaster and defeat, they have risen superior
to fortune, and stand to-day with their banners all
tattered and soiled in the humble service of the
whole country. No matter what fortune may be-

tide us in the future, while life lasts, I have a hand that will succor and a heart ready to embrace the humblest soldier of this noble band."

At that time there were thirty-three States in the Union. The committee on platform consisted of one from each State. The delegates from California and Oregon, voting with the South, gave them seventeen votes in committee. The resolutions were quickly framed, with the exception of the one on slavery. Here was the deadlock. The majority plank declared that the right to settle in the Territories with slaves "was not to be destroyed nor impaired by Territorial legislation." The minority proposed once more to leave the question to the Supreme Court. The compromise was not accepted. The two reports came before the convention, and, the Douglas men being in the majority on the floor, the minority, or squatter-sovereignty report, was adopted by a vote of 165 to 138. Here came the crisis. The delegates from Alabama, Mississippi, Florida, Louisiana, Arkansas, Texas, and a part of Delaware, withdrew from the convention. Hon. William L. Yancey of Alabama led this movement. He was a man of courage and decision, with unrivaled powers of oratory. He had been a member of Congress, and his influence in the South was large. So far back as June 15, 1858, he had written a famous letter to James M. Slaughter that "no national party can save us; no sectional party can ever do it; but if we would do as our fathers did, organize committees of safety all over the cotton States— and it is only to them that we can hope for any effectual movement—we shall fire the Southern heart, instruct the Southern mind, give courage to each other, and, by one concerted action, we can precipitate the cotton States into a revolution." This was called the "Scarlet Letter," and was widely scattered and read.

The seceding delegates organized a second assemblage over which the Hon. James A. Bayard presided. The Douglas men were left in control of the first convention, but could not secure the two-thirds vote necessary for his nomination. More than fifty ballots were taken, the full strength of the Illinois candidate being 152. On the 3d of May the convention adjourned to meet in Baltimore on the 18th of June, when it was hoped a spirit of compromise might be inspired by the seriousness of the situation.

On the night of the break in that body Mr. Yancey made a speech in Charleston, when in prophetic words he declared, "Perhaps even now the pen of the historian is nibbed to inscribe the history of a new revolution."

The seceding delegates called for a convention to be held in Richmond, Va., on the second Monday in June.

When the seven States had withdrawn from the convention, the Georgia delegation was split up. A majority left the convention, a small minority remained. This action created great excitement in Georgia. The Democratic executive committee called a State convention to meet in Milledgeville on June 4. A committee of prominent citizens, headed by Hon. J. J. Gresham of Macon, addressed letters to public men asking their views in this alarming situation. Howell Cobb indorsed the seceders; he was opposed to Douglas. Alexander H. Stephens thought Georgia should appoint delegates to the Baltimore convention, withdraw the demand for a new plank in the Cincinnati platform, abide by the doctrine of non-intervention, and nominate a good man for President. "If we must quarrel with the North," said he, "let us base it on the aggressive acts of our enemies and not on the supposed shortcomings of our friends."

Hon. Robert Toombs did not come South during the Charleston convention. He watched from his post in the Senate the great struggle between the Democratic factions. On May 10, he wrote, in reply to the letter of the Macon committee:

Perhaps the time may not have come for the attainment of the full measure of our constitutional rights ; it may not have been prudent on the part of the representatives of the seventeen States to have sanctioned and presented as much truth on the slavery issue as is contained in what is commonly called the majority platform ; but when it was thus sanctioned, approved, and presented to the convention, it was well to stand by and defend it, especially against the platform of the minority. The seceding delegates did this with manly firmness, and I approve their action.

Mr. Toombs advised, however, that the seceding delegates ought to meet with the convention at Baltimore and endeavor to obtain such a satisfactory adjustment of difficulties as could be secured. "This course requires no sacrifice of principles." This plan had been proposed by the delegates from New York to the delegates from the Southern States. "The proposed Richmond convention, if it shall be found necessary to hold it," he said, " can be held after, as well as before the Baltimore convention, and I think with clearer lights for its guidance."

"It is sometimes wise," said Mr. Toombs, "to accept a part of our just rights, if we can have the residue unimpaired and uncompromised, but nothing can justify a voluntary surrender of principle, indispensable to the safety and honor of the State.

"It is true we are surrounded with danger, but I do not concur in the opinion that the danger to the Union is even one of our greatest perils. The greatest danger, to-day, is that the Union will survive the Constitution. The body of your enemies in the North, who hate the Constitution, and daily trample it under their feet, profess an ardent attachment to the Union, and I doubt not, feel such attachment for a Union unrestrained by a Constitution. Do not mistake your real danger! The Union has more friends than you have, and will last, at least, as long as its continuance will be compatible with your safety."

Prior to the reassembling of the Democratic convention, the resolutions introduced by the Hon. Jefferson Davis, containing the Southern exposition of principles, came up in the Senate. Mr. Toombs had opposed the policy of introducing those resolutions, but as they were then before the country, he said they should be met. He ridiculed the idea of popular sovereignty. He declared that Congress should protect slavery in the Territories. The Federal Government, he claimed, did protect its citizens, native and naturalized, at home and abroad, everywhere except on the soil of our own territory, acquired by common blood and treasure.

This speech of Senator Toombs marked an epoch in his career. It separated him entirely from Stephen A. Douglas, to whom he had been closely allied, in spite, as he said, of Douglas having wandered after strange gods. Douglas absented himself from the Senate when Toombs spoke. For the first time in twenty years, Toombs and Stephens took divergent paths. They were

called in Georgia the "Siamese twins." From the
election of Harrison to the Democratic split in
1860, they had been personal friends and firm
political allies. Mr. Stephens was for Douglas
and the Union; Mr. Toombs feared lest "the
Union survive the Constitution."

The Democratic party in Georgia met on June
4, and parted on the lines of the Charleston division. The Union element in Georgia was led by
Herschel V. Johnson, a man of power and influence. He had been Governor of the State, was a
man of learning, profound in thought and candid in expression. His wife was a niece of President Polk. His state papers were models of
clear and classical expression. Governor Johnson was, however, better fitted for the bench or the
Cabinet than for a public leader.

Both wings of the Georgia convention appointed
delegates to the Baltimore convention. That body
admitted the delegation which had seceded from
the Charleston convention. As the seceding delegates from the other States were rejected, the
Georgia delegates refused to go in. Missouri was
the only Southern State which was represented
entirely in the body, composed of 190 delegates.
Massachusetts withdrew and Caleb Cushing resigned the chair. Stephen A. Douglas was nominated for President of the United States. Governor Fitzpatrick of Alabama declined the vice

presidency, and Herschel V. Johnson of Georgia
was chosen for vice president. The seceders immediately organized a national convention, Mr.
Cushing presiding. It was composed of 210 delegates. The majority or anti-Douglas platform of
the Charleston convention was adopted. John
C. Breckenridge of Kentucky was nominated for
President, and Joseph C. Lane of Oregon for vice
president. Mr. Breckenridge was at that time vice
president of the United States, and Mr. Lane was
a senator. Meanwhile, a Constitutional Union
party had been formed in Georgia, and had elected
delegates to a convention of that party in Baltimore. This body nominated for President and vice
president, John Bell of Tennessee and Edward
Everett of Massachusetts. Mr. Bell had been
United States Senator at the time of the passage
of the Kansas-Nebraska bill, in 1854, and had been
arraigned by Mr. Toombs for opposing the party
policy. He was one of the thirteen who voted
against it in the Senate.

The contest in Georgia waged with much vigor.
Robert Toombs supported Breckenridge. He was
a delegate to the Democratic State convention
which put out a Breckenridge and Lane electoral
ticket. He cut out the business of that convention, and declared that the Constitution and equality of the States was the only bond of everlasting
union. Mr. Stephens headed the Douglas ticket.

Senator Douglas himself came to Georgia and spoke during the campaign. The Bell and Everett ticket was championed by Benjamin H. Hill. The vote in Georgia was: Breckenridge, 51,893; Douglas, 11,580; Bell, 42,855.

Of these three Georgians, so strikingly arrayed against each other in this critical campaign, Mr. Vincent, a gifted Texan, thus wrote with dramatic power: "Hill, Stephens, Toombs—all eloquent, all imbued with the same lofty patriotism. They differed widely in their methods; their opinions were irreconcilable, their policies often diametrically opposite. Hill was quick, powerful, but unpersistent; Stephens, slow, forcible and compromising; Toombs, instantaneous, overwhelming, and unyielding. Hill carried the crowd with a whirlwind of eloquence; Stephens first convinced, then moved them with accelerating force; Toombs swept them with a hurricane of thought and magnetic example. Hill's eloquence was in flights, always rising and finally sublime; Stephens' was argumentative with an elegant smoothness, often flowing in sweeping, majestic waves; Toombs' was an engulfing stream of impetuous force, with the roar of thunder. Hill was receptive, elastic, and full of the future; Stephens was philosophical, adaptable, and full of the past; Toombs was inexhaustible, original, inflexible, and full of the now. It was Hill's special forte to close a cam-

paign ; Stephens' to manage it ; Toombs' to originate it.   In politics as in war, he sought, with the
suddenness of an electric flash, to combat, van-
quish, and slay.   Hill's eloquence exceeded his
judgment; Stephens' judgment was superior to
his oratorical power; in Toombs these were equi-
pollent.   Hill considered expediency ; Stephens,
policy ; Toombs, principle always ; Hill would perhaps flatter, Stephens temporize, Toombs neither
—never.   At times Hill would resort to the arts of
the dialectician ; Stephens would quibble over the
niceties of construction ; Toombs relied on the im-
pregnability of his position, the depth of his thought,
the vigor of his reasoning.   Hill discussed with opponents ; Stephens debated with them ; Toombs
ignored them.   Hill refuted and vanquished his
adversaries ; Stephens persuaded and led them ;
Toombs magnetized them, and they followed him.
Their enemies said that Hill was treacherous in
politics ; Stephens selfishly ambitious ; and that
Toombs loaned like a prince and collected like a
Shylock.

"In those days Georgia did not put pygmies on
pedestals.   Hill will be remembered by his 'Notes
on the Situation'; Stephens by his 'War between
the States'; Toombs had no circumstantial superiority.   He is immortal, as the people are
eternal."

CHAPTER XVII.

TOOMBS AS A LEGISLATOR.

GEORGIA had taken a leading hand in the momentous events. Alexander H. Stephens had been prominently mentioned for President; so had Howell Cobb. When Senator Toombs had attacked the doctrine of Mr. Douglas, the followers of the latter charged that Mr. Toombs had deserted his old ally, and was himself making a bid for the presidency. Especially was this the case, they urged, as Mr. Toombs had recommended the seceding delegates to go back to the Baltimore convention, and endeavor to effect an honorable adjustment. The Augusta *Chronicle and Sentinel*, a leading Union organ, took up the charge and asked: "What of it? He is certainly as much entitled to it as any citizen in the republic. Were he elected, he would be such a President as the country needs, giving no countenance to corruption or fraud, but, with a will of his own, setting aside all dictation and acting as President of all the people. We doubt if there is a man that could arouse such a furor in his behalf, North or South, as Robert Toombs."

Close friends of Mr. Toombs at that time believed he was not without his ambition to occupy the Executive chair. Never an office-seeker, he had gone easily to the front rank of national politics and had won his honors in Georgia in a kingly way. He realized, however, that he was not politic enough to gain support from Northern States. His convictions were overmastering passions; his speech was fervid and fearless; and his bold, imperturbable expression had placed him in a fierce white light, which barred him from the promotion of party conventions. While his enemies were accusing him of a desire to destroy the Union and embroil the sections, Robert Toombs was probably cherishing in his heart a vague hope that one day he might be called to the presidency of a common country.

Senator Toombs was very active in attending to his public duties. He was interested in every species of legislation. His remarks upon the different matters of national business exhibited versatility, study, and interest in everything that affected the public welfare. Those who believe him to have been a conspirator, using his high position to overthrow the government, have only to look over the debates in Congress to see how active and conscientious were his efforts to promote every real interest of the Union.

In the United States Senate, on July 31, 1854,

Mr. Toombs gave an elaborate exposition of his views upon the policy of internal improvements. He said he had maintained opposition to this system as a fundamental principle. Since he entered public life, he had sustained President Polk's veto of the River and Harbor bill in 1847. He believed that Congress had no constitutional power to begin or carry on a general system of internal improvements. He wanted to know where this power of the Constitution could be found. Madison and Jefferson had opposed this system. Monroe, Jackson, and Clay had yielded to the popular pressure and sanctioned it. "Instead of leaving the taxes or the money in the pockets of the people," he said, "you have spent nine months in endeavoring to squander and arranging to have more to squander in the next Congress. I should like to use a polite term," said he, "for I am a good-natured man, but I think it is corruption.

"In this bill you offer me seventy thousand dollars for the Savannah river. Ships were sunk in that river for the common defense of the country during the Revolutionary War. You are bound to abate your nuisance at common law. You might offer me this Capitol full of gold, and I would scorn the gift just less than the giver. You ought to have removed these obstructions long ago. When we come and ask of you this act of justice, you tell me to go with you into

your internal improvement bill and take pot-luck
with you."

Mr. Toombs claimed that the power given to
Congress to regulate commerce, simply meant to
prescribe the rules by which commerce could be
carried on, and nothing else. "The people of
Maryland," he said, "had never asked that the
harbor of Baltimore should be cleaned at the expense of the people of Georgia. They did not
ask that other people should pay their burdens.
They came here and asked the privilege of taxing
their own commerce for their own benefit, and we
granted it. I hold it to be a fundamental principle in all governments, and especially in all free
governments, that you should not put burdens on
the people whenever you can discriminate and
put them on those who enjoy the benefits. You
started with that principle with your post-office
establishments.

"Senators, is it just? I tell you, as God
lives, it is not just, and you ought not to do it.
There is manhood in the people of the Mississippi
Valley. Let them levy tonnage duties for their
own rivers and ports and put up their own lighthouses, and charge the people who use them for
the benefits conferred. Let the honest farmer
who makes his hay, who gathers his cheese, who
raises his meal in Vermont, be not taxed to increase your magnificent improvements of nature

and your already gigantic wealth. Senators, it is unjust."

During the session of Congress of 1856-57, Senator Toombs again arraigned the whole system of internal improvements. He carefully differentiated between building a lighthouse and clearing out a harbor by the Federal Government. He said in course of the debate: " Where lighthouses are necessary for the protection of your navy, I admit the power to make them; but it must be where they are necessary, and not merely for the benefit and facilitation of commerce. Foreign and domestic commerce ought to be charged, as in England and France, for the benefit they receive. I would make the shipowners, the common carriers of this country, who are constantly using the power of this government to make money out of the products of honest industry and agriculture, submit to this rule.

"The power to found a navy is found in the only fountain of power in this country, the Constitution. The defense of one is the defense of all. The destruction of nationality is the destruction of the life of all.

"I say if you take away the property of one man and give it to a thousand, or if you take away the property of a million and give it to nineteen millions, you do not create national wealth by transferring it from the pockets of

honest industry to other people's pockets. This
is my principle. It is immovable. The more
commerce there is on the Mississippi the more
they are able and competent to pay the expenses
of transporting it, and I only ask that they shall
do it."

Mr. Toombs sustained the veto of President
Pierce of the Mississippi River bill.

In July, 1856, he said that he had for eleven
years maintained the vetoes of Mr. Polk. "I
have perceived that this mischief is widespread,
this corruption greater, this tendency to the
destruction of the country is more dangerous.
The tendency to place the whole government
under the money power of the nation is greater
and greater. The danger may be all of my
imagination; but whether that be so, or whether
I see in a bolder light the evil that will grow by
letting this sluice from the public treasury and
making it run by the will of the majority, I
deem it so important that it may be worth an
empire. We are called on, upon the idea of
everybody helping everybody's bill, to vote for
them all. There certainly can be no greater
abandonment of public principle than is here
presented."

Senator Toombs, while a member of the Georgia
Legislature, opposed the omnibus bill, granting
State aid to railroads, and one of the first devices

to fall under his criticism was a scheme to build a road to his own town. He was by nature progressive. He championed the cause of the State railroad of Georgia. In general terms he believed that the States and the people should carry out works of internal improvement. It is said that the first office ever held by Mr. Toombs was that of commissioner of the town of Washington, Ga. The election hinged upon a question of public improvement, the question being "ditch or no ditch"; Toombs was elected commissioner, and the ditch was dug.

He was nothing of a demagogue. He did not attempt to belittle the public service. He championed the provision for higher pay for the United States Judges, and for increasing the stipend of army officers, although he denounced the system of double rations as vicious. He did not hesitate to hit an unnecessary expense in every shape. All overflowing pension grabs found in him a deadly enemy. In December, 1856, while speaking on the subject of claims, he said: "In 1828, when half a century had passed over the heads of the men who fought your battles, when their generation was gone, when Tories and jobbers could not be distinguished from the really meritorious, the agents came here and attempted to intimidate public men." He alluded to pension agents as men who prowl about and make fortunes by peddling in the pretended patriotism and sufferings of their fathers.

"It is," said he, "a poor pretext for an honorable man to come and tell the government, ' My ancestor fought for his own and the public liberty; he did not choose to be a slave to a foreign despotism; but with manliness, and honor, and patriotism, he fought during the war; now pay me for this. I want to be paid in hard dollars for the honor, and chivalry, and patriotism of my ancestor.' I tell you, Mr. President, it is not good money; it is bad money; it is dishonorable to the memory of those who fought your battles."

In February, 1857, the electoral vote for President was counted by the two Houses of Congress. The vote of the State of Wisconsin (five ballots) had been cast on a day other than that fixed by the States for the meeting of the Electoral College. If counted, it gave Frémont 114 votes; if omitted, Frémont would have 109.

In the debate which followed, Senator Toombs discussed very closely a point which has since been the subject of sharp contention. He said: "The duty of counting the vote for President devolves on the Senate and House of Representatives. They must act in their separate capacities; but they alone can determine it, and not the President of the Senate and the tellers of the two Houses.

It is a high privilege, a dangerous one to the liberties and Constitution of this country. The Senate and House must determine the votes to be counted, and the President of the Senate can only announce those to be votes which are thus decided by competent authority, and any attempt of the presiding officer to declare what votes he may deem to be legal, or to decide which are the votes, no matter whether it affects the result or not, or even to say that the question shall not be decided, however highly I respect the chair, I submit is not a power given to the presiding officer by the Constitution and the laws."

In 1850 Senator Toombs found it necessary to oppose an appropriation for an experiment with the Atlantic cable. He was not prepared to say that the experiment would not be successful, but he boldly declared, despite the importance of the work and the high character of the men who were supporting it, that there was no power in the Federal Constitution for such an appropriation. Because the government establishes post roads, it could not be inferred that the government had the power to aid in transmitting intelligence to all quarters of the globe. He did not believe in going beyond the constitutional guarantees. He declared of these questions, as he had in the debate upon the Kansas bill, that in hunting for power and authority he knew but one place to go

—to the Constitution. When he did not find it there, he could not find it anywhere.

Senator Toombs favored the purchase of Cuba, because he considered it advantageous to the republic. "I will accept Canada as readily, if it can be honestly and fairly done," he said. "I will accept Central America and such part of Mexico as, in my judgment, would be advantageous to the republic."

The question of the slave population of Cuba should not come into this discussion, he declared. "I will not trammel the great constitutional power of the Executive to deal with foreign nations, with our internal questions; and I will not manacle my country, I will not handcuff the energies of this mighty republic, by tying up our foreign diplomacy with our internal dissensions. At least to the rest of the world, let us present ourselves as one people, one nation." He spurned the idea that he wanted Cuba to strengthen the slave power in Congress. He said, "Some may think we go for it because by this means we shall have one more slave State in the Union. I know that the senator from New York (Mr. Seward) at the last session alluded to the comparative number of slaveholding and non-slaveholding States; but I never considered that my rights lay there; I never considered that I held my rights of property by the votes of senators. It is too feeble a tenure.

If I did, I have shown by my votes that I have not feared them. Whenever any State, Minnesota or Oregon, or any other, came, no matter from where, if she came on principles which were sufficient in my judgment to justify her admission into this great family of nations, I never refused her the right hand of fellowship. I did not inquire whether you had seventeen or eighteen free States. If you had fifty, it would not alter my vote. The idea of getting one slave State would have no effect on me. But Cuba has fine ports, and with her acquisition, we can make first the Gulf of Mexico, and then the Carribean Sea, a *mare clausum.* Probably younger men than you or I will live to see the day when no flag shall float there except by permission of the United States of America. That is my policy. I rose more with a view to declare my policy for the future; that development, that progress throughout the tropics was the true, fixed, unalterable policy of the nation, no matter what may be the consequences with reference to European powers."

Mr. Toombs believed that much bad legislation resulted from trusting too much to committees. He rarely failed to question such reports, and never voted unless he thoroughly understood the subject. He thought this whole machinery was a means of " transferring the legislation of the country from those into whose hands the Constitution had placed it to irresponsible parties." He said it was a common newspaper idea that Congress was wasting time in debating details. His opinion was that nine-tenths of the time the best thing to be done in public legislation was to do nothing. He thought Congress was breaking down the government by its own weight in "pensioning all the vagrants brought here. All that a man has to do is to make affidavit and get a pension."

In 1859 he refused to vote to appropriate $500,000 for the improvement of Buffalo harbor, because he held he had no right to spend the money of the whole Union for a particular locality; for this reason he voted to abolish the mint at Dahlonega, in his own State.

Mr. Toombs opposed the policy of buying the outstanding debt at a premium. He criticised Senator Simon Cameron for asking that the government give employment to 50,000 laborers out of work. He said, " Sir, government cannot do it and never did do it. There never was a government in the world which did not ruin the people they attempted to benefit by such a course. Governments do not regulate wages."

Senator Toombs contended that the Postal Department stood on a different footing from the army and navy. Postal service, he thought, was no part of the national duty. " It is of no more importance to the people of the United States

that this government should carry my letters than
that it should carry my cotton." He claimed that
he had some old-fashioned ideas, but they were
innate. "I do not think it right, before God, for
me to make another man pay my expenses."

In discussing the financial report, he said, " You
have as much time to appropriate money intelli-
gently as you have to give it lavishly. While
there is a general cry for retrenchment, when any
practical movement is made, the answer always is
that this is not the right time or the right place.
I am afraid we shall never find the right time, or
the right place, until the popular revolution becomes strong enough to send here men who will
do the public business better than we have done
it."

CHAPTER XVIII.

ELECTION OF LINCOLN.

In the election of November, 1860, Mr. Lincoln received 1,857,610 votes, and the combined opposition 2,787,780 votes, the successful candidate being in a minority of nearly a million votes. The new House of Representatives was Democratic, and the Senate had not been won over to the antislavery party. But the trend of Northern politics was unmistakably toward the extinction of slavery. As Mr. Lincoln said in his letter to Mr. Stephens: "You think slavery is right and ought to be extended, while we think it is wrong and ought to be restricted. There, I suppose, is the rub." Mr. Buchanan's message to Congress was full of conservative counsel, but the Northern pressure was too strong. His Cabinet was soon dissolved, and the places of Southern men were taken by Northern representatives, whose influence was not assuring to Southern people.

Just before his departure for Congress Mr. Toombs, in response to an invitation, wrote a conservative letter to his constituents in Danburg, Wilkes County, Ga. It bore date of December

13, 1860. The General Assembly of Georgia had unanimously passed a resolution calling for a State convention to meet on January 16, 1861. Mr. Toombs took the ground that separation, sooner or later, was inevitable. The time when the remedy was to be applied was the point of difference. He opposed delay longer than March 4, but declared that he would certainly yield that point "to earnest and honest men who are with me in principle but are more hopeful of redress from the aggressors than I am. To go beyond March 4, we should require such preliminary measures to be taken as would, with reasonable certainty, lead to adequate redress, and in the meantime, we should take care that the delay gives no advantage to the adversary." Mr. Toombs declared that he believed the policy of Mr. Lincoln was to ultimately abolish slavery in the States, by driving slavery out of the Territories, by abrogating Fugitive-slave laws, and by protecting those who stole slaves and incited insurrections. The only way to remedy these evils, in the Union, was by such constitutional amendments as can be neither resisted nor evaded. "If the Republican party votes for the amendments, we may postpone final action. This will be putting planks where they are good for something. A cartload of new planks in the party platform will not redress one wrong nor protect one right."

As strong and unmistakable as this letter seemed, the great body of the people of Georgia did not think it sufficiently aggressive. Secession now amounted to a furor. It was not the work of leaders, but the spirit which pervaded the ranks of the people, who clamored because events did not move fast enough. The "minute-men" declared Mr. Toombs' letter was a backdown. They called him a traitor, and wanted to vote him a tin sword.

Congress, upon reassembling, devoted itself to measures of compromise. The situation was one of the deepest gravity. In the House a committee of thirty-three was raised, and in the Senate a committee of thirteen, to look into the situation. But there was no Henry Clay to interpose, with tact and broad statesmanship, at the supreme moment.

Twice before in our history, the "Great Pacificator" had proven equal to a desperate emergency. Adjusting the tariff in 1832 when South Carolina threatened nullification, he had kept the peace between Calhoun and Jackson. Proposing his omnibus bill in 1850, he had silenced all calls for disunion by the territorial concession. Equally lacking was the example of Webster to face the prejudices of the North and calm the apprehensions of the South. Perhaps it was because these men had postponed the conflict then that it reappeared now with irrepressible power.

The House Committee reported propositions to amend the Fugitive-slave laws, and accepted Mr. Toombs' demand that a law should be enacted by which all offenses against slave property, by persons fleeing to other States, should be tried where the offense was committed.

Mr. Toombs was a member of the committee of thirteen in the Senate. The five Southern members submitted the Crittenden Compromise, demanding six amendments to the Constitution. These recognized slavery south of the old Missouri line, prohibited interference by Congress with slavery in the District of Columbia, or with transportation of slaves from one State to another, and provided for the payment for fugitive slaves in cases where the marshal was prevented from arresting said fugitive. The sixth amendment guaranteed the permanence of these provisions.

The House adopted the report of the committee of thirty-three. In the Senate a resolution was adopted declaring that the provisions of the Constitution were already ample for the preservation of the Union; that it needed to be obeyed rather than amended. This, upon a test vote of twenty-five to twenty-three, was substituted for the Crittenden Compromise. Mr. Toombs and five other Democratic members refused to vote, as they appropriately declared that no measure could be of value to the South, unless it had the support of

Republican senators from the North. They sat still and waited to see whether those senators offered any guarantees. The twenty-five votes showed that the Republicans were not in a conciliatory mood. This, in the opinion of Senator Toombs, was conclusive that the best interests of the South lay in immediate separation.

Once convinced that this was the proper course, Senator Toombs bent all his powers to bring about that result. He saw that if the Southern States must secede, the quicker they did so the better. If the North cared to recall them, a vigorous policy would react more promptly upon the Republicans. He did not go into this movement with foreboding or half-heartedness. There was no mawkish sentiment—no melancholy in his make-up. His convictions mastered him, and his energy moved him to redoubled effort. On the 22d of December he sent his famous telegram to his "fellow-citizens of Georgia." He recited that his resolutions had been treated with derision and contempt by the Republican members of the committee of thirteen. The amendments proposed by Mr. Crittenden had "each and all of them been voted against unanimously by the Republican members of the committee." These members had also declared that they had no guarantees to offer. He believed that the House Committee only sought to amuse the South with delusive hope, "until your election, in order that you may defeat the friends of secession. If you are deceived by them it shall not be my fault. I have put the test fairly and frankly. It has been decided against you, and now I tell you upon the faith of a true man, that all further looking to the North for security for your constitutional rights in the Union, ought to be instantly abandoned. It is fraught with nothing but menace to yourselves and your party. Secession by the 4th of March next should be thundered forth from the ballot-box by the united voice of Georgia. Such a voice will be your best guaranty for liberty, security, tranquillity, and glory."

CHAPTER XIX.

ON the 7th of January, 1861, Robert Toombs delivered his farewell speech to the United States Senate. It received profound attention. It was full of brief sentences and bristling points. In epigrammatic power, it was the strongest summary of the demands of the South. As Mr. Blaine said, it was the only speech made by a congressman from the seceding States which specified the grievances of the South and which named the conditions upon which the States would stay in the Union. Other Senators regarded secession as a fixed fact. Mr. Toombs declared what, in his opinion, would prevent it. And yet, as he stood at his desk, where for seven years he had been a recognized leader, his earnestness and deliberation revealed a man whose hand did not hesitate to lead a revolt and whose heart did not fail in the face of a certain revolution. He acted up to his own words, repeated a short while later: " He who dallies is a dastard ; he who doubts is damned."

This speech was bold, succinct, definite. " Senators," said Mr. Toombs, " my countrymen have demanded no new government. They have demanded no new Constitution. The discontented States have demanded nothing but clear, distinct, constitutional rights, rights older than the Constitution. What do these rebels demand? First, that the people of the United States shall have an equal right to emigrate and settle in the Territories with whatever property (including slaves) they may possess. Second, that property in slaves shall be entitled to the same protection from the government as any other property (leaving the State the right to prohibit, protect, or abolish slavery within its limits). Third, that persons committing crimes against slave property in one State and flying to another shall be given up. Fourth, that fugitive slaves shall be surrendered. Fifth, that Congress shall pass laws for the punishment of all persons who shall aid and abet invasion and insurrection in any other State."

He said: "We demand these five propositions. Are they not right? Are they not just? We will pause and consider them; but, mark me, we will not let you decide the questions for us. I have little care to dispute remedies with you unless you propose to redress our wrongs.

"But no matter what may be our grievances, the honorable senator from Kentucky (Mr. Crittenden) says we cannot secede. Well, what can we do? We cannot revolutionize. He will say that is treason. What can we do? Submit? They say they are the strongest and they will hang us. Very well! I suppose we are to be thankful for that boon. We will take that risk. We will stand by the right; we will take the Constitution; we will defend it with the sword, with the halter around our necks. Will that satisfy the honorable senator from Kentucky? You cannot intimidate my constituents by talking to them of treason.

"You will not regard confederate obligations; you will not regard constitutional obligations; you will not regard your oaths. What, then, am I to do? Am I a freeman? Is my State a free State? We are freemen; we have rights; I have stated them. We have wrongs; I have recounted them. I have demonstrated that the party now coming into power has declared us outlaws, and is determined to exclude thousands of millions of our property from the common territory; that it has declared us under the ban of the Union, and out of the protection of the laws of the United States everywhere. They have refused to protect us from invasion and insurrection by the Federal power, and the Constitution denies to us, in the Union, the right to raise fleets and armies for our own defense. All these charges I have proven by the record; and I put them before the civilized world and demand the judgment of to-day, of to-morrow, of distant ages, and of Heaven itself upon the justice of these causes. I am content, whatever it be, to peril all in so holy a cause. We have appealed, time and again, for these constitutional rights. You have refused them. We appeal again. Restore us those rights as we had them; as your Court adjudges them to be; just as our people have said they are. Redress these flagrant wrongs—seen of all men—and it will restore fraternity, and unity, and peace to us all. Refuse them, and what then? We shall then ask you, 'Let us depart in peace.' Refuse that, and you present us war. We accept it, and, inscribing upon our banners the glorious words, 'Liberty and Equality,' we will trust to the blood of the brave and the God of battles for security and tranquillity."

This speech created wide attention. It closed the career of Robert Toombs as a member of the national councils. For sixteen years he had served in the two Houses in Washington, holding his rank among the first men in the country.

He was then fifty-one years old, full of strength and confidence. His leadership among Southern men was undisputed; his participation in public business had been long and honorable; upon matters of home and foreign policy his word had been law in the Senate; his influence had been preponderating.

RESIDENCE OF GENERAL TOOMBS, WASHINGTON, GA.

CHAPTER XX.

On the 16th of January, the State Sovereignty convention met in Milledgeville, Ga. The election had taken place shortly after the delivery of Senator Toombs' farewell address, and Georgia had answered to his call in the election of delegates by giving a vote of 50,243 in favor of secession, and 39,123 against it. The convention was presided over by George W. Crawford, who had lived in retirement since the death of President Taylor in 1850, and who was called on to lend his prestige and influence in favor of the rights of his State. The convention went into secret session, and when the doors were opened, Hon. Eugenius A. Nisbet of Bibb offered a resolution, "That in the opinion of this convention, it is the right and duty of Georgia to secede from the Union." On the passage of this, the yeas were 165 and the noes 130. Mr. Toombs voted "yes," and Messrs. Hill, Johnson, and Stephens, "no." Next day the committee of seventeen, through Judge Nisbet, reported the Ordinance of Secession. It was short and pointed; it simply declared that the people of the

State of Georgia, in convention assembled, repealed the ordinance of 1788, whereby the Constitution of the United States was ratified and adopted. The Union was declared dissolved, so far as the State of Georgia was concerned, and the State to be in full possession of all those rights of sovereignty that belonged to a free and independent State. On the passage of this ordinance, the yeas were 208, and the noes, 89. Messrs. Toombs and Hill "yes," and Mr. Stephens "no." At 2.15 P. M. on the 19th of January, a signal gun was fired, and the "Stars and Stripes" lowered from the State Capitol. One moment later, the white colonial flag of Georgia fluttered to the winds, and the State was in uproar. The news flashed to the utmost corners of the commonwealth. Guns were fired, bells rung, and men were beside themselves. The night only intensified this carnival of joy. There were some men who shook their heads and doubted the wisdom of this step, and there were women and little children who regarded these demonstrations with awe. They did not comprehend what was meant by "going out of the Union," and by some inscrutable instinct feared the result of such an act. The old Union sentiment was, perhaps, stronger in Georgia than in any other Southern State. Georgia was the youngest of the thirteen States, the last of the commonwealth to come into the national compact. Her charter from the Crown

had originally barred slavery from her limits, but
the success of the institution in Carolina, the progress of other States in subduing land and in cul-
tivating indigo and tobacco in the Southern sa-
vannas, rendered white labor unavailable, and
left Georgia a laggard in the work of the younger
colonies. Finally, slaves were admitted, and commerce and agriculture seemed to thrive. But if
the State had preserved its original charter restrictions, it is not certain that, even then, the Union
sentiment would have prevailed. As Senator
Toombs had declared: "The question of slavery
moves not the people of Georgia one-half so much
as the fact that you insult their rights as a community. Abolitionists are right when they say
that there are thousands and tens of thousands of
people in Georgia who do not own slaves. A very
large portion of the people of Georgia own none
of them. In the mountains there are but a few of
them; but no part of our people is more loyal to
race and country than our bold and hardy mountain population, and every flash of the electric
wire brings me cheering news from our moun-
tain-tops and our valleys that these sons of Georgia
are excelled by none of their countrymen in loyalty
to their rights, the honor and glory of the commonwealth. They say, and well say, this is our
question: we want no negro equality; no negro
citizenship; we want no mongrel race to degrade

our own, and, as one man, they would meet you
upon the border with the sword in one hand and
the torch in the other. They will tell you, 'When
we choose to abolish this thing (slavery), it must
be done under our direction, according to our will.
Our own, our native land shall determine this
question, and not the Abolitionists of the North.'
That is the spirit of our freemen."

The spirit of the people was plainly manifested
by the zeal and ardor of Thomas R. R. Cobb.
He was a young man who went into the secession
movement with lofty enthusiasm. He had all the
ardor and religious fervor of a crusader. He had
never held public office, and had taken no hand in
politics until the time came for Georgia to secede.
He was the younger brother of Howell Cobb. He
declared that what Mr. Stephens said was the de-
termining sentiment of the hour, that "Georgia
could make better terms out of the Union than in
it." The greater part of the people was fired with
this fervor, which they felt to be patriotic. Gray-
bearded men vied with the hot blood of youth, and
a venerable citizen of Augusta, illuminating his
residence from dome to cellar, blazoned with
candles this device upon his gateway—"Georgia,
right or wrong—Georgia!" Never was a movement so general, so spontaneous. Those who
charged the leaders of that day with precipitating
their States into revolution upon a wild dream of

power, did not know the spirit and the temper
of the people who composed that movement.
Northern men who had moved South and engaged
in business, as a general thing, stood shoulder to
shoulder with their Southern brethren, and went
out with the companies that first responded to the
call to war. The South sacrificed much, in a
material point of view, in going into civil conflict.
In the decade between 1850 and 1860, the wealth
of the South had increased three billions of dollars,
and Georgia alone had shown a growth measured
by two hundred millions. Her aggregate wealth
at the time she passed the Ordinance of Secession
was six hundred and seventy-two millions, double
what it is to-day. In one year her increase was
sixty-two millions. Business of all kinds was pros-
pering. But her people did not count the cost
when they considered that their rights were invaded. Georgia was the fifth State to secede.
South Carolina, Mississippi, Alabama, and Florida
had preceded her. Of the six States which formed
the Provisional Government, Georgia had relatively
a smaller number of slaves than any, and her State
debt was only a little more than two and a half
millions of dollars. Her voting population was
barely 100,000, but she furnished, when the test
came, 120,000 soldiers to the Confederate army.

As a contemporary print of those times remarked, "The Secession convention of Georgia

was not divided upon the subject of rights or
wrongs, but of remedies." Senator Toombs declared that the convention had sovereign powers,
"limited only by God and the right." This policy
opened the way to changing the great seal and
adopting a new flag. Mr. Toombs was made
chairman of the committee on Foreign Relations
and became at once Prime Minister of the young
Republic. He offered a resolution providing that
a congress of seceded States be called to meet in
Montgomery on the 4th of February. He ad-
monished the convention that, as it had destroyed
one government, it was its pressing duty to build
up another. It was at his request that commissioners were appointed from Georgia to the other
States in the South. Mr. Toombs also introduced
a resolution, which was unanimously adopted,
"That the Convention highly approves the energetic and patriotic conduct of Governor Brown in
seizing Fort Pulaski."

The Ordinance of Secession was, on the 31st of
January, signed by all the members of the convention, in the open air, in the Capitol grounds. The
scene was solemn and impressive. Six delegates
entered their protests, but pledged "their lives,
their fortunes, and their sacred honor" in defense
of Georgia against coercion and invasion.

When the time came for the election of delegates to the Provisional Congress at Montgomery,

Robert Toombs was unanimously selected as the first deputy from the State at large. His colleague, Howell Cobb, was chosen on the third ballot. The district selected Francis S. Bartow, Martin J. Crawford, E. A. Nisbet, B. H. Hill, A. R. Wright, Thomas R. R. Cobb, A. H. Kenuan, and A. H. Stephens.

The address to the people of Georgia adopted by this convention, was written by Mr. Toombs. It recited that "our people are still attached to the Union from habit, national tradition, and aversion to change." The address alluded to our "Northern Confederates" and declared that the issue had been "deliberately forced by the North and deliberately accepted by the South. We refuse to submit to the verdict of the North, and in vindication we offer the Constitution of our country. The people of Georgia have always been willing to stand by this compact; but they know the value of parchment rights in treacherous hands." The report charged that the North had outlawed three thousand millions of our property, put it under a ban, and would subject us, not only to a loss of our property, but to destruction of our homes and firesides. It concludes: "To avoid these evils, we withdraw the powers that our fathers delegated to the government of the United States, and henceforth seek new safeguards for our liberty, security, and tranquillity."

On the 4th of February, 1861, forty-two delegates met at Montgomery, Ala. The States of Alabama, Florida, Georgia, Louisiana, Mississippi, and South Carolina were represented. Howell Cobb of Georgia was chosen President of the Provisional Congress. Mr. Stephens said it was the most intellectual body of men he had ever seen. One of the first duties of this convention was to elect a President and vice president of the new Confederacy. All eyes were turned to Robert Toombs. It was by common consent agreed that Georgia, owing to her commanding position, her prominence in the movement, and her wealth of great men, should furnish the President. Toombs towered even above the members of that convention. Bold, imperious, and brainy, he had guided the revolution without haste or heat, and his conservative course in the Georgia convention had silenced those critics who had called him "the genius of the revolution," but denied to him the constructive power to build upon the ruins he had made. He had, in the choice of delegates to the Provisional Congress, boldly advocated the election of Mr. Stephens from his own district, although the latter was a Union man and, at that time, was not on good terms with Toombs. Toombs declared that Alexander Stephens was a patriot notwithstanding his views against secession. He had secured the recommitment of a dangerous resolution upon slavery which, he declared, would injure the South by the announcement of an ultra policy. He had written a very conservative letter to Senator Crittenden. He had been a prominent Secessionist, and had contemplated the movement as unavoidable when men were talking with bated breath. But in the opening of the revolution, he had proven a safe counselor. Mr. Toombs was approached, and announced that he would accept the presidency if it were offered with unanimity. He was surprised to learn that the delegates from four States had agreed on Jefferson Davis. When this report was confirmed, Mr. Toombs, ignorant of the real cause of this sudden change of sentiment, forbade further canvass of his own claims, and cordially seconded the nomination of Mr. Davis. Mr. Toombs was a man of rare magnanimity. He was absolutely without envy or resentment, and turning to Mr. Stephens, pressed him to accept second place on the ticket. The announcement of a Georgian for vice president effectually disposed of his own chance for the presidency. The fact was that Mr. Toombs was the first choice of Georgia, as he was thought to be of Florida, Carolina, and Louisiana. Jefferson Davis had not been presented by Mississippi. He had been selected by that State as the commander-in-chief of the military forces and himself preferred a military station. He was not in

Montgomery when his nomination was confirmed. A messenger had to be dispatched to inform him of his election as President of the Confederate States of America.

The sudden selection of Mr. Davis by four States probably carries a bit of secret history. Old party antagonisms arose at the last moment to confront the candidacy of Mr. Toombs. Toombs had summarily left the Whig party in 1850, to join the great Constitutional Union movement. Jefferson Davis had always been a States' Rights Democrat, and had been defeated for Governor of Mississippi by the Constitutional Union party. Thus it would seem that, at the eleventh hour, party lines were drawn against Robert Toombs, and his boast that he had saved the Union in 1850 probably cost him the presidency of the new republic. There was a story, credited in some quarters, that Mr. Toombs' convivial conduct at a dinner party in Montgomery estranged from him some of the more conservative delegates, who did not realize that a man like Toombs had versatile and reserved powers, and that Toombs at the banquet board was another sort of a man from Toombs in a deliberative body.

At all events, the recognized leader of the Confederacy was set aside, and with rare unanimity the election of officers was accepted with unselfish patriotism.

At that time a curious and remarkable incident in the life of Mr. Toombs was related. Within thirty days he had performed journeys to the extent of fifteen hundred miles, largely by private conveyance, and during that brief period he served under four distinct governments: as senator in the Congress of the United States, as delegate from his native county (Wilkes) to the convention of the sovereign republic of Georgia, as deputy from his State to the Congress of seceding States, which instituted a Provisional Government, and finally in the permanent government which he aided in framing for the Confederate States of America.

In the perfection of a permanent government and the new-molding of a Constitution, Mr. Toombs was now diligently engaged. The principal changes brought about by him may be briefly recalled. It was specified, in order to cut off lobby agents, that Congress should grant no extra compensation to any contractor after the service was rendered. This item originated with Mr. Toombs, who had noted the abuses in the Federal Government. Congress was authorized to grant to the principal officer of each of the executive departments a seat upon the floor of either house, without a vote, but with the privilege of discussing any measure relating to his department. This was an old idea of Mr. Toombs, and during his visit abroad, he had attended sessions of the British Parliament in company with Mr. Buchanan, then Minister to England. He had been impressed with the value of the presence in Parliament of the Ministers themselves. During a debate in the United States Senate in 1859, Mr. Toombs had said: "My own opinion is that it would be a great improvement on our system if the Cabinet officers should be on the floor of both Houses, and should participate in the debate; I have no doubt that we should thus get rid of one of the greatest difficulties in our Constitution."

Mr. Toombs also incorporated into the organic law a prohibition of the payment of bounties and of the internal improvement system. There was a tax upon navigation for harbors, buoys, and beacons, but this was adjusted upon the Toombs principle of taxing the interest for which the burden was levied. Mr. Toombs was made chairman of the Finance Committee of the Provisional Congress. This appointment was received with general satisfaction. His long legislative experience, his genius for finance, and his executive power, fitted him for this position. To provide ways and means for the new nation which was, as yet, without resources or a system of taxation, involved no little difficulty. It was important that the young Confederacy should exhibit resources sufficient to equip her armies and maintain herself before she could sue for independence or foreign recognition. It was for these admitted qualities of Mr. Toombs for details and management, that President Davis preferred him to take the position of Secretary of the Treasury. Next to the presidency this was his real place, but it was suggested that a man like Toombs deserved the first position in the new Cabinet. A telegram from President Davis, offering him the portfolio of Secretary of State, reached Mr. Toombs in Augusta. He at first declined, but being urged by Mr. Stephens, finally consented to serve. The Cabinet was then made up as follows. Robert Toombs of Georgia, Secretary of State; C. G. Memminger of South Carolina, Secretary of the Treasury; L. P. Walker of Alabama, Secretary of War; J. H. Reagan of Texas, Postmaster-General; J. P. Benjamin of Louisiana, Attorney-General; S. B. Mallory of Florida, Secretary of the Navy.

CHAPTER XXI.

ONE of the first acts of the new Confederate Government was to send three commissioners to Washington. John Forsyth of Alabama, Martin J. Crawford of Georgia, and A. B. Roman of Louisiana, were intrusted by the Secretary of State, Mr. Toombs, with a speedy adjustment of questions growing out of the political revolution, upon such terms of amity and good will as would guarantee the future welfare of the two sections. Mr. Toombs instructed Mr. Crawford, whom he had especially persuaded to take this delicate mission, that he should pertinaciously demand the evacuation of Fort Sumter and the maintenance of the status elsewhere.

Secretary Seward declined to receive the commissioners in any diplomatic capacity, or even to see them personally. He acknowledged the receipt of their communication and caused the commissioners to be notified, pointedly, that he hoped they would not press him to reply at that time. Mr. Seward was represented as strongly disposed in favor of peace, and the Confederate Government was semi-officially informed that Fort Sumter would probably be evacuated in a short time, and all immediate danger of conflict avoided. There is no doubt that such were Mr. Seward's intentions. He had cordially agreed with General Winfield Scott that the possession of Fort Sumter amounted to little in a strategical way, and that the peace-loving people, North and South, should not be driven into the war party by premature shock over the provisioning of a fort that no Federal force could have held for a week. Mr. Lincoln's Cabinet took this position and, by a vote of five to two, favored the abandonment of Sumter. The commissioners were apprised of this feeling, and in a dispatch to Secretary Toombs, on the 20th of March, declared that there was no change in the status. "If there is any faith in man," they wrote, "we may rely on the assurances we have as to the status. Time is essential to the principal issue of this mission. In the present posture of affairs, precipitation is war."

On the 26th of March the commissioners, having heard nothing more, asked the Confederate Secretary whether they should delay longer or demand an answer at once. Secretary Toombs wired them to wait a reasonable time and then ask for instructions. He gave them the views of President Davis, who believed that the counsels of Mr. Seward would prevail in Washington.

"So long as the United States neither declares war nor establishes peace, it affords the Confederate States the advantage of both positions, and enables them to make all necessary arrangements for public defense and the solidification of government more safely, cheaply, and expeditiously than if the attitude of the United States was more definite and decided."

Meanwhile new pressure was brought to bear on President Lincoln. On the 2d of April, the commissioners, who kept up pretty well with the situation, telegraphed Secretary Toombs: "The war party presses on the President; he vibrates to that side." The rumor was given that the President had conferred with an engineer in regard to Fort Sumter. "Watch at all points." Three days later they telegraphed that the movement of troops and the preparation of vessels of war were continued with great activity. "The statement that the armament is intended for San Domingo," they said, "may be a mere ruse." "Have no confidence in this administration. We say, be ever on your guard. . . . . Glad to hear you are ready. The notice promised us may come at the last moment, if the fleet be intended for our waters."

On the 6th of April Governor Pickens of South Carolina was informed that the President had decided to supply Fort Sumter with provisions, and on the 10th, Hon. Levi P. Walker, Secretary of

War at Montgomery, notified General Beauregard,
then in command of the Confederate forces at
Charleston, to demand the evacuation of Fort
Sumter, and, if refused, to proceed to reduce it.

There is no doubt that the Lincoln Cabinet re-
versed its position about Sumter. The pressure
of New England and the West became too strong.
What Sumter lacked in military importance, it
made up in political significance. The Lincoln
Government had already been taunted with weakness by the people who had placed it in office.
Mr. Lincoln decided, against the better judgment
of Mr. Seward, to make the issue in Charleston
Harbor.

Seward's mind was of finer and more reflective
cast than Mr. Lincoln's. He had all the points of
a diplomatist, ingenuity, subtlety, adroitness. He
was temporizing over the natural antipathy of the
North to war and the probable transient nature of
the secession feeling in the South. At that very
moment he was assuring England and France that
" the conservative element in the South, which was
kept under the surface by the violent pressure of
secession, will emerge with irresistible force." He
believed " that the evils and hardships produced
by secession would become intolerably grievous to
the Southern States."

Mr. Lincoln was not temporizing at all. He was
looking the crisis in the face. What he wanted

was support at the North, not at the South. He
was willing to force the fighting at Sumter, knowing that the mere act of the Confederates in firing
upon the flag would bring to his aid a united North.

Secretary Toombs was one man in the Montgomery Cabinet who was not deceived by Seward's
sophistries. He knew the temper of Mr. Lincoln
better than Mr. Seward did. He appreciated the
feeling at the North, and gave his counsel in the
Davis Cabinet against the immediate assault upon
Sumter. There was a secret session of the Cabinet
in Montgomery. Toombs was pacing the floor
during the discussion over Sumter, his hands behind him, and his face wearing that heavy, dreamy
look when in repose. Facing about, he turned
upon the President and opposed the attack. " Mr.
President," he said, " at this time, it is suicide, murder, and will lose us every friend at the North.
You will wantonly strike a hornet's nest which
extends from mountains to ocean, and legions, now
quiet, will swarm out and sting us to death. It is
unnecessary ; it puts us in the wrong ; it is fatal."
He clung to the idea expressed in his dispatches
to the commissioners, that " So long as the United
States neither declares war nor establishes peace,
the Confederate States have the advantage of both
conditions." But just as President Lincoln overruled Secretary Seward, so President Davis overruled Secretary Toombs.

No event in American history was more portentous than the first gun fired from Fort Johnson at 1.30 o'clock in the morning of April 12, 1861. As the shell wound its graceful curve into the air and fell into the water at the base of Sumter, the Civil War was an accomplished fact. Major Anderson replied with his barbette guns from the fort. He had but little more than 100 men, and early in the engagement was forced to rely entirely upon his casemate ordinance. The Confederate forces numbered about five thousand, with thirty guns and seventeen mortars, and served their guns from the batteries on Mount Pleasant, Cummings Point, and the floating battery. Fort Sumter was built on an artificial island at the mouth of Charleston Harbor, and was about three and a half miles from the city. It had cost the government one million dollars, and had not been entirely completed at the time of the bombardment.

The excitement in Charleston at the opening gun was very great. People rushed from their beds to the water-front, and men and women watched the great duel through their glasses. The South had gone into the war with all the fervor of conviction. The gunners in Moultrie and on Morris Island would leap to the ramparts and watch the effect of their shots, and jump back to their guns with a cheer. There was all the pomp and sound, but few of the terrors of

war. On the morning of the second day the
quarters in the fort caught fire and the whole
place was wrapped in flames and smoke, but Major
Anderson's men won the admiration of their
enemies by standing by their guns and returning
the fire at regular intervals. The battle lasted
thirty-two hours; more than fifty tons of cannon-
balls and eight tons of powder were expended
from weapons the most destructive then known
to warfare; not a life was lost on either side.
Sumter and Moultrie were both badly damaged.
Major Anderson surrendered on Saturday, April
13.

The London *Times* treated this remarkable
event in humorous style. The proceedings at
Charleston were likened to a cricket match or a
regatta in England. The ladies turned out to
view the contest. A good shot from Fort Sumter
was as much applauded as a good shot from Fort
Moultrie. When the American flag was shot
away, General Beauregard sent Major Anderson
another to fight under. When the fort was found
to be on fire, the polite enemy, who had with
such intense energy labored to excite the confla-
gration, offered equally energetic assistance to
put it out. The only indignation felt throughout
the affair was at the conduct of the Northern
flotilla, which kept outside and took no part in
the fray. The Southerners resented this as an

act of treachery toward their favorite enemy, Major Anderson. "Altogether," says the *Times*, "nothing can be more free from the furious hatreds, which are distinctive of civil warfare, than this bloodless conflict has been." Another London paper remarked " No one was hurt. And so ended the first, and, we trust, the last engagement of the American Civil War."

Mr. Toombs' prediction, that the attack upon Fort Sumter would " open a hornet's nest " in the North, was sustained. The effect of the assault at that time and the lowering of the national flag to the forces of the Confederacy acted, as Mr. Blaine has stated, "as an inspiration, consolidating public sentiment, dissipating all differences." In fact it brought matters to a crisis all around, and prepared the two sections for the great drama of the War.

An important part of the work of Secretary Toombs was the selection of a commission to proceed to Europe and present the Confederate position to England and France, in order to secure recognition of the new nation. Mr. William L. Yancey was placed at the head of this commission, and with him were associated Mr. A. D. Mason of Virginia, and Mr. A. P. Rost of Louisiana. The first month of the term of the Confederate Secretary of State was occupied in the issue of letters of marque. On the 19th of April President Lincoln proclaimed a blockade of Southern ports, and declared that privateers with letters of marque from the Southern Confederacy should be treated as pirates. This gave Secretary Toombs a strong point in dealing with foreign powers. The new government had been organized with promptness and ability. Great energy was shown in getting the civil and military branches equipped. The Southern position had been presented with great strength abroad, and France and England were not slow in framing proclamations recognizing the Confederate States as belligerents. Next to immediate recognition as a separate nationality, this step was significant, and was the first triumph of the diplomacy of Secretary Toombs over Secretary Seward. Then came the demand from the foreign powers that the blockade must be effectual, imposing a heavy burden upon the Northern States. Lord Lyons, acting in Washington in concert with the French Government, declared that " Her Majesty's Government would consider a decree closing the ports of the South, actually in possession of the Confederate States, as null and void, and they would not submit to measures on the high seas pursuant to such a decree." Mr Seward bitterly complained that Great Britain "did not sympathize with this government." The British Minister accordingly charged the British Consul at Charleston with the task of obtaining from the Confederate Government securities concerning the proper treatment of neutrals. He asked the accession of the Lincoln government and of the Davis government to the Declaration of Paris of 1856, which had adopted as articles of maritime law that privateering be abolished; that the neutral flag covers enemy's goods, with the exception of contraband of war; that neutral goods, with the exception of contraband of war, are not liable to capture under the enemy's flag; that a blockade, in order to be binding, must be effectual, that is, must be maintained by a force sufficient to prevent access to the coast of the enemy. These conditions, except the first, were accepted by the Confederate Government.

The Southern Confederacy thus became parties, as Mr. Blaine says, to " an international compact"; and when, a few months later, Mr. Seward offered to waive the point made by Secretary Marcy many years before, and accept the four articles of the Paris convention, he found himself blocked, because the Confederate States had not accepted the first article, abolishing privateering, and her privateers must, therefore, be recognized. It was by these privateers that great damage was inflicted upon American shipping.

The Confederate States had no regular navy, and but few vessels; they were an agricultural community, not a commercial or a ship-building people. Quite a number of vessels were put in commission under letters of marque, and these reached the high seas by running the blockade. Many prizes were taken and run into Southern ports. Later on steamers were fitted out and sent to sea under command of experienced officers. This naval militia captured millions of the enemy's property, and produced a great sensation at the North. A Southern agent was sent abroad by the naval department to get ships and supplies. "In three years' time," says Mr. Blaine, "fifteen millions of property had been destroyed by Southern privateers, given to the flames, or sunk beneath the waters. The shipping of the United States was reduced one-half, and the commercial flag of the Union fluttered with terror in every wind that blew, from the whale fisheries of the Arctic to the Southern Cross."

On the 21st of May, the Confederate Congress, after providing for the disposition of these naval prizes, and the treatment of prisoners of war brought into Southern ports, adjourned to meet on the 20th of July in the City of Richmond, now selected as the permanent seat of Government of the Confederacy.

The powers of Europe never recognized the Confederate States as a separate nation. The leaders of the English Government were, no doubt, inclined to this step, but the rank and file of the Liberal party, under the leadership of John

Bright, refused to sanction such a course toward a government whose corner stone was slavery. Mr. Seward ingeniously pressed the point that Southern success meant a slave oligarchy around the Gulf of Mexico. Russia remained the strong ally of the Northern States. England, with the Crimean War fresh upon her hands, hesitated before engaging Russia again or imperiling India in the East. France could not afford to take the step without the aid of England. Secretary Toombs dispatched a Minister to Mexico to look into the interesting tumult then going on. Louis Napoleon was filled with his desire of establishing Maximilian in Mexico, but his movement did not succeed. Maximilian was defeated and executed, and Napoleon found himself too much engaged with the House of Hohenzollern in Germany to follow any new or original policy in America.

Carlyle declared with dyspeptic acrimony that the Civil War was the foulest chimney of the century, and should be allowed to burn out.

Secretary Toombs had issued credentials to commissioners to the unseceded Southern States. On the 17th of April Virginia seceded; on the 28th of May North Carolina went out of the Union; these were followed by Tennessee and Arkansas. The border States of Kentucky and Missouri did not formally secede, but indignantly declined to

furnish troops in response to Mr. Lincoln's proclamation. They appointed delegates to a Peace
Congress to meet in Washington.

The tedious routine of the State Department
did not suit the restless spirit of Robert Toombs.
He had established relations abroad as belligerents, and had placed the new government in
touch with its Southern neighbors. His dispatches were remarkable for brevity, clearness, and
boldness; his public papers are models of nervous
style, but he longed for a more active field in the
revolution. He chafed under red-tape and convention. Toombs charged the new administration
with too much caution and timidity. He declared
that ninety per cent. of war was business, and that
the South must organize victory rather than trust
entirely to fighting. He urged the government to
send over cotton to England and buy arms and
ships forthwith. "Joe Brown," he impatiently
declared, "had more guns than the whole Confederacy. No new government," said he, "ever
started with such unlimited credit." Mr. Toombs
believed that the financial part of the Confederacy was a failure. "We could have whipped the
fight," said he, in his impetuous way, "in the first
sixty days. The contest was haphazard from
the first, and nothing but miraculous valor kept
it going." Mr. Toombs said that had he been
President of the Confederacy, he would have

mortgaged every pound of cotton to France and England at a price that would have remunerated the planters, and in consideration of which he would have secured the aid of the armies and navies of both countries.

But Robert Toombs concluded that his place was in the field, not in the Cabinet. Too many prominent men, he explained, were seeking bombproof positions. He received a commission as brigadier general, and on the 21st of July, 1861, joined Generals Beauregard and Johnston at Manassas.

CHAPTER XXII.

WHEN Robert Toombs resigned the Cabinet and took the field, he still held the seat, as was his prerogative, in the Confederate Congress. This body, like the British Parliament, sat in chairs, without desks. One morning Congress was discussing the Produce Loan. By this measure, invitations were given for contributions of cotton and other crops in the way of a loan. By the terms of the act these articles were to be sold and the proceeds turned over to the Secretary of the Treasury, who was to issue eight per cent. bonds for them. This was an extraordinary measure, and never really amounted to much. Colonel A. R. Lamar, at one time Secretary of the Provisional Congress, relates that during this debate General Toombs walked into the hall. "He was faultlessly attired in a black suit with a military cloak thrown over one shoulder and a military hat in his left hand. He made a rattling speech against the measure. Drawing himself up, he said: "Mr. Speaker, we have been told that Cotton is King, that he will find his way to the vaults of the

bankers of the Old World; that he can march up
to the thrones of mighty potentates, and drag
from the arsenals of armed nations the dogs of
war; that he can open our closed ports, and fly
our young flag upon all the seas. And yet, before
the first autumnal frost has blighted a leaf upon
his coronet, he comes to this hall a trembling
mendicant, and says, 'Give me drink, Titinius, or I
perish.'" The effect was magical; Colonel Lamar,
in commenting upon this dramatic incident, sums
up the whole character of Robert Toombs:

"He was cautious and safe in counsel, while
wild and exasperating in speech."

When Mr. Toombs was once asked by an Englishman, where were the files of the State Department, he answered that "He carried the archives in
his hat." When he resigned the position of Secretary of State, Hon. Robert M. T. Hunter of Virginia
was appointed in his stead. General William
M. Browne had been Assistant Secretary under
Mr. Toombs. He was an Englishman, who came
to this country during Buchanan's administration and edited a Democratic paper in Washington. When General Toombs joined the Army his
staff was made up as follows; D. M. Dubose, Adjutant General; R. J. Moses, Commissary General;
W. F. Alexander, Quartermaster Major; DeRosset
Lamar, Aid-de-camp.

General Toombs' entry into the field, just after

the first battle of Manassas, found the army of the Confederacy flushed with victory, but badly scattered after the first serious engagement of the war. General Johnston had declared that even after the decisive advantage at Bull Run, pursuit was not to be thought of, for his troops were almost as much disorganized by victory as the Federals by their defeat. Many soldiers, supposing the war was over, had actually gone home. "Our men," said General Johnston, "had in a larger degree the instincts of personal liberty than those of the North, and it was found very difficult to subordinate their personal wills to the needs of military discipline."

The battle of Manassas had a powerful effect upon the Northern mind. The Lincoln Cabinet was seized with fear for the safety of Washington. New troops were summoned to that city, and the materials for a magnificent army were placed in the hands of General McClellan, who had succeeded McDowell, the luckless victim of Manassas. More than one hundred thousand men were now massed in front of Washington, while Joseph E. Johnston, with fifty-four thousand, advanced his outposts to Centreville, and at Munson's Hill Toombs' brigade was in sight of the national capital. His troops could easily watch the workmen building one of the wings of the Capitol, and the victorious Confederates, with prestige in their ranks, were actually flaunting their flag in the face of Mr. Lincoln. This movement, we are told by good generals, was of no military value, but it kept the Northern administration in a white heat. It confused the Union commanders by crossing their counsels with popular clamor and political pressure, and it crippled McClellan when he finally moved down the Chesapeake to the peninsula, by detaining a large part of his force to pacify the authorities in Washington.

When McClellan and Mr. Lincoln were disputing over their change of base, the military situation was suddenly shifted by the evacuation of Manassas by the Confederate army, and its retirement first behind the Rappahannock, then along the Rapidan. Johnston, it seems, wanted to be nearer his base, and on the 8th of March skillfully managed his withdrawal, so that the enemy had no idea of his movements. General Toombs' brigade started in retreat from Centreville. He did not relish this movement. He writes home from Culpepper :

This has been a sad and destructive business. We were ordered to send off all our heavy baggage, but so badly did they manage that none of it was sent back, and every particle of that baggage, blankets, and every imaginable useful article, was burned up to prevent its falling into the hands of the enemy. My brigade must have lost half a million of property and all the rest were in the same condition. Millions of stores with guns and ammunition were destroyed. Never was any business worse managed. The enemy had no more idea of attacking us in Centreville than they had of attacking the Peaks of Otter. Of course, when we retreated, they sent marauding parties in our trail to watch our retreat and take possession of the country, and now the whole of the beautiful Counties of Loudon, Fauquier, Prince William, Fairfax, and the Lord only knows how many more, are in the possession of the enemy. It was a sad, distressing sight, all the way along, and one that frequently drew tears from my eyes. I do not know what it means, but I would rather have fought ten battles than thus to have abandoned these poor people. We have got to fight somewhere, and if I had my way, I would fight them on the first inch of our soil they invaded, and never cease to fight them as long as I could rally men to defend their homes. The great body of the army is now in the neighborhood, and I suppose we shall abandon these people and retreat back toward Richmond. . . . . My command is in excellent condition. A few broke down on the way, but I managed to have them taken care of there and lost none of them on the march.

One of the great features of General Toombs' control of his brigade was the excellent care he took of his men. He never allowed them to be imposed upon by the officers or by other commands.

This letter betrays the impatience of General Toombs over any mismanagement. He was the soul of business, and as the transportation facilities at Manassas were meager, he chafed under the heavy loss to which his brigade was subjected in this retreat. With impetuous ardor he calls for resistance, not retreat. He did not approve of the "Fabian policy" of Joseph E. Johnston. As General Longstreet afterward remarked, "Toombs chafed at the delays of the commanders in their preparations for battle. His general idea was that the troops went out to fight, and he thought that they should be allowed to go at it at once." Near Orange Court House, he wrote to his wife on the 19th of March, 1862, "I know not what is to become of this country. Davis' incompetency is more apparent as our danger increases. Our only hope is Providence."

In January, 1862, the General Assembly of Georgia elected Robert Toombs a member of the Confederate States Senate. Benjamin H. Hill was to be his colleague. But General Toombs had a different conception of his duty. He realized that he had been prominent in shaping the events that had led to the Civil War, and he did not shirk the sharpest responsibility. He felt that his duty was in the field. He had condemned the rush for civil offices and what he called "bomb-proof positions," and he wished at least to lead the way to active duty by remaining with his army.

Two months later an effort was made by some of his friends to have him appointed Secretary of War. This would have brought him in close contact with the army, which he was anxious to serve. The parties behind this movement believed that the great abilities of Mr. Toombs should not be hidden behind the command of a brigade. He would have made an ideal war minister. His genius for details and his ability to manage affairs and plan campaigns would have overmatched Edwin M. Stanton. But Mr. Toombs promptly cut off this movement in his behalf.

On 22d March, 1862, he wrote to his wife from Orange Court House, Va. :

I thought I had been very explicit on that point. I would not be Mr. Davis' chief clerk. His Secretary of War can never be anything else. I told my friends in Richmond to spare me the necessity of declining if they found it in contemplation. I have not heard that they had any occasion to interfere. . . . . So far as I am concerned, Mr. Davis will never give me a chance for personal distinction. He thinks I pant for it, poor fool. I want nothing but the defeat of the public enemy and to retire with you for the balance of my life in peace and quiet in any decent corner of a free country. It may be his injustice will drive me from the army, but I shall not quit it until after a great victory, in which I shall have the opportunity of doing something for the country. The day after such an event I shall retire, if I live through it. I have grievances enough now to quit, but I shall bide my time. I get along very well with the army. I have not seen Johnston but once ; he was polite and clever. George W. Smith I see every day. He is a first-rate gentleman and a good officer. I hear from Stephens constantly, but from nobody else in Richmond. . . . . You say you pray for me daily. I need it. Put it in your prayers that if it be the will of God that I shall fall, a sacrifice in this great conflict, that I may meet it as becomes a gentleman.

An instance of General Toombs' impatience under red-tape rules may be recalled. A member of his brigade was taken ill, and he secured for him entrance into the hospital of Richmond. The hospital was crowded; regulations were stringent, and under some technical ruling his sick soldier was shipped back to his brigade. Toombs was fired with indignation. He proceeded to sift the affair to the bottom, and was told that General Johnston had fixed the rules. This did not deter him. Riding up to the commander's tent and securing admission, he proceeded to upbraid the general as only Toombs could do. When he returned to his headquarters he narrated the circumstance to Dr. Henry H. Steiner, his brigade surgeon and lifelong friend. Dr. Steiner, who had been a surgeon in the regular army, and had served in the Mexican war, was a better tactical officer than Toombs. He was himself fearless and upright, but full of tact and discretion. "General," said Dr. Steiner, "you have been too rash; you will be arrested." Toombs replied that he thought so, too. He held himself in anticipation for two or three days, but he was not disturbed. When he was finally summoned to General Johnston's tent, it was to consult over a plan of movement, and it was noticed that Toombs was the only brigadier in counsel. General Johnston subsequently remarked that Toombs was the biggest brained man in the Confederacy. The boldness and clearness of the impetuous Georgian had captured the grim hero of Manassas, who forgave the affront in the face of the overmastering mind of the man.

General McClellan reached Fortress Monroe, April 2, 1862, and commenced his march up the peninsula. The country is low and flat, and the season was unusually wet and dismal. The objective point was Richmond, seventy-five miles away, and the first obstruction met by the Federal army was at Yorktown. The defense adopted by General Magruder was a series of dams extending along the Warwick River, which stretched across the peninsula from the York to the James River, a distance of thirteen miles. The fords along the Warwick had been destroyed by dams defended by redoubts, and the invader and defender were stationed in dense swamps. At dam No. 1 Toombs' troops were often under fire. They fought with spirit. Each detachment was on duty defending the dam forty-eight hours, and between long exposure in the trenches, the frequent alarms, and sharp sorties, the service was very exhausting. It was only possible to change troops at night. On the 16th of April Toombs writes:

One of my regiments, the 17th Georgia, had a skirmish day before yesterday. They acted splendidly, charging the Yankees, and driving them from the rifle-pits, killing, wounding, and taking prisoners over one hundred of the enemy. I lost but two killed and a few wounded.

At the siege of Yorktown in the early part of May, 1862, General Toombs commanded a division consisting of his own and Semmes' brigades. He had 2357 men in his own and 2342 in Semmes' brigade, making about 4700 troops in line. During this siege General Magruder reports that General Toombs supported Cobb's brigade, and promptly and energetically led the remainder of his command under fire, arriving just before the enemy ceased their attack, and in time to share its danger. General Magruder had only 11,000 men under him in the peninsula, and General Huger but 8000, to oppose McClellan's march with 80,000. Johnston and Lee both pronounced the peninsula untenable, and on the 4th of May Yorktown was evacuated.

After the retreat from the peninsula, General Johnston concentrated his entire army behind the Chickahominy River, sixteen miles from Richmond. On the 12th of May General Toombs writes home that his command near the Chickahominy was "resting easily after a disagreeable march from Yorktown. I hear that there is great consternation in Richmond. . . . . The loss of New Orleans gives us a terrible blow, and, followed by Norfolk, makes it necessary for us to strike a decisive blow somewhere." On 19th of May, 1862, he writes home from the camp near Richmond:

We seem to have come up here to defend this city. You ask me my opinion of the present state of the country. It is bad enough. The utter incompetency of Mr. Davis and his West Point generals have brought us to the verge of ruin. If McClellan is unwise enough to fight us here, we shall whip and drive him out of Virginia. . . . . As to Richmond, it will never be taken while this army is here.

General Toombs' estimate of the army and of the futility of an attack from McClellan was justified when, after the 26th of June, the Army of the Potomac, almost in sight of the spires of Richmond, was forced to reel back, in the deadly clinch of a seven days' combat, to the James River. The Confederate army changed its position from one of retreat to a brilliant and aggressive policy, and the subtle tactics of Johnston gave way to the bold strokes of Lee. The South was thrilled with victory.

General Toombs frequently referred to the incompetency of Mr. Davis. The letters which have just been quoted were written to his wife, and were not made public then, but he did not hesitate to express his opinion openly. Jefferson Davis and Mr. Toombs had some differences while the former was Secretary of War under Franklin Pierce and Mr. Toombs was in the Senate. Mr. Toombs believed that President Davis was too partial to West Point, at which school Mr. Davis had been trained, and that in his man-

agement of the army he showed the tenacity of a
martinet rather than the breadth of a statesman.

In February, 1859, the Army Appropriation bill
had come up before the United States Senate.
Mr. Toombs attacked, and Mr. Davis defended the
whole system. Mr. Toombs contended that the
compensation of army officers was too great. It
was more than the same talent could command in
any other walk of life. It was upon a wrong basis.
"You take a boy of sixteen and send him to West
Point, and when he comes out you give him $1400
a year. In the course of a few years you carry
him up to $3000, $6000, or $8000. Take the gen-
eral employment of the youths of the country who
are educated at the different colleges for all civil
purposes. You may have the highest amount of
genius and intellect, and you get nothing like such
average there. It will take them many years to
make that much money." Mr. Toombs declared
that a brigadier general's commission was higher
than that of a United States Senator. "I think,"
said he, "it requires as great qualifications to govern
this country as it does to be a brigadier general."
Officers had increased far beyond the wants of
the country. Members of Congress appoint cadets
for the different districts; "they are generally
associated in some way, as brothers, sons, or
cousins, with the governing power." He thought
a salary of $600 or $900 for the West Point grad-

uates enough. According to the way army commissions were valued in England, the commission of a lieutenant who graduated at West Point could not be worth less than $50,000. The pay of a captain was higher than that of a judge. That position required the highest ability and integrity, and the average salary of a judge was but $2000, without traveling expenses. Mr. Toombs contended that West Point men seldom reflected any opinions but those of the government which employed them. They seldom sympathized with the people, and he wanted a government of the people. "You take a boy to West Point," he said, "give him quarters, and fuel, and clothes, and maintain him, and you say he has rendered service. When the citizens of this country send their sons to college they pay their expenses or work their way through; but when a boy is carried to West Point he is taken care of; a house is provided for him; clothes are provided for him; instructors are provided for him, and that is called being in service. I lay down the proposition that the true theory of wages, if you employ these people to keep the peace, is exactly the same—a constable's pay—you ought to pay them what they can be had for."

Mr. Davis held that army officers were constantly tempted to resign by offers of higher pay. It was the training of these men in the service, not for the service, it was their attachment for the country which made them so valuable. It was better to instruct men for officers' places and then appoint them, than to appoint them and then instruct them. He thought appointments were free from partisan selection. A soldier's devotion was as broad as the continent. A West Point cadet is a warrant officer; he goes there to serve the government as it may direct. It directs him to stay there until he has sufficient elementary instruction to properly discharge the duties of an officer.

The debate showed the views of the two men, and indicated the differences which, from points of public policy, soon deepened into personal dislike. On the 30th of May, Toombs wrote from the army, "Davis is polite and formal; so am I."

In the latter part of 1862 it was evident that the two armies must meet and contend for the mastery in Virginia. The day before the seven days' fighting commenced, Dr. Steiner said to General Toombs, his intimate friend: "General, I have a favor to ask of you. Keep your mind unclouded during these important operations." Dr. Steiner knew that during the heat and excitement of battle, temptation was great among soldiers to take ardent spirits, a practice that had grown somewhat upon General Toombs during his service in the field, and which at times deprived him of his best powers. "Why, doctor, I gladly promise," said the great Georgian. Nor did he, during the week, take a glass of any sort of liquor.

General Toombs' brigade was the First Brigade, First Division, Army of Northern Virginia, and during the campaign of the peninsula, was in Magruder's division. On June 15, 1862, Toombs occupied the most exposed position, which was held for nine days. Magruder recommended relief for his troops, which had been suffering from lack of rest and care. Just before the seven days' fight Toombs' brigade was placed in D. R. Jones' division and Magruder commanded his own, Jones', and McLaw's divisions, holding about 13,000 men. Toombs' brigade was composed of the 1st, 15th, 17th, and 20th Georgia regiments.

On the 26th of June Toombs' brigade was posted upon the east of Garnett's House, on Golding's farm, just in front of the enemy. Both sides threw up breastworks so near that neither could advance its picket line. "Just before dark," says Dr. Steiner, "Mr. Toombs received orders to charge the enemy, firing having been heard on the left. The position was a dangerous one. A charge at that time of the evening was perilous. Just in front lay a deep gulch—Labor-in-Vain Ravine—which was alive with the enemy, and the charge must be through an unprotected field of wheat and clover. General

Toombs was astonished at the order. His first instructions had been to put himself near Garnett House, to hold his position and to take advantage of any retreat of the enemy. He doubted the authenticity of the order, and sent word that he would not obey unless in writing. Pretty soon written instructions were returned and General Toombs prepared for what he believed to be a forlorn hope. He advanced seven companies of the 2d Georgia Regiment, 750 men, under Colonel B. M. Butt, toward the enemy in the face of a heavy front and flank fire. Colonel Williams' regiment crossed the field at double-quick under a galling fire from the opposite side of the ravine. Unshaken by fearful odds, they held their ground and replied with spirit. The 15th Georgia Regiment, under Colonel McIntosh then entered the fight, and this gallant officer was mortally wounded. The 17th Georgia charged on the left and the 20th on the right. The engagement was a very bloody one. Over 200 of Toombs' men were lost and several valuable officers were killed. The opposing troops were a part of General Hancock's command, and the firing ceased only with the night. Next morning the enemy retreated, and Toombs' men pressed forward and held their position. General Toombs was censured for this engagement, for which, it seems, he was in no wise responsible.

On the 1st of July, about three o'clock in the afternoon, commenced one of the famous battles of the war. McClellan's army had gotten away from its perilous position astride the Chicka-hominy, and now found itself united and strongly intrenched on the heights of Malvern Hill. All hope of destroying that army was gone, and it was evident that an engagement must ensue, with the odds in favor of the Union army. It was in many respects like the battle of Gettysburg, ex-cept that the Confederate forces were not handled with the precision and effectiveness of the historic sorties against Cemetery Heights. The battlefield was in plain range of the enemy's gunboats, and there was much surprise that General Lee should have sanctioned an engagement at that point. General D. H. Hill misunderstood the signal for attack at Malvern Hill, and late in the afternoon ordered the charge. Toombs' brigade had been marching and countermarching all day, and went into action much thinned from the effects of the sharp fighting at Labor-in-Vain Ravine. There was no concerted attack. The charge seems to have been made by brigades, even single regiments being thrown forward. They advanced through a swamp, and the difficulties of the charge, owing to a murderous fire which raked the plain from the hills, 600 yards away, cannot be exaggerated. Toombs' brigade was one of the first to reach the

plateau swept by fifty guns. It advanced with
Anderson's brigade, but obliqued to the left about
half-way up the hill, and took position near a
fence, where the troops, suffering fearfully from
the cool, deadly aim of the Federal gunners, were
ordered to lie down and secure some shelter from
the cannon-shot. It was at this time that General
D. H. Hill rode up to General Toombs and ordered his brigade forward. Some sharp words
ensued between these officers, and the men moved
forward handsomely to the brow of the hill. At
this time, however, the steady stream of fugitives
pressing back from the charge, broke the alignment
of the brigade and separated the regiments. Colonel Butt's regiment went forward with Kershaw's
brigade. The whole Confederate charge was soon
checked and the troops fell back in disorder.
Their loss was fully 5000 men, and the loss in
Toombs' brigade was 219 men, making his losses
in the two engagements over one-third of his entire number. Malvern Hill was a blunder which
was never repeated, but it was a disastrous one
for the Georgia troops.

The subjoined correspondence will be understood in the light of the meeting of General D. H.
Hill and General Toombs near Malvern Hill during the progress of the charge of the Confederate
forces.

HEADQUARTERS FIRST BRIGADE, FIRST DIVISION,
In the Field, July 6, 1862.

MAJOR GENERAL D. H. HILL.

Sir: Military movements since Tuesday last have prevented an earlier reply to your conversation with me on the battlefield that evening. I understood you to say, among other things, that "Your (my) brigade would not fight"; that you "always knew it would not fight" ; that it "pretended to want to fight, but would not"; " Where were you when I was riding in front on my horse trying to rally your brigade?" I desire first to know whether I am correct in my understanding of your language, and if not, wherein I am mistaken.

And secondly, to request of you such explanation of that language as you may choose to give.

I am sir,

Your obedient servant,

ROBERT TOOMBS.

July 6, 1862.

General: Your note has just been received. My remarks were personal to yourself and not to your brigade. I did not in the slightest degree reflect on your men. What I said was in substance this : " You have been wanting to fight, and now that you have one, you have got out of it." There were witnesses to our conversation, and if my remarks were severer, I will let you know.

It may be well to suggest to you that, as the commanding officer on the field, I have an official report to make which will not be modified by your note.

It is notorious that you have a thousand times expressed your disgust that the commanding general did not permit you to fight. It is equally notorious that you retired from the field. These are the two facts of which I reminded you on Tuesday. I made no comment upon them, and if the simple truth has been offensive, the interpretation of it has been your own.

Yours truly,

D. H. HILL,

BRIGADIER GENERAL TOOMBS.   Major General.

HEADQUARTERS FIRST BRIGADE, FIRST DIVISION,
GENERAL D. H. HILL.   July 6, 1862.

Sir : Your note of this date has just been received. It is scarcely necessary for me to say it is not satisfactory. It would be inappropriate to comment upon it properly in this note, and for that reason alone I waive it for the present. As to your remark that you were the commanding officer on the field on the 1st inst., I never before heard of it, nor do I now think so, but, however that fact may be, I am at a loss to know for what reason you state it unless it was to menace and intimidate me in the pursuit of proper satisfaction for the unprovoked insult you have cast upon me. If that was your object, this note will satisfy you that you have failed in your object. I now demand of you personal satisfaction for the insult you cast upon my command and myself on the battlefield on the 1st inst., and for the repetition and aggravation thereof in your note of this day. I refer you to my friend Colonel Benning for all necessary arrangements.

Your obedient servant,

ROBERT TOOMBS.

CAMP NEAR RICHMOND, VA.,

July 12, 1862.

General: Your note of the 6th was received yesterday. I must again enter my protest against your second declaration that I reflected upon your brigade in the battle of

Malvern Hill. Witnesses to our interview affirm that my remarks were entirely personal to yourself.

In regard to your demand for satisfaction, I construe it to mean either that I must apologize to you for the language used by me on the battlefield, or that I must grant you a hostile meeting. If the first interpretation be correct, I will state that I will make full, public, and ample concessions when satisfied that I did you injustice ; and this I would do without any demand. I certainly thought that you had taken the field too late, and that you left it too early. You may, however, have done your whole duty, and held your ground as long as it was possible for a brave and skillful officer to hold it. If the facts prove this to be so, no one will be more gratified than myself, and my acknowledgment of error will be cordial and complete.

But if your demand means a challenge, its acceptance, when we have a country to defend and enemies to fight, would be highly improper and contrary to the dictates of plain duty, without reference to higher grounds of action. I will not make myself a party to a course of conduct forbidden alike by the plainest principles of duty, and the laws which we have mutually sworn to serve.

Yours truly,

D. H. Hill, Major General.

Brigadier General Robert Toombs.

Just what General Toombs replied to this is not known. The letter has not been preserved in this correspondence. It evidently declared that the explanation was not satisfactory. Major R. J. Moses, Jr., a member of General Toombs' staff, submitted in writing the following report of his recollection of

General Hill's words to General Toombs at Malvern Hill:

Where is your brigade, sir ?   I told you that I wanted a fighting brigade, and your brigade will not fight.   I knew it would not, and you are the man who pretends to have been spoiling for a fight.   For shame !   Rally your troops !   Where were you when I was riding up and down your line rallying your troops ?

Major Moses adds:

As aid-de-camp of General Robert Toombs, I remained with him until some time after this conversation.   Previous to this conversation General Toombs had been about fifteen yards to the rear of the center of his line and his troops were unbroken.   There were many men coming by us, but I saw not over ten from General Toombs' brigade. The order was given " Forward, left oblique," and General Toombs moved to the left of his line.   When General Hill met him and commenced this attack on the character of himself and his brigade without the slightest provocation, General Toombs had not only been rallying the troops, but continued to use his best endeavors to rally them till late at night.   I was with General Toombs the whole time from the commencement of the action until half or three-quarters of an hour after the conversation.

The following is the concluding letter of the correspondence:

July 15, 1862.

General: I regret that my last note, which was intended to be conciliatory, has been misunderstood or misappreciated.   I take it for granted that you know enough of my previous history to be aware that a hostile meeting, under any circumstances, would be abhorrent to my principles and character. At this time it would be in the highest degree improper. I have offered you the only redress which I could make even after a meeting, viz., an acknowledgment of error when convinced of that error. As no good can result from a continued correspondence, it will close on my part with this communication.

Yours truly,

D. H. HILL, Major General.

BRIGADIER GENERAL ROBERT TOOMBS.

General Hill was a good man and a brave soldier. His devotion to the Confederate cause was undoubted, but his zeal sometimes made him harsh, and more than once he placed himself in the position of reflecting upon the conduct of others. On one occasion at the battle of Chickamauga, where General Hill was in command of the extreme right of the Confederate line, on the second day of the battle information was brought to him of the sudden and unexpected advance of a strong Federal force against his line. It proved to be the division of the Federal General Gordon Granger. General Hill and General W. H. T. Walker, who commanded two divisions under General Hill, proceeded at once to the threatened point, to ascertain the situation of affairs, accompanied by some members of their staff. Arrived at a point where this new arrival of Federal forces could be seen, General Walker deferred to General Hill and asked him, " What do you wish me to do ? "

"What do I want you to do?" said Hill with severity, and even with something like a snarl, "I want you to fight."

General Walker flushed up in a moment. He was not a man to deserve any reflection upon his courage or to bear it when offered. No man in the old army had a higher and more deserved reputation for dashing courage. He had been desperately wounded in Florida, and again wounded, supposed to be mortally, in leading the assault on Chapultepec in the Mexican War, and had, on many occasions, given undoubted evidence of his valor and fidelity. He answered hotly, "Of course I will fight; you know that, General Hill, well enough; but, by God! sir, there are two ways of fighting, one to whip and the other to get whipped."

The point was a good one. Major Joseph B. Cumming, chief of General Walker's staff, who related this incident, says it had the desired effect.

When Longstreet marched against Pope he stationed General Toombs' brigade to guard one of the fords of the Rapidan. Toombs was absent at the time and when he rode up ordered them back to camp. General Longstreet heard of Toombs making stump speeches and "referring in anything but complimentary terms of his commander." He sent General Toombs to Gordonsville. Afterward he received an apology from Toombs and directed him to join his command. As we were preparing for the charge at Manassas (second battle), Toombs got there, riding rapidly with his hat in his hand, and was much enthused. I was just sending a courier to his command with a dispatch. 'Let me take it,' he exclaimed. 'With pleasure,' I responded, and handed him the paper. He put spurs to his horse and dashed off, accompanied by his courier. When he rode up and took command of his brigade there was wild enthusiasm, and, everything being ready, an exultant shout was sent up, and the men sprang to the charge. I never had any more trouble with Toombs. We were afterward warm personal friends."

On the 30th of August, 1862, Hon. A. H. Stephens wrote to Mrs. Toombs that General Toombs was still at Gordonsville. He said:

How long he will remain, I do not know. I thought at first that it would only be for a day or two, or until General Longstreet could receive and reply to two notes he had written, explaining to my mind very fully and satisfactorily his acts and conduct, which, it seems to me, General Longstreet had misunderstood. Such is still my opinion, and yet I may be mistaken. I do not know much of General Longstreet. I only know that General Toombs, who does know him, always expressed very high admiration of him as an officer.

At the second battle of Manassas, August 29, 1862, Toombs' brigade in Jones' division held the

rear of Longstreet's corps. Early in the morning
the brigade took up the march in the direction of
the old battlefield of Manassas, where heavy firing was heard. Arriving at noon it was stationed
on the extreme right, or upon the Manassas Gap
railroad. The brigades formed in echelon. General Longstreet in his published report commended especially General Toombs for gallant
conduct at Manassas Plain.

General D. R. Jones, in his report of Manassas,
says:

> General Toombs, released from arrest, under which he
> had been since the 18th of August, came upon the field
> shortly after his brigade went in under fire and accompan-
> ied it in action.

Captain H. L. French, of the 17th Georgia Regiment, says: "Soon after our engagement, to our
great satisfaction, we unexpectedly met our
gallant commander, Brigadier General Robert
Toombs, who, anticipating the fight, had ridden
hard all day. He was greeted with hearty cheers.
and said, 'Boys, I am proud of the report given of
you by General Jones. I could not be with you
to-day, but this was owing to no fault of mine.
To-morrow I lead you.'"

One report of this engagement declares that as
Toombs dashed into the fire and joined his men.
he waved his hat and shouted, "Go it, boys! I am

with you again. Jeff Davis can make a general, but it takes God Almighty to make a soldier ! "

The expulsion of Pope only accelerated the momentum of the Army of Northern Virginia. From the front of Richmond, the theater of operations was transferred at once to the front of Washington, and the Union army was again on the defensive. General Lee, freed from the necessity of guarding the Confederate capital, resolved to invade Maryland. He reasoned that the prestige of the invasion would advance the cause of the young nation abroad; that it would relieve Virginia from incursions during the winter, and that the presence of the army in Maryland would raise the standard of revolt and cause the liberation of that State from the Union cause. Lee's army, however, was not equal to such an expedition. It was not well clothed or armed, and barely numbered 40,000, while McClellan had 80,000.

Toombs' brigade accompanied Longstreet's corps in its counter-march from Hagarstown to Hill's support. On the 14th of September these were withdrawn to the valley of the Antietam. The creek of Antietam runs obliquely to the source of the Potomac, and empties into that river six miles above Harper's Ferry. The Confederate lines were, on the 15th, drawn up in front of

Sharpsburg, Longstreet being on the right of the road from Sharpsburg.

In this place the creek is crossed by four stone bridges, and three of these were strongly guarded by the Confederates. Burnside's army corps was stationed on the Sharpsburg Turnpike, directly in front of bridge No. 3. The preliminary deploy occupied the 16th of September, an artillery duel enlivening the time before the battle. Burnside lay behind the heights on the east bank of the Antietam and opposite the Confederate right, which, Swinton says, it was designed he should assail, after forcing the passage of the Antietam by the lower stone bridge. The part assigned to General Burnside was of the highest importance, for a successful attack by him upon the Confederate right, would, by carrying the Sharpsburg Crest, force Lee from his line of retreat by way of Shepherdstown. Swinton says this task should have been an easy one, for the Confederate forces at this point had been drawn upon to recruit the left where Hooker had made his furious assaults.

There was left in the right wing of the Confederate army but a single division of 2500 men under General D. R. Jones, and the force actually present to dispute the passage of the stone bridge did not exceed 400. These troops were under the direction of General Robert Toombs, and this engagement made his reputation as a fighter and was one of the most brilliant and memorable of the Civil War. It was one o'clock before Burnside charged. General Lee, in his report of the battle, said :

In the afternoon the enemy advanced on our right, where General Jones' division was posted, who handsomely maintained his position. General Toombs' brigade, guarding the bridge on Antietam Creek, gallantly resisted the approach of the enemy, but his superior number enabling him to extend his left, he crossed below the bridge and assumed a threatening attitude on our right, which fell back in confusion. By this time, between 3 and 4 o'clock P.M., A. P. Hill, with five of his brigades, reached the scene of action and drove the enemy from the position they had taken. The bridge was defended with two regiments of Toombs' brigade (2d and 20th) and the batteries of General Jones. General Toombs' small command repulsed five different assaults made by greatly superior forces, and maintained its position with distinguished gallantry. . . . . Toombs charged the flank of the enemy, while Archer moved upon the front of the Federal line. The enemy made a brief resistance and then ran in confusion.

Such commendation from the commander-in-chief of the Confederate army speaks for itself.

Speaking of the last charge, when the Federals were driven back over the creek in the counter-attack, General Jones says:

General Toombs, whom I had sent for, arriving from the right with a portion of his brigade (11th Georgia Regiment) was ordered to charge the enemy. This he did most gallantly, supported by Archer's brigade, delivering fire at less than fifty yards, dashing at the enemy with the bayonet, forcing him from the crest and following him down the hill.

General Garnett's report credits Toombs with having "reënforced the right just after it had been driven back, and restored the fortunes of the day in that quarter."

From the report of General Toombs it appeared that when he first moved into Maryland he was assigned to command a division composed of Toombs', Drayton's, and Anderson's brigades, and took possession of Hagerstown. On September 14 he was ordered to Sharpsburg, two of his regiments having been sent to Williamsport to protect the wagon trains. With two small regiments left, General Toombs took position near the bridge over the Antietam on the road to Harper's Ferry. He took possession of the ground with the 20th Georgia Regiment, commanded by Colonel Jonathan B. Cumming, and the 2d Georgia Regiment, commanded by Colonel Holmes. The creek was comparatively straight by this bridge. He formed his regiments along the creek in more open order than was desirable on account of the smallness of his number. Subsequently the 50th Georgia, with scarcely 100 men, was placed under his command. Colonel Eubanks' battery was by

order of General Longstreet placed in his rear.
The enemy opened on his position on Tuesday
evening, the 16th of September. On Wednesday
morning, his pickets were driven in and the enemy
menaced his position. The ground descended
gently to the creek covered with a narrow strip of
woods, affording slight protection. The enemy approached by the road parallel with his line of
battle, he says, exposing his flank to a destructive
fire. Between 9 A. M. and 1 P. M. the Federals
made five attempts to carry the bridge, and were
repulsed by the 2d and 20th Georgia regiments.
Failing to wrest the bridge from its heroic defenders, the enemy turned his attention to the
fords. "Not being able to get reënforcements,
and seeing that the enemy would cross and attack
my front, right flank, and rear, Colonel Holmes
having been killed, Major Harris wounded, both
regiments having suffered heavily, ammunition
nearly exhausted, and the battery withdrawn, I
withdrew my command to a position, designated
by Longstreet, opposite the lower fords. This
change of position was made very satisfactorily
and without serious loss. The 15th and 17th
Georgia regiments and part of the 11th, previously
detached, now came up and occupied the new
position. The 20th and 2d went to the ammunition
train to replenish their cartridge boxes. The
enemy moved through the bridge and ford with

extreme caution, and lost nearly two hours in crossing, about which time A. P. Hill's division came
from Harper's Ferry. I was ordered by Longstreet
to put my command in motion to meet the enemy.
I found them in possession of the ground I was
ordered to occupy, including the bridge road and
the suburbs of Sharpsburg. With less than one-
fifth the numbers of the enemy and within
100 paces of his lines I determined to give battle.
I had instantly to determine either to retreat or
to fight. A retreat would have left the town of
Sharpsburg and General Longstreet's rear open to
the enemy. The enemy advanced in good order
to within sixty or eighty paces, when the effectiveness of the fire threw his column into considerable
confusion, perceiving which I instantly ordered a
charge, which was brilliantly executed by my
whole line. The enemy fled in confusion toward
the river, making two or three efforts to rally,
which were soon defeated. The enemy brought
over the bridge a battery. I ordered Richardson's
battery to open upon it, and at the same time the
15th and 20th Georgia charged upon it and compelled it to rejoin the flying infantry. I desired
to pursue the enemy across the river, but, being
deficient in artillery, I sent to General Lee for a
battery, which came up too late. I then determined
to move my troops to my first position along the
river, but received the order to occupy the heights

on the opposite side of the road leading to the bridge from Sharpsburg, and there the troops bivouacked for the night."

The gallant conduct of Toombs' brigade at Sharpsburg was the theme on both sides. The country rang with its exploits and the fiery Georgia brigadier became the toast of the army. Burnside's heavy losses abundantly proved the stoutness of the resistance and the deadliness of the charges of the Georgia troops.

The next evening, on the edge of Sharpsburg, General Toombs and his aids crossed a little branch on his way to the headquarters of Colonel Benning. General Toombs rode his famous mare "Gray Alice," so well known to his command. He was not very far over when a troop of calvary rode up. He challenged them, and they answered "We are friends." Captain Troup of his staff, however, detected the ruse and fired into them. The squad returned the fire. General Toombs was shot through the hand with which he was holding the reins. The gray mare at once became unmanageable and ran back across the branch. As soon as he could control the mare, General Toombs rode back to Colonel Benning and, reporting his wound, turned his brigade over to Colonel Benning. When it became known that General Toombs was wounded his men were deeply pained. Always solicitous for their welfare, his soldiers were devotedly attached to him. He took care of his brigade even to the extremity of violating army discipline. He exacted the utmost consideration for his men, and the officer who periled their safety, or disputed their efficiency, was quickly called to account. Whether against Johnston, Longstreet, or Hill, the First Brigade, First Division, was sure of a fearless champion in the person of its commander.

The battle of Sharpsburg was a very bloody one. The losses on the Federal side were nearly 12,500, while the Confederates lost 8000. Lee withdrew into Virginia, and McClellan was too much demoralized to follow. Longstreet, in summing up the Manassas and Maryland campaign, declared that in one month the troops had marched over two hundred miles upon little more than half rations and fought nine battles and skirmishes. They had " killed, wounded, and captured nearly as many men as we had in our ranks, besides taking arms and other munitions of war in large quantities." General Longstreet compliments Brigadier General Toombs for his "gallant defense at the bridge of Antietam and his vigorous charge upon the enemy's flank ; he was severely wounded at the close of the engagement."

General Toombs returned to his home after Sharpsburg, and remained several months. He rejoined his command near Fredericksburg, but in March, 1863, wrote a touching farewell to his brigade and resigned his commission in the army of Northern Virginia. It seemed to him that he did not have justice done him at Richmond. He aspired, with the ambition of a soldier, to be promoted in his country's service. His conduct at Sharpsburg, where he wrung admiration from his superior officers, appeared to call for recognition from the President, but he did not receive his major-generalship, and, although more than once in the actual command of a division, did not secure that title. It is true that he would have liked the promotion; but he did not expect it. He had written to his wife that he would not be driven from the army until after some great battle, when he should have the opportunity of doing something for his country. "The day after such an event, I will retire if I live through it." The battle had occurred, his record was written upon the stone bridge of Antietam, and his work was at an end.

Postmaster-General Reagan was one of those who recognized the merits of General Toombs. Twice did he approach President Davis with the request that General Toombs be promoted to the command of a division. That official replied promptly that he did not oppose it himself, but that he could not do it without the recommendation of the army officers, and that recommendation had not been given. Possibly the field officers believed the suggestion would have been ungracious to Mr. Davis. General Toombs had not hesitated to criticise the policy and appointments of the Richmond administration. That practice had strained his relations with the Confederate Government, but Toombs was a man who " would not flatter Neptune for his trident."

General Toombs was not a trained soldier, but he had some fine points of a great commander. He was the soul of energy and common sense. He was bold, dashing, magnetic. He had the quality of infusing his spirit into his men. His quick mind seized the points of a campaign, and his intellect was broad and overmastering. It is related of · him that one day in Virginia he hurried to the rear for a conference with Jefferson Davis, to which the President had summoned him, upon some point of civil administration. This business over, he dashed back to the front, where he had an engagement with General Lee over a plan of attack. General Longstreet said Toombs had the kindling eye and rare genius of a soldier, but lacked the discipline of a military man. This was the serious flaw in his character. He had what General Johnston declared was the great drawback about the Southern soldier, " a large endowment of the instinct of personal liberty," and it was difficult to subordinate his will to the needs of military discipline. He had been accustomed to priority, and in whatever company, under whatever conditions he found himself, his had been the part to lead and to rule. As Colonel Thomas W. Thomas had said of him, "Toombs has always been the big frog in the pond." Men conceded to him this prestige. Under the cast-iron rule of the army he found himself subordinated to men intellectually beneath him, but trained and skilled in the art of war. He was swift to detect error, and impatient in combating blunder. The rule of mediocrity, the red tape of the service, the restraints of the corps, the tactics of the field galled his imperious spirit. He commanded his brigade as he had represented his State in the Senate—as a sovereign and independent body, and like the heroic Helvetian had blazoned on his crest, "No one shall cross me with impunity."

Robert Toombs made a mistake in sinking himself in the routine of a brigade commander. He should have taken the War Department, or, like Pitt, have pushed the war from the floor of the Senate. Swinton says that Abraham Lincoln brought the habits of a politician to military affairs, in which their intrusion can only result in confusion of just relations. There is ineradicable antagonism between the maxims which govern politics and those which govern war.

During General Toombs' absence in the field, he opposed the Conscript Acts of the Confederate administration. He believed them arbitrary and unjust. He considered that this was a tendency toward centralization which the Confederate Government was fighting; that it placed too much power in the hands of one man; that it was deadly to States' Rights and personal liberty, and that it would impair the efficiency of the army by lowering its patriotism. The champion of this anti-administration policy in Georgia was Linton Stephens, the brother of the vice president. Toombs in the field, the elder Stephens in Congress, and Linton Stephens in the Georgia Legislature, fought the Conscription and Impressment Acts. Hon. Joseph E. Brown, the war Governor of Georgia, was also a vigorous opponent of this policy. This influence gave rise, in the early part of 1864, to the Peace Resolutions of Linton Stephens, who sustained Governor Brown in his policy, to inaugurate State action for " the preservation of rights and the attainment of peace." Linton Stephens, in a strong letter to General Toombs at that time, called attention to the fact that since the war began neither side had made any effort to stop the effusion of blood. He believed that the professional soldiers and West Point generals would never permit the cessation of hostilities. Such men, he thought, would not, in human nature, desire peace. " How can it be explained," he wrote, " that both governments have fought on during these long years of blood and tears and desolation, without either one offering terms of peace, and with both running a swift race of rivalry in usurping the most despotic power under the ever-recurring and false plea of necessities of war? Have both governments formed designs that cannot be accomplished in peace, and which seek opportunity and shelter in the confusion and panic of war?"

Mr. Linton Stephens was a leading lawyer and legislator in Georgia. He was a man of great ability. He had started the practice of law in the office of Robert Toombs, and had been a political follower and close friend of the great Georgian. He had served upon the bench of the Supreme Court of his State, and at the close of the war his political influence was probably greater than that of any man at home. He was fearless, inflexible, high-toned, and full of power. He did not hesitate to condemn the legislation asked for by Mr. Davis, and joined Mr. Toombs in opposing the appointment of General Bragg as supervisor of all military operations. Mr. Stephens believed that the next step after the Impressment Act would be the organization of all labor into a military system under government control.

The result of the policy of Mr. Davis justified the protest of the Georgians, but there is nothing to warrant the belief that Mr. Davis was moving toward military despotism or that he relished the continuance of strife. He saw that the South was in for the war. Desperate situations required desperate remedies. He grasped the government with a strong hand, and lacked neither nerve nor patriotism. The principles of this policy were unsound, but the motives of Jefferson Davis were pure. Nor was there reason to sustain the wholesale denunciation of West Point. That school of soldiers was the backbone of the army, and the fact that so many Southern men gave up commissions in the United States army and came South when their States seceded, overthrew the idea that they were tools of the general government and had lost identity or sympathy with people at home. But General Toombs was bold and impatient in his positions.

Equally opposed was he to the policy adopted in Georgia of recommending the planting of all grain and no cotton. From Richmond he wrote in March, 1864, directions to his brother Gabriel Toombs, who managed his plantations in Washington:

I do not care to change my crops. I wish to raise an abundant provision crop and then as much cotton as I can. . . . Brown's and Chambers' policy is all foolishness. . . . As to what I shall choose to plant on my own estates, I shall neither refer it to newspapers, nor to public meetings, nor to legislatures. I know what sort of people compose these classes. Let them take up arms and come with me to drive the intruders away from our soil, and then we will settle what sort of seed we will put into it.

CHAPTER XXIII.

GENERAL TOOMBS' next appearance in the field was as adjutant and inspector-general of General G. W. Smith's division of Georgia militia. He was present during the battles before Atlanta, the engagement at Peachtree Creek, and the siege of the city. General J. E. Johnston had just been relieved from command of the Confederate forces, and General J. B. Hood placed in charge. General Toombs wrote from Atlanta:

The tone of the army has greatly improved. We are now receiving reënforcements from the West. Davis, having kicked Johnston out, now feels obliged to sustain Hood, so the country is likely to get good out of evil. General Hood is displaying great energy and using his best exertions for success. I think very well of him. He is a most excellent man, and undoubtedly of great military talent. Whether equal or not to this great struggle, time must prove.

The militia are coming up finely. Twelve hundred of them arrived here this evening, armed and tolerably well equipped. Poor fellows! They are green and raw, undisciplined and badly officered. It keeps us at work day and night to bring order out of this confused mass, and we have but a poor chance. They march right into the trenches, and are immediately under the enemy's fire all day. We shall trust to a kind Providence alone to preserve them from a great disaster, and make them useful to the army and the country. The pressure is so great that we are compelled to put them to the work of veterans without an hour's preparation. I am doing my utmost to get them in the best possible position. Georgians are all coming up well except the cities.

Speaking of men who try to shirk duty, Mr. Toombs wrote, "Poor creatures! What do they want to live for?"

General Toombs had the task of organizing the recruits and getting them ready for the field. He writes to his wife: "Since I began this letter, the Yankees have begun an attack on a part of our line and I was obliged to ride with General Hood to look after our defenses." General Toombs alludes to General E. C. Walthall of Mississippi, as "a splendid officer and a gentleman." He says: "The enemy are evidently intending to starve us rather than to fight us out. I have, at the request of General Hood, not less than twenty letters to write on that very subject. Sherman shells the town furiously every day. Not much damage yet."

It has been customary to speak in light terms of the Georgia militia, who, late in the day, took the field to man the defenses when Sherman was marching to the sea. They were frequently made up of old men and boys who had been exempt from the

regular service, and these were hurried into action
with poor equipment and scant preparation. General Toombs, in a letter written to his wife, July
25, 1864, says:

> The militia have behaved with great gallantry. This is
> sincerely true. They have far exceeded my expectations,
> and in the fight on Thursday equaled any troops in the line
> of battle. If they will stand and fight like men, our homes
> will be saved. God give them the spirit of men, and all
> will be well !

In another place he writes:

> We have a mixed crowd, a large number of earnest,
> brave, true men ; then all the shirks and skulks in Georgia
> trying to get from under bullets.

General Toombs commended and endorsed the
policy of Governor Brown during his six years'
administration of the office from 1857 to 1863.
These two men were warm friends and political
allies. When Governor Brown's third term was
drawing to a close, he preferred the selection of
General Toombs as his successor. But Toombs
declined to make the race. His game now was
war, not politics. He preferred the field to the
Cabinet. He writes with considerable feeling this
letter to his wife:

> Whatever fate may befall me, I feel that this is my place,
> in the field and with the militia, with the men who own the
> country and who are struggling to preserve it for their
> children. I am truly thankful to God for the health he
> has given me to enable me to perform my part of this work.

He called all the sons of Georgia to come, even
to "die together rather than let the Yankee over-
run and conquer Georgia." He concludes a letter
of appeal:

> Better be
> Where the unconquered Spartans still are free,
> In their proud charnel of Thermopylæ.

General Toombs' last military service, after the
fall of Atlanta, was on the 20th of December,
1864, when as adjutant and inspector-general he
served in General G. W. Smith's division, Georgia
militia, at the siege of Savannah. General Dick
Taylor, in his "Destruction and Reconstruction,"
gives a very graphic description of General
Toombs' energy. The Georgia militia had left
Macon for Savannah, and to avoid capture by the
resistless column of Sherman's army, then marching to the sea, was shipped by way of Thomas-
ville. The trains were sometimes slow in moving,
and to General Taylor, who was anxious to mass
all forces at Savannah, the delay was galling.
When Toombs came up, he "damned the dawdling
trainmen, and pretty soon infused his own nervous force into the whole concern. The wheezing
engines and freight vans were readily put in motion, and Governor Brown's 'army' started toward Savannah." News reached General Taylor
about that time that the Federal forces at Port
Royal were coming up to capture Pocotaligo on

the Charleston and Savannah road. This was a dangerous move, as General Taylor was anxious to hold this line for coast defense. He needed reënforcements to hold this point, and at once thought of "Joe Brown's Army." The position of Governor Brown was, however, as General Taylor understood it, that Georgia troops were to be held to guard Georgia soil. This was one of the points in his discussion with Mr. Davis. General Taylor consulted with General Toombs, however, and they arranged to have the Georgia militia "shunted off at a switch near Savannah and transported quietly to Carolina." At Pocotaligo these troops had a lively brush with the Union forces and succeeded in holding the railroad. The Georgians were plucky whether at home or abroad, but General Taylor declared that Toombs enjoyed his part in making them "unconscious patriots."

Sherman's march to the sea was the concluding tragedy of the Civil War. The State which had been at the forefront of the revolution had become the bloody theater of battle. From the Tennessee River to Atlanta, Sherman and Johnston had grappled with deadly fury down the mountain defiles; then Cheatham and Wheeler harassed him at Macon and united for a final siege of Savannah. The granaries and workshops of the Confederacy were gone when Georgia was devastated—as General Lord Wolseley said, Sherman's invasion was a swordthrust through the vitals of the young nation. Robert Toombs had followed his own idea of meeting the invader as soon as he struck an inch of State soil and fighting him as long as a man remained. From the fruitless defense of Savannah, Toombs hastened to discuss the situation with Governor Brown. He happened to be dining with him that April day when the news came of the surrender at Appomattox. The two men looked at each other intently, when they realized that all was over.

Toombs and Brown had been closely allied since the day that the latter was nominated for Governor in 1857. They had fought campaigns together. Toombs had sustained Governor Brown's war policy almost to the letter. Now they shook hands and parted. Henceforth their paths diverged. Days of bitterness put that friendship to an end. Both men worked his course during reconstruction as he saw fit. But political differences deepened almost into personal feud.

General Toombs repaired to his home in Washington and, on the 4th of May, 1865, Jefferson Davis, his Cabinet and staff, having retreated from Richmond to Danville, thence to Greensboro, N. C., and Abbeville, S. C., rode across the country with

an armed escort to Washington, Ga. Here, in the
old Heard House, the last meeting of the Confederate Cabinet was held. ·The members separated,
and the civil government of the Southern Confederacy passed into history. There were present
John C. Breckenridge, Secretary of War; John
H. Reagan, Postmaster-General, besides the members of Mr. Davis' staff. The Confederate President was worn and jaded. He looked pale and
thin, but was plucky to the last. After the surrender of Lee and Johnston, he wanted to keep up
the warfare in the mountains of Virginia, and in
the country west of the Mississippi, but he was
finally persuaded that the Confederacy must cease
to struggle. On the public square of Washington
the little brick house, with its iron rail and its red
walls, is still pointed out to the visitor as the spot
where the Davis government dissolved. It was a
dramatic fate which determined its dissolution at
the home of Robert Toombs. He had been present
at its birth. His had been one of the leading
spirits of the revolution. He had served it in the
Cabinet and field, he had been pressed for the position of its chief magistracy, and now in the shadow
of his own rooftree its concluding council was
held. General Reagan was a guest of General
Toombs during his stay in Washington, as was
General St. John and Major Raphael J. Moses,
who had been a member of Toombs' staff. In

the evening General Toombs called General Reagan into a room by himself and inquired whether the latter needed any money. General Reagan said he had money enough to take him to Texas. Then General Toombs inquired after Mr. Davis, and asked whether he had any money. "I told him no," says General Reagan, "but that I had money enough to take us both West of of the Mississippi, and had told Mr. Davis so. I had no doubt but that he would rely on that." General Toombs then asked if Mr. Davis was well mounted. "I told him yes, that he had his bay horse Kentucky, and that after the surrender General Lee had sent his fine gray Traveler, by his son Robert, around through Lynchburg to Mr. Davis at Greenesboro, N. C." "Well," said General Toombs, with thoughtfulness, "Davis and I had a quarrel once, but that is over now. I am at home and can command money and men, and if Mr. Davis wants anything, I shall be glad to furnish it." General Toombs added that under terms of the convention between Sherman and Johnston, Mr. Davis was entitled to go where he pleased between that point and the Chattahoochee River. "I wish you would say to Mr. Davis," said Toombs, in his bluff way, "that, if necessary, I will call my men around me and see him safe to the Chattahoochee at the risk of my life."

On his return to the hotel Mr. Reagan gave

General Toombs' message to Mr. Davis, and told the latter of the inquiries and offers. "That is like Toombs," said Mr. Davis. "He was always a whole-souled man."

The four men whom the Washington government wanted to arrest and hold responsible for the war were Toombs, Davis, Slidell, and Howell Cobb. Their friends understood this perfectly, and each man was urged to make his escape. Jefferson Davis was arrested in Irwin County, Ga., on May 10. He was rapidly making his way to the West, and was trying to reach Texas. How General Toombs finally escaped must be reserved for a more extended recital.

General Toombs and Mr. Davis never met but once after the war. It was unexpected, dramatic. Some years after General Toombs had returned from his long exile, and Mr. Davis was just back from his trip to England, the ex-president visited Lookout Mountain, Tennessee, the guest of the poet Sidney Lanier. He here appeared at his best in the company of sympathetic and admiring friends, and charmed everyone by his polish and learning. The day before Jefferson Davis left, General and Mrs. Toombs arrived at the mountain. Mr. Davis was, at that time, absent on a horseback trip. He was fond of riding, and had gone over to see some of the fine views of the mountain and to inspect the fields where recent battles had raged with so much fury. The hotel was kept by a Northern man who knew nothing of the relations between Mr. Davis and General Toombs, and he believed the thing to do was to put General and Mrs. Toombs in a vacant room of the cottage occupied by Mr. Davis. It was a small house, with a piazza extending along the front. It so happened that the Toombses, who had just learned of Mr. Davis' presence at the hotel, were sitting on the piazza chatting with friends when Mr. Davis came up. Mr. Davis had also heard of General Toombs' arrival at the hotel, but neither knew that the other was domiciled in the same cottage. To General Toombs the appearance was as if Mr. Davis had come at once to make a cordial call. No one could be more hospitable and polite than Toombs, and this apparent challenge to friendship brought out the best side of his nature. The men met with considerable warmth. From General Toombs Mr. Davis advanced to Mrs. Toombs. Between these two the meeting was profoundly affecting. He embraced her tenderly. Toombs and Davis had been friends and neighbors years ago in Washington City, and Mr. Davis had been extremely fond of Mr. Toombs' family. The distinguished party soon fell into friendly conversation. Next day Mr. Davis left Lookout Mountain. He never met Robert Toombs again.

CHAPTER XXIV.

TOOMBS AS A FUGITIVE.

At the conclusion of the war, Secretary Stanton issued specific orders for the arrest of Jefferson Davis, Alexander H. Stephens, and Robert Toombs. Mr. Stephens was arrested quietly at his own home in Crawfordville on the 12th of May, 1865, two days after Mr. Davis had been overtaken. On the same day a squad of soldiers, most of them negroes, reached Washington, Ga. They were commanded by General Wilde, and their orders were to take General Toombs in charge. One of the colored troops marched up town with the photograph of Toombs, which they had procured to identify him, impaled upon his bayonet. General Toombs was, at the time, in his private office at his residence. Hearing the noise in his yard, he walked out of his basement to the corner of his front steps. There he perceived the squad and divined their purpose. "By God, the bluecoats!" was all he said. Walking quickly through his back lot, he strode across his plantation and disappeared. By this time the guard was clamoring at the front door, and Mrs. Toombs went out to meet them. "Where is General Toombs?" the

286

commander asked. " He is not here," the lady answered firmly. A parley ensued, during which Mrs. Toombs managed to detain the men long enough to enable her husband to get out of sight. " Unless General Toombs is produced, I shall burn the house," retorted the officer. Mrs. Toombs blanched a little at this, but, biting her lip, she turned on her heel, and coolly replied : " Very well, burn it." Among the listeners to this colloquy was a young man just returned from the Confederate army. He was moved with indignation. He still wore the gray jacket, and was deeply anxious for the Toombs family. He had been a neighbor to them all his life, as had his father before him, and he shared the pride which the village felt for its most distinguished resident.

He was the son of Hon. I. T. Irvin, a prominent public man and lifelong friend of General Toombs. Preparations were made for the threatened fire. General Toombs did not come out. Furniture was moved and papers destroyed, but the young Confederate was soon convinced that the threat was a mere bluff. Relieved on that point, his loyal spirit yearned toward the fugitive. Charles E. Irvin was the name of the young man, and he had seen service in the artillery under Longstreet. Not yet twenty-one years of age, he was fired with ardor and devotion, and had already resolved to aid General Toombs in escaping.

Riding over to a neigbor's house, Mr. J. T. Wingfield, he failed to find his friend, but left word for General Toombs to let him know where to meet him with his horses. That night about two o'clock Lieutenant Irvin got word from General Toombs to bring his horse to Nick Chenault's by seven o'clock in the morning. This was a farm about eighteen miles from Washington, near the Broad River. Here General Toombs mounted his trusted horse and felt at home. It was the famous mare Gray Alice, which had carried him through all his campaigns. He had ridden her during the charges at Antietam, and she had borne him from the fire of the scouts the night he had received his wound. Once more he pressed her into service, and Robert Toombs, for the first time in his life, was a fugitive. This man, who commanded men and had gained his own way by sheer brain and combativeness, fled by stealth from a dreaded enemy. It was a new rôle for Toombs. His plucky young guide was resolved to accompany him in his flight—it might be to his death ; it was all the same to Lieutenant Irvin. Riding swiftly into Elbert County, the two men crossed over to Harrison Landing, a picturesque spot on the Savannah River. Here dwelt an old man, Alexander LeSeur, who led something of a hermit's life. Before the war he had been a " Know-nothing," and had been exposed to Toombs' withering fire upon that class

RESIDENCE OF GENERAL B. W. HEARD, WASHINGTON, GA., WHERE JEFFERSON DAVIS HELD
LAST MEETING OF CABINET, APRIL, 1865.

of politicians. LeSeur met the fugitive with a
laugh and a friendly oath. "You have been
fighting me for forty years," he said, "and now
that you are in trouble, I am the first man you
seek for protection."

General Toombs had not traveled too fast. The
country was swarming with raiders. News of the
capture of Davis and Stephens had fired these
men with desire to overhaul the great champion
of secession. A Federal major, commanding a
force of men, put up at Tate's residence, just opposite the hermit's island. While there, a negro
from the LeSeur place informed the officer that
some prominent man was at the house. "If it
ain't Jeff Davis, it is just as big a man," said he.
The hint was taken. The island was surrounded
and carefully watched, but when the party went
over to capture Toombs, the game was gone.

General Toombs now started out carefully up
the Savannah River. In Elbert, he was in the
hands of his friends. This county, which had
first encouraged the struggles of the young lawyer, which had followed him steadfastly in his
political fortunes, which had furnished soldiers
for his brigade, now supplied protectors at every
step. Before leaving this county he was initiated
into a Masonic lodge, and took the first degrees of
the order. More than once the signs and symbols
of the mystic brotherhood stood him in good stead

on this eventful trip. He was afterward a high Mason, and remained to his death a devoted friend of the order.

Continuing his journey alone he stopped at the Tugaloo River in Habersham County, and remained at the house of Colonel Prather until Lieutenant Irvin, whom he had sent back to Washington with letters, could rejoin him with funds and clothing. Here his young companion soon found him, bringing, besides letters from home, some astonishing news.

"General," said Lieutenant Irvin, "what do you think? Your friend General Joseph E. Brown has sold out the State of Georgia, and gone over to the Republican party."

Toombs glared at him savagely.

"For the first time on this trip," says Lieutenant Irvin, "he looked like he wanted to kill me. He brought his fist down heavily upon the table and said: 'By God, I don't believe it!'   •

"'Well here it is in black and white.'"

Lieutenant Irvin gave him the paper in which was printed Governor Brown's famous address to the people of Georgia.

"This news," said Lieutenant Irvin, "absolutely sent the old man to bed."

Toombs remained a week at Colonel Prather's, and in the meantime sent Lieutenant Irvin to Savannah with important letters. He desired to escape, if possible, through the port of Savannah. The Savannah friends were not at home, however, and Lieutenant Irvin, bearing these important letters, actually fell into the hands of the enemy.

He was a high-strung, plucky young fellow, and was reproved by a Federal officer for continuing to wear brass buttons. Irvin retorted sharply, and was hurried into prison. Fearing that he would be searched and his papers found, he slipped them to a friend, undetected by the guard. After remaining in prison for several hours, Lieutenant Irvin was released and censured by the officer, who reminded him that there were bayonets about him.

"Yes," retorted young Irvin, "and brave men always avail themselves of such advantages."

Trudging back from Savannah, Lieutenant Irvin found General Toombs at the Rembert place, near Tallalah Falls. This was a beautiful home in a wild, picturesque country, where Toombs was less liable to capture than in middle Georgia, and where he was less known to the people. General Toombs had already procured the parole papers of Major Luther Martin, of Elbert County, a friend and member of his former command. He traveled under that name, and was so addressed by his young companion all along the route. General Toombs passed the time deer-hunting in Habersham. He had the steady hand and fine eye of

a sportsman, and he was noted for his horseman-
ship and endurance.

Returning toward Washington through Elbert
County, General Toombs decided to spend a night
with Major Martin. Lieutenant Irvin stoutly opposed this and warned him that if the enemy were
to look for him anywhere, it would certainly be
at Martin's house. Turning down the road, he
finally concluded to put up at the house of Colonel
W. H. Mattox. It was well he did. That night
a party of thirty soldiers raided the Martin plantation on a hot trail, and searched thoroughly for
Toombs.

During his travels General Toombs did not wear
a disguise of any sort. Dressed in a checked suit,
and riding his gray mare, he was a prominent object, and to most of the people was well known.
One day he wore green goggles, but soon threw
them away in disgust. The nearness of troops
forced General Toombs to abandon his plan of
going home for his family before leaving the country. He dispatched Lieutenant Irvin to Washington with letters to his wife, telling her that he
would not see her again until he had gone abroad,
when he would send for her to join him. He himself passed through Centreville, twelve miles from
his home, and directed his young guide where to
meet him in middle Georgia. This Lieutenant
Irvin found it very hard to do. General Toombs

was very discreet as to whom he took into his confidence. Once or twice he cautioned his companion against certain parties, to the surprise of the young man. Toombs, however, read human nature pretty well, and, later, when the real character of these persons developed, Irvin understood the counsels of his older friend. So carefully did General Toombs cover his tracks that Lieutenant Irvin, after his detour to Washington, was a long time in overtaking him. Traveling straight to Sparta, Lieutenant Irvin called on Judge Linton Stephens and asked about the general. This shrewd Georgian came to the door and flatly denied knowing anything about Toombs.

"He questioned me closely," said Lieutenant Irvin, "and finding that I was really who I pretended to be, finally agreed to take me to Toombs. Riding down to Old-Town, in Jefferson County, we failed to find Toombs, but receiving a clew that he had passed through the David Dickson plantation in Hancock County, I accosted Mr. Worthen, the manager. 'Has an old man riding a gray horse passed this way,' Worthen was asked. He promptly answered, 'No.' Believing that he was deceiving me, I questioned him more closely."

Worthen tried to persuade the young man to get down and take some plums. He was evidently anxious to detain him. Finally he eyed the stranger more closely, and, convinced that he was the com-

panion whom Toombs expected, he confessed that
General Toombs had been at his place and was
then at the home of Major Gonder in Washington County.

Lieutenant Irvin had ridden over two hundred
miles in this search and lost two or three days out
of his way. Toombs covered his trail so carefully that it was difficult even for his friends to
find him. Small wonder that he was not captured
by the enemy.

Lieutenant Irvin was not yet "out of the
woods." Reaching the home of Major Gonder
late in the evening, he rode up to the front fence,
fifty yards from the dwelling. Mrs. Gonder and her
daughter were sitting on the piazza. Lieutenant
Irvin asked the usual question about the old
man and the gray horse. The lady replied that
she knew nothing about them.

Lieutenant Irvin said: "But I was directed to
this place."

Mrs. Gonder: "I should like to know who sent
you."

Lieutenant Irvin: "But has no one passed or
stopped here, answering my description?"

Both ladies were now considerably worked up;
the younger scarcely suppressed her amuse-
ment.

"Come, ladies," said Lieutenant Irvin, "I see
you both know more than you will confess."

"If I do, I will die before I tell it," naïvely replied the elder.

"Now I know you know where General Toombs is."

"Then get it out of me if you can."

Finally the young man persuaded her that he was the friend of Toombs, and Mrs. Gonder reluctantly directed him to Colonel Jack Smith's over on the Oconee River.

Riding up to Colonel Smith's, his valiant pursuer spied General Toombs through the window. The head of the house, however, denied that Toombs was there at all.

"But that looks very much like him through the window" said Lieutenant Irvin.

"Young man," retorted Colonel Smith, "what is your name?"

Of course this disclosure led to the reunion of the fugitive and his friend.

Toombs realized that he was in almost as much danger from his own friends as from the enemy. He was careful to whom he disclosed his identity or his plans, for fear that they might indiscreetly comment on his presence or embarass him even by their willingness to befriend him. So it was that he proceeded secretly, picking his way by stealth, and actually doing much of his travel by night.

At the home of Colonel Jack Smith, the two men remained a week to rest their horses and take

their bearings. General Toombs spent much
time on the Oconee trolling for trout, while bodies
of Union cavalry were watching the ferries
and guarding the fords, seining for bigger fish.

Passing into Wilkinson County, General
Toombs stopped at the home of Mr. Joseph Deas.
When Lieutenant Irvin asked if the pair could
come in, Deas replied, " Yes, if you can put up
with the fare of a man who subsists in Sherman's
track."

A maiden sister of Deas lived in the house.
With a woman's sensitive ear, she recognized General Toombs' voice, having heard him speak at
Toombsboro seventeen years before. This discov-
ery, she did not communicate to her brother until
after the guests had retired. Deas had been discussing politics with Toombs, and his sister asked
him if he knew to whom he had been talking all
night? Deas said he did not.

" Joe Deas," she said, " are you a fool? Don't
you know that is General Toombs ? "

Strange to say, a negro on the place, just as
they were leaving, cried out " Good-by, Marse
Bob." He had driven the family to the speaking
seventeen years before, and had not forgotten the
man who defended slavery on that day.

" Good Lord ! " said Toombs, " go give that
negro some money."

This same negro had been strung up by the

thumbs by Sherman's troops a few months before because he would not tell where his master's mules were hidden. He piloted General Toombs through the woods to the home of Colonel David Hughes, a prominent and wealthy farmer of Twiggs County. Colonel Hughes had been in Toombs' brigade, and the general remained with him a week.

General Toombs was sitting on the piazza of Colonel Hughes's house one afternoon when an old soldier asked permission to come in. He still wore the gray, and was scarred and begrimed. He eyed General Toombs very closely, and seemed to hang upon his words. He heard him addressed as Major Martin, and finally, when he arose to leave, wrung the general's hand.

"Major Martin," he said, brushing the tears from his eyes, "I'm mighty glad to see you. I wish to God I could do something for you."

At the gate he turned to Colonel Hughes and said: "I know who that is. It is General Toombs. You can't fool me."

"Why do you think so?" Colonel Hughes asked.

"Oh, I remember Gray Alice jumping the stone walls at Sharpsburg too well to forget the rider now."

"Colonel," he continued, "this morning a man near here, who is a Republican and an enemy of General Toombs, thought he recognized him near your house. He saw him two hundred yards away. I heard him say he believed it was Toombs and he wished he had his head shot off. I came here to-night to see for myself. You tell General Toombs that if he says the word, I will kill that scoundrel as sure as guns."

The veteran was persuaded, however, to keep quiet and do nothing of the sort.

It was at this time that Lieutenant Irvin found that the ferries of the Ocmulgee River were guarded from one end to the other. Near this place Davis had been captured and the Union troops were on a sharp lookout for Toombs. Convinced that further travel might be hazardous, General Toombs and his friend rode back to the mountains of North Georgia, and there remained until the early fall. It was in the month of October that the fugitives again started on their checkered flight. The May days had melted into summer, and summer had been succeeded by early autumn. The crops, planted when he started from home that spring day, were now ripening in the fields, and Northern statesmen were still declaring that Toombs was the arch-traitor, and must be apprehended. Davis was in irons, and Stephens languished in a dungeon at Fortress Monroe.

Passing once more near Sparta, Ga., Toombs met, by appointment, his friends, Linton Stephens, R. M. Johnson, W. W. Simpson, Jack Lane, Edge

Bird, and other kindred spirits. It was a royal reunion, a sort of Lucretia Borgia feast for Toombs
—"eat and drink to-day, for to-morrow we may
die."

Traveling their old road through Washington
County, they crossed the Ocmulgee, this time in
safety, and passed into Houston County. The
Federals believed Toombs already abroad and had
ceased to look for him in Georgia. After the passage was made General Toombs said: "Charlie,
that ferryman eyed me very closely. Go back and
give him some money."

Lieutenant Irvin did return. The ferryman
refused any gift. He said: "I did not want to
take what you did give me." Irvin asked the
reason. The ferryman said: "Tell General
Toombs I wish to God I could do something
for him."

General Toombs had a wide personal acquaintance in Georgia. He seldom stopped at a house
whose inmates he did not know, and whose rela-
tives and connections he could not trace for generations. Sometimes, when incognito, the two men
were asked where General Toombs was. They
answered, "Cuba."

At Oglethorpe, in Macon County, General
Toombs rode right through a garrison of Federal soldiers. As one of his regiments came from
this section, General Toombs was afraid that some

of his old soldiers might recognize him on the road. A Federal officer advanced to the middle of the street and saluted the travelers. Their hearts bounded to their throats, and, instinctively, two hands stole to their revolvers. Pistols and spurs were the only resources. Chances were desperate, but they were resolved to take them. The officer watched them intently as they rode leisurely through the town, but he was really more interested in their fine horses, "Gray Alice" and "Young Alice," than in the men. Jogging unconcernedly along until the town was hidden by a hill, General Toombs urged his horse into a run, and left "his friends, the enemy," far in the rear. It was a close call, but he did not breathe freely yet. There was possibility of pursuit, and when the party reached the residence of a Mr. Brown, a messenger was sent back to the town to mislead the soldiers should pursuit be attempted. From the hands of the enemy, General Toombs and his friend were now inducted into pleasanter scenes. The house was decorated with lilies and orange blossoms. A wedding was on hand, and the bride happened to be the daughter of the host. Brown was a brave and determined man. He assured General Toombs that when the wedding guests assembled, there would be men enough on hand, should an attack be made, to rout the United States garrison, horse, foot, and dragoons. At

Dr. Raines' place, on the Chattahoochee River, a horse drover happened to say something about Toombs. He gave the statesman a round of abuse and added: "And yet, they tell me that if I were to meet General Toombs and say what I think of him, I would either have a fight or he would convince me that he was the biggest man in the world."

Tired of the long horseback ride, having been nearly six months in the saddle, the men now secured an ambulance from Toombs' plantation in Stewart County, and crossed the river into Alabama. His faithful mare, which he was forced to leave behind, neighed pathetically as her master rode away in a boat and pulled for the Alabama shore. At Evergreen they took the train, and it seemed that half the men on the cars recognized General Toombs. General Joseph Wheeler, who was on board, did not take his eyes off him. Toombs became nervous under these searching glances, and managed to hide his face behind a paper which he was reading. At Tensas Station he took the boat for Mobile. There was a force of Federal soldiers on board, and this was the closest quarters of his long journey. There was now no chance of escape, if detected. The soldiers frequently spoke to General Toombs, but he was not in the slightest way molested.

At Mobile General Toombs took his saddle-

bags and repaired to the home of his friend Mr.
Evans, about four miles from the city. There
he was placed in the care of Howard Evans and
his sister, Miss Augusta J. Evans, the gifted Southern authoress. Anxious to conceal the identity
of their guest, these hospitable young people
dismissed their servants, and Miss Evans herself cooked and served General Toombs' meals
with her own hands. She declared, with true
hospitality, that she felt it a privilege to contrib-
ute to the comfort and insure the safety of the
brilliant statesman. She was a Georgian herself,
and with her this was a labor of love.

These were among the most agreeable moments
of General Toombs' long exile. He loved the
companionship of intellectual women, and the conversation during these days was full of brilliant
interest. Miss Evans was a charming talker, as
bright as a jewel, and Toombs was a Chesterfield
with ladies. The general would walk to and fro
along the shaded walks and pour forth, in his
matchless way, the secret history of the ruin of
Confederate hopes.

General Toombs wrote home, in courtly enthusiasm, of his visit to Mobile. Mr. Stephens sent
Miss Evans a warm letter of thanks for her attentions to his friend. "I have," said he, "just received a letter from General Toombs, who has
been so united with me in friendship and destiny

all our lives, giving such account of the kind attentions he received from you and your father while in Mobile, that I cannot forbear to thank you and him for it in the same strain and terms as if these attentions had been rendered to myself. What you did for my friend, in this particular, you did for me."

While General Toombs was in Mobile, General Wheeler called upon the Evans family and remarked that he thought he had seen General Toombs on the train. Miss Evans replied that she had heard General Toombs was in Cuba.

Lieutenant Irvin went to New Orleans and secured from the Spanish Consul a pass to Cuba for "Major Luther Martin." At Mobile General Toombs took the boat *Creole* for New Orleans. He seemed to be nearing the end of his long journey, but it was on this boat that the dramatic incident occurred which threatened to change the course of his wanderings at last. While General Toombs was at supper, he became conscious that one of the passengers was eying him closely. He said to Lieutenant Irvin: "Charlie, don't look up now, but there is a man in the doorway who evidently recognizes me."

"General, probably it is someone who thinks he knows you."

"No," replied Toombs quietly, "that man is a spy."

Lieutenant Irvin asked what should be done. General Toombs told him to go out and question the man and, if convinced that he was a spy, to throw him over the stern-rail of the steamer. Lieutenant Irvin got up and went on deck. The stranger followed him. Irvin walked toward the rail. The stranger asked him where he was from. He answered " North Carolina."

" Who is that with you ? " he questioned.

"My uncle, Major Martin," said Irvin.

The man then remarked that it looked very much like Robert Toombs. Irvin answered that the likeness had been noted before, but that he could not see it.

" Young man," said the stranger, " I don't want to dispute your word, but that is certainly Toombs. I know him well, and am his friend."

Irvin then gave up the idea of throwing him overboard. Had the brave young officer not been convinced that the party questioning him was Colonel M. C. Fulton, a prominent resident of Georgia, he says he would certainly have pitched him into the Gulf of Mexico.

General Toombs, when informed of the identity of Colonel Fulton, sent for him to come to his room, and the two men had a long and friendly conversation.

Arriving at New Orleans General Toombs drove

up to the residence of Colonel Marshal J. Smith. On the 4th of November, 1865, he boarded the steamship *Alabama*, the first of the Morgan line put on after the war between New Orleans, Havana, and Liverpool. A tremendous crowd had gathered at the dock to see the steamer off, and Lieutenant Irvin tried to persuade General Toombs to go below until the ship cleared. But the buoyant Georgian persisted in walking the deck, and was actually recognized by General Humphrey Marshall of Texas, who had known him in the Senate before the war.

"No," said Toombs to his companion's expostulations, "I want fresh air, and I will die right here. I am impatient to get into neutral waters, when I can talk. I have not had a square, honest talk in six months."

By the time the good ship had cleared the harbor, everybody on board knew that Robert Toombs, "the fire-eater and rebel," was a passenger, and hundreds gathered around to listen to his matchless conversation.

Lieutenant Irvin never saw General Toombs again until 1868. He himself was an officer of the Irvin artillery, Cutts' battalion, being a part of Walker's artillery in Longstreet's corps. Entering the army at seventeen years of age, Charles E. Irvin was a veteran at twenty-one. He was brave, alert, tender, and true. He recalls that when his company joined the army in Richmond, Robert Toombs, then Secretary of State, gave them a handsome supper at the Exchange Hotel. "I remember," said he, "with infinite satisfaction, that during the seven months I accompanied General Toombs, in the closest relations and under the most trying positions, he was never once impatient with me." Frequently, on this long and perilous journey, Toombs would say; "Well, my boy! suppose the Yankees find us to-day; what will you do?" "General, you say you won't be taken alive. I reckon they will have to kill me too."

General Toombs often declared that he would not be captured. Imprisonment, trial, and exile, he did not dread; but to be carried about, a prize captive and a curiosity through Northern cities, was his constant fear. He was prepared to sell his life dearly, and there is no doubt but that he would have done so.

During all these trying days, Toombs rode with the grace and gayety of a cavalier. He talked incessantly to his young companion, who eagerly drank in his words. He fought his battles over again and discussed the leaders of the Civil War in his racy style. He constantly predicted the collapse of the greenback system of currency, and speculated facetiously each day upon the chances of capture. He calculated shrewdly enough his routes and plans, and when he found himself on *terra firma*, it was under the soft skies of the Antilles with a foreign flag above him.

CHAPTER XXV.

FROM Cuba General Toombs proceeded to Paris. It was early in July before he reached his new stopping place. He found himself somewhat restricted in funds, as he had not had time to turn his property into gold to make his trip abroad. It is related that just after the departure of the famous " specie train," through Washington in the wake of Mr. Davis' party, a Confederate horseman dashed by the residence of General Toombs and threw a bag of bullion over the fence. It was found to contain five thousand dollars, but Toombs swore he would not even borrow this amount from his government. He turned it over to the authorities for the use of disabled Confederate soldiers, and hurriedly scraped up what funds he could command in case he should be compelled to fly. Arriving in Paris, General Toombs succeeded in selling one of his plantations, realizing about five dollars an acre for it. He used to explain to the astounded Frenchmen, during his residence abroad, that he ate an acre of dirt a day.

308

General Toombs repaired to Enghien, where he took a course of sulphur baths for the benefit of his throat. Constant exposure with the army and in his flight had brought on his old enemy, the asthma. He had been a healthy man, having long passed the limit of manhood before he tasted medicine. Late in life, an attack of scarlet fever left his throat in a delicate condition.

Mrs. Toombs joined him in Paris in July, 1865, and he passed eighteen months quietly with her in Europe. It was in marked contrast to his tour in 1855, when, as United States Senator, he had gone from place to place, observed, honored, and courted. He was now an exile without a country. He had seen his political dreams wiped out in blood and his home in the hands of the enemy. From the dignity and power of a United States Senator and a possible aspirant to the Presidency, he had been branded as a conspirator, and forced, like Mirabeau, to seek shelter in distant lands.

France was, at that time, in a state of unrest. Louis Napoleon was watching with anxiety the eagles of Prussia hovering over the German Confederation. Austria had already succumbed to Prussian power, and Napoleon had been blocked in his scheme to secure, from this disorder, his share of the Rhenish provinces. Toombs, who had fled from a restored Union in America, now watched the march of consolidation in Europe, and predicted its final success.

General Toombs was an object of interest in Europe. His position toward the American government prevented his public recognition by the rulers, but he used to relate with zest his interviews with Carlyle, the Empress Eugenie, and other notables. He was a man to attract attention, and his talk was fascinating and bright.

He was sometimes sought in a legal way by prominent financiers, who asked his opinions upon fiscal matters in America. There is no doubt but that, like Judah P. Benjamin, he could have built up a large practice abroad, had he cared to do so; but permanent residence away from home was entirely out of his mind.

In December, 1866, General and Mrs. Toombs received a cable message telling them of the death of their only daughter, Mrs. Dudley M. DuBose, in Washington, Ga. Mrs. Toombs at once returned home, leaving the grief-stricken father alone in Paris. Anxious to go back with her, he was advised that matters were still unsettled in the United States. The impeachment of Andrew Johnson was in progress, and his conviction meant restored martial law for the South. So the days were full of woe for the lonely exile.

On December 25, 1866, he writes a beautiful and pathetic letter to his wife. While the deni-

zens of the gay city were deep in the celebration
of the joyous Christmas feast, the Southern wan-
derer, "with heart bowed down," was passing
through the shadows, and suffering in silence the
keenest pangs of affliction. Around him the vo-
taries of fashion and wealth were flushed with
gayety. Paris was in the ecstasy of Christmas-
tide. But the depths of his soul were starless
and chill, and in the midst of all this mirth one
heart was tuned to melancholy. He writes to
his wife :

The night you left I retired to the room and did not go
to sleep until after two o'clock. I felt so sad at parting
with you and could not help thinking what a long dreary
trip you had that night. I shall have a long journey of
five thousand miles to Havana, and do not know that I
shall meet a human being to whom I am known, but if I
keep well I shall not mind that, especially as I am home-
ward bound ; for my hearthstone is desolate, and clouds
and darkness hover over the little remnant that is left of
us, and of all our poor friends and countrymen ; and, when
you get home, Washington will contain nearly all that is
dear to me in this world. I remained alone yesterday after
I got up and went to my solitary meal. I immediately
came back to my room, and have seen nothing of Christmas
in Paris.

On January 1, 1867, he writes :

This is the first of the new year. How sad it opens upon
me ! In a foreign land, with all that is dear to me on earth
beyond the ocean, either on the way to a distant home or
at its desolate fireside. Well, I shall not nurse such gloomy

ideas. Let us hope that the new year may be happier and that we may grow better. God knows I cannot regret that 1866 is gone. I hope its calamities will not enter with us into 1867. I had hoped to hear from New York of your safe arrival on the other side of the ocean.

The loss of his daughter Sallie was a severe blow to General Toombs. But two of his children lived to be grown. His eldest daughter Louise died in 1855, shortly after her marriage to Mr. W. F. Alexander. General Toombs had a son who died in early childhood of scarlet fever. This was a great blow to him, for he always longed for a son to bear his name. Away off in Paris his heart yearned for his four little grandchildren, left motherless by this new affliction. He writes again from Paris:

I almost determined to take the steamer Saturday and run the gauntlet to New York. I would have done so but for my promise to you. I know everything looks worse and worse on our side of the ocean, but when will it be any better? Is this state of things to last forever? To me it is becoming intolerable. . . . . Kiss the dear little children for me. Bless their hearts! How I long to see them and take them to my arms. God bless you! Pray for me that I may be a better man in the new year than in all the old ones before in my time.

Early in January General Toombs decided to sail for Cuba and thence to New Orleans. If he found it unsafe to remain in the South he concluded he could either go back to Cuba or extend his travels into Canada. He had promised his wife he would remain abroad for the present. But he writes:

The worst that can happen to me is a prison, and I don't see much to choose between my present condition and any decent fort. I feel so anxious about you and the children that it makes me very wretched.

From Paris, January 16, 1867, he writes:

My preparations are all complete, and I leave to-morrow on the *New World* for Havana and New Orleans, *via* Martinique. I am well; except my throat. I shall have a long and lonesome voyage, with not much else to cheer me but that I shall find you and our dear little ones at the end of my journey. If I am permitted to find you all well, I shall be compensated for its fatigues and dangers. God grant that we may all meet once more in this world in health!

Yours truly and affectionately, as ever,

TOOMBS.

General Toombs returned to America and after a short residence in Canada went to Washington, where he had a long interview with his old senatorial colleague, President Andrew Johnson. He went home from Washington and was never again molested. He made no petition for relief of political disabilities. He was never restored to citizenship. When Honorable Samuel J. Randall proposed his General Amnesty Act in 1875, Mr. Blaine and other Republicans desired to exclude from its provisions the names of Davis and Toombs. The Democrats would not accept this amendment, and the bill was never passed. Once, when Senator Oliver P. Morton asked General Toombs why he did not petition Congress for pardon, Toombs quietly answered, " Pardon for what ? I have not pardoned you all yet."

CHAPTER XXVI.

COMMENCING LIFE ANEW.

WHEN General Toombs finally returned to Georgia it was with a great part of his fortune gone, his political career cut off by hopeless disability, and his household desolate. These were serious calamities for a man fifty-seven years of age. He found himself forced under new and unfavorable conditions to build all over again, but he set about it in a vigorous and heroic way. His health was good. He was a splendid specimen of manhood. His once raven locks were gray, and his beard, which grew out from his throat, gave him a grizzly appearance. His dark eye was full of fire and his mind responded with vigor to its new work.

When General Toombs arrived at Washington, Ga., he consulted some of his friends over the advisability of returning to the practice of law, which he had left twenty-five years before. Their advice was against it. Things were in chaos; the people were impoverished, and the custodians of the courts were the creatures of a hostile government. But Robert Toombs was made of different stuff. Associating himself in the practice of his profession with General Dudley M. DuBose, who had been his chief of staff, and was his son-in-law, an able and popular man in the full vigor of manhood, General Toombs returned actively to the practice of law. He was not long in turning to practical account his great abilities. Success soon claimed him as an old favorite. Business accumulated and the ex-senator and soldier found himself once more at the head of the bar of Georgia. Large fees were readily commanded. He was employed in important cases in every part of Georgia, and the announcement that Robert Toombs was to appear before judge and jury was enough to draw large crowds from city and country. His old habits of indomitable industry returned. He rode the circuits like a young barrister again. He was a close collector of claims, an admirable administrator, a safe counselor, and a bold and fearless advocate. In a short time General Toombs' family found themselves once more in comfort, and he was the same power with the people that he had always been.

Cut off from all hope of official promotion, scorning to sue for political pardon, he strove to wield in the courts some of the power he forfeited in politics. He figured largely in cases of a public nature, and became an outspoken tribune of the people. He did not hesitate to face the Supreme

Court of Georgia, then made up of Republican judges, and attack the laws of a Republican legislature. Among the bills passed at that time to popularize the legislature with the people, was a series of liberal homestead and exemption laws. They were the relief measures of 1868. By these schemes, at once rigorous and sweeping, millions of dollars were lost in Georgia. They were intended to wipe out old debts, especially contracts made during the war, and Governor Bullock had appointed a Supreme Court which sustained them. These laws were abhorrent to Toombs. He thundered against them with all the powers of his learning and eloquence. When he arose in court, there stood with him, he believed, not only the cause of his client, but the honor of the whole State of Georgia. It was much easier to seduce a poverty-stricken people by offering them measures of relief than to drive them by the bayonet or to subject them to African domination. In the case of Hardeman against Downer, in June, 1868, he declared before the Supreme Court that these homestead laws put a premium on dishonesty and robbed the poor man of his capital. "But we must consider the intention of the Act," said the Court. "Was it not the intention of the legislature to prevent the collection of just such claims as these you now bring?" "Yes, may it please the Court," said

Toombs, shaking his leonine locks, "there can be no doubt that it was the intention of the legislature to defraud the creditor; but they have failed to put their intention in a form that would stand, so it becomes necessary for this Court to add its own ingenuity to this villainy. It seems that this Court is making laws rather than decisions."

In one of his dissenting opinions upon these laws, Justice Hiram Warner declared that he would not allow his name to go down to posterity steeped in the infamy of such a decision. General Toombs lost his case, but the decision was subsequently overruled by the Supreme Court of the United States.

The times were full of evil. The legislature was dominated by adventurers and ignorant men, and public credit was freely voted away to new enterprises. The State was undeveloped, and this wholesale system of public improvement became popular. Unworthy men were scrambling for public station, and the times were out of tune. In the midst of this demoralization Toombs was a pillar of fire. He was tireless in his withering satire, his stinging invective, his uncompromising war upon the misgovernment of the day.

Here was a fine field and a rare occasion for his pungent criticism and denunciation. His utterances were not those of a political leader. He was not trimming his sails for office. He did not shape his conduct so as to be considered an available man by the North. He fought error wherever he saw it. He made no terms with those whom he considered public enemies. He denounced radicalism as a "leagued scoundrelism of private gain and public plunder."

In opposing the issue of State bonds to aid a certain railroad, he declared that if the legislature saddled this debt upon the taxpayers, their act would be a nullity. "We will adopt a new constitution with a clause repudiating these bonds, and like Ætna spew the monstrous frauds out of the market!"

"You may," he said, "by your deep-laid schemes, lull the thoughtless, enlist the selfish, and stifle for a while the voices of patriots, but the day of reckoning will come. These cormorant corporations, these so-called patriotic developers, whom you seek to exempt, shall pay their dues, if justice lives. By the Living God, they shall pay them."

"Georgia shall pay her debts," said Toombs on one occasion. "If she does not, I will pay them for her!" This piece of hyperbole was softened by the fact that on two occasions, when the State needed money to supply deficits, Toombs with other Georgians did come forward and lift the pressure. Sometimes he talked in a random way, but responsibility always sobered him. He was impatient of fraud and stupidity, often full of exaggerations, but scrupulous when the truth was relevant. Always strict and honorable in his engagements, he boasted that he never had a dirty shilling in his pocket.

The men who "left the country for the country's good" and came South to fatten on the spoils of reconstruction, furnished unending targets for his satire. He declared that these so-called developers came for pelf, not patriotism. "Why, these men," he said, "are like thieving elephants. They will uproot an oak or pick up a pin. They would steal anything from a button to an empire." On one occasion he was bewailing the degeneracy of the times, and he exclaimed: "I am sorry I have got so much sense. I see into the tricks of these public men too quickly. When God Almighty moves me from the earth, he will take away a heap of experience. I expect when a man gets to be seventy he ought to go, for he knows too much for other people's convenience."

"I hope the Lord will allow me to go to heaven as a gentleman," he used to say. "Some of these Georgia politicians I do not want to associate with. I would like to associate with Socrates and Shakespeare."

During his arguments before the Supreme Court, General Toombs used to abuse the Governor and the Bullock Legislature very roundly. The Court adopted a rule that no lawyer should be allowed, while conducting his case, to abuse a coördinate branch of the government. General Toombs was informed that if he persisted in this practice he would be held for contempt. The next time Toombs went before the Court he alluded to the fugitive Governor in very sharp terms. "May it please your Honors, the Governor has now absconded. Your Honors have put in a little rule to catch me. In seeking to protect the powers that be, I presume you did not intend to defend the powers that were."

The papers printed an account of an interview between General Gordon and Mr. Tilden in 1880, Gordon told Tilden that he was sorry he could not impart to Tilden some of his own strength and vitality. "So my brother told me last year," answered Mr. Tilden. "I have since followed him to the grave." Toombs read this and remarked that Tilden did not think he was going to die. "No one expects to die but I. I have got sense enough to know that I am bound to die."

On one occasion Toombs was criticising an appointment made by an unpopular official. "But, General," someone said, "you must confess that it was a good appointment." "That may be, but that was not the reason it was made. Bacon was not accused of selling injustice. He was eternally damned for selling justice."

General Toombs was once asked in a crowd in

the Kimball House in Atlanta what he thought
of the North. "My opinion of the Yankees is
apostolic. Alexander the coppersmith did me
much evil. The Lord reward him according to
his works." A Federal officer was standing
in the crowd. He said: "Well, General, we
whipped you, anyhow." "No," replied Toombs,
"we just wore ourselves out whipping you."

He spoke of the spoliators in the State Legislature as "an assembly of manikins whose object
is never higher than their breeches pockets;
seekers of jobs and judgeships, anything for pap
or plunder, an amalgamation of white rogues and
blind negroes, gouging the treasury and disgracing Georgia."

He was a violent foe of exemptions, of bounties,
and of all sorts of corruption and fraud. He was
overbearing at times, but not more conscious of
power than of honesty in its use. He was generous to the weak. It was in defense of his ideas
of justice that he overbore opposition.

General Toombs kept the issues before the people. He had no patience with the tentative policy.
He forfeited much of his influence at this time by
his indiscriminate abuse of Northern men and
Southern opponents, and his defiance of all the
conditions of a restored Union. He could have
served his people best by more conservative conduct, but he had all the roughness and acerbity of

a reformer, dead in earnest. It was owing to his constant arraignment of illegal acts of the post-bellum régime that the people finally aroused, in 1870, and regained the State for white supremacy and Democratic government. He challenged the authors of the Reconstruction measures to discuss the constitutionality of the amendments. Charles J. Jenkins had already carried the cause of Georgia into the courts, and Linton Stephens, before United States Commissioner Swayze in Macon, had made an exhaustive argument upon the whole subject. Toombs forced these issues constantly into his cases, and kept public interest at white heat.

CHAPTER XXVII.

In July, 1868, the people of Georgia made the first determined stand against the Republican party. John B. Gordon was nominated for Governor, and Seymour and Blair had been named in New York as National Democratic standard-bearers. A memorable meeting was held in Atlanta. It was the first real rally of the white people under the new order of things. Robert Toombs, Howell Cobb, and Benjamin H. Hill addressed the multitude. There was much enthusiasm, and crowds gathered from every part of Georgia. This was the great "Bush Arbor meeting" of that year, and old men and boys speak of it to-day with kindling ardor. "Few people," said Toombs in that speech, "had escaped the horrors of war, and fewer still the stern and bitter curse of civil war. The histories of the greatest peoples of earth have been filled with defeats as well as victories, suffering as well as happiness, shame and reproach as well as honor and glory. The struggles of the great and good are the noblest legacies left by the past to the present

generation, trophies worthy to be laid at the feet
of Jehovah himself. Those whose blades glittered
in the foremost ranks of the Northern army on
the battlefield, with a yet higher and nobler purpose denounce the base uses to which the victory
has been applied. The old shibboleths of victory
are proclaimed as living principles. Whatever
else may be·lost, the principles of Magna Charta
have survived the conflict of arms. The edicts of
the enemy abolish all securities of life, liberty,
and property; defeat all the rightful purposes of
government, and renounce all remedies, all laws.

General Toombs denounced the incompetency
of the dominant party in Georgia—"In its tyranny,
its corruption, its treachery to the Caucasian
race, its patronage of vice, of fraud, of crime and
criminals, its crime against humanity and in its
efforts to subordinate the safeguards of public security and to uproot the foundations of free government it has forfeited all claims upon a free
people."

Alluding to General Longstreet, who had been
a member of the Republican party, General
Toombs said: "I would not have him tarnish his
own laurels. I respect his courage, honor his devotion to his cause, and regret his errors." He denounced the ruling party of Georgia as a mass of
floating putrescence, "which rises as it rots and
rots as it rises." He declared that the Reconstruc-

tion Acts "stared out in their naked deformity, open to the indignant gaze of all honest men."

The campaign at that time was made upon the illegality of the amendments to the Constitution. Enthusiasm was fed by the fiery and impetuous invective of Toombs. The utterances of most public men were guarded and conservative. But when Toombs spoke the people realized that he uttered the convictions of an unshackled mind and a fearless spirit. Leaders deprecated his extreme views, but the hustings rang with his ruthless candor.

The conclusion of his Bush Arbor effort was a fine sample of his fervid speech: "All these and many more wrongs have been heaped upon you, my countrymen, without your consent. Your consent alone can give the least validity to these usurpations. Let no power on earth wring that consent from you. Take no counsel of fear; it is the meanest of masters; spurn the temptations of office from the polluted hands of your oppressors. He who owns only his own sepulcher at the price of such claims holds a heritage of shame. Unite with the National Democratic party. Your country says come; honor says come; duty says come; liberty says come; the country is in danger; let every freeman hasten to the rescue."

It was at this meeting that Benjamin H. Hill, who made so much reputation by the publication of a series of papers entitled, " Notes on the

Situation," delivered one of the most memorable speeches of his life. It was a moving, overmastering appeal to the people to go to the polls. When this oration was over, the audience was almost wild, and Robert Toombs, standing on the platform, in his enthusiasm threw his hat away into the delighted throng. A young bright-faced boy picked it up and carried it back to the speakers' stand. It was Henry Grady.

The defeat of the National Democratic party in 1868 disheartened the Southern people, and the old disinclination to take part in politics seized them stronger than before. In 1870, however, General Toombs delivered, in different parts of Georgia, a carefully prepared lecture on the Principles of Magna Charta. It was just the reverse in style and conception to his fervid Bush Arbor oration. It was submitted to manuscript and was read from notes at the speakers' stand. With the possible exception of his Tremont Temple lecture, delivered in Boston in 1856, it was the only one of his public addresses so carefully prepared and so dispassionately delivered. In his opinion the principles of free government were drifting away from old landmarks. The times were out of joint, the people were demoralized. The causes which afterward led to the great revolt in the Republican ranks in 1872 were already marked in the quick perception of Toombs, and this admir-

able state paper was framed to put the issue
before the public in a sober, statesmanlike way,
and to draw the people back to their old moor-
ings. This lecture was delivered in all the large
cities and many of the smaller towns of Georgia,
and had a great effect. Already there had been
concerted appeal to Georgians to cease this political opposition and "accept the situation." Even
statesmen like Mr. Hill had come round to the
point of advising the people to abandon "dead
issues." The situation was more desperate than
ever.

In his Magna Charta lecture Mr. Toombs said
that Algernon Sidney had summed up the object
of all human wisdom as the good government of
the people. "From the earliest ages to the present time," said he, "there has been a continued
contest between the wise and the virtuous who
wish to secure good government and the corrupt
who were unwilling to grant it. The highest duty
of every man, a duty enjoined by God, was the
service of his country." This was the great value
of the victory at Runnymede, with its rich fruits
—that rights should be respected and that justice
should be done. "These had never been denied
for seven hundred years, until the present evil
days," said Toombs. Magna Charta had been
overridden and trampled underfoot by brave ty-
rants and evaded by cowardly ones. There had

been ingenious schemes to destroy it. The men of '76 fought for Magna Charta. These principles had been prominent in our Constitution until a Republican majority attempted destruction and civil war. Kings had made efforts to destroy its power and subvert its influence. Not a single noble family existed in England but which had lost a member in its defense. Society was organized to protect it, and all good and true men are required to maintain its teachings. " The assassins of liberty are now in power, but a reaction is coming. Stand firm, make no compromise, have nothing to do with men who talk of dead issues. It is the shibboleth of ruin. Push forward, and make a square fight for your liberties."

The plain but powerful summary of public obligation had a more lasting effect than his more fiery appeals. General Toombs was a potent leader in the campaign, though not himself a candidate or even a voter. General D. M. DuBose, his law partner, was elected to Congress this year, and the Democratic party secured a majority in the State Legislature. Among the men who shared in the redemption of the State Robert Toombs was the first and most conspicuous.

Some of the best speeches made by General Toombs at this time were delivered to the farmers at the various agricultural fairs. These were frequent and, as Judge Reese declared, abounded with wisdom which caused him years of reflection and observation. He had been reared upon a farm. His interests, as his sympathies, were with these people. He remained in active management of his large plantation, Roanoke, in Stewart County, during the period when he was a member of Congress and even when he was in the army. Two or three times a year he made visits to that place and was always in close communication with his overseers. He loved the work and was a successful farmer. A fondness for gardening and stock-raising remained with him until his last years. Even in a very busy and tempestuous life, as he characterized it in speaking to Judge Reese, a spacious garden, with orchards and vineyards, was to him an unfailing source of recreation and pleasure.

He writes to his wife of the disasters of the army at Orange Court House, Va., but finds time to add: "The gardens and fruit are great additions to the family comfort, and every effort should be made to put them in the best condition." Writing from Richmond of the condition of Lee's army in March, 1862, he does not forget to add: "I am sorry to know that the prospects of the crops are so bad. One of the best reliances now is the garden. Manure high, work well, and keep planting vegetables." From Roanoke, in 1863, he writes; "My plantation affairs are not in as good condition as I would wish. I have lost a great many sheep, have but few lambs and little wool; cattle poor—all need looking after." In the midst of the shelling of Atlanta in 1864, he writes from the trenches to his wife : "Tell Squire to put your cows and Gabriel's in the volunteer oatfield. Every day we hear cannonading in front."

It was in 1869 that General Toombs made one of his great speeches at the State fair in Columbus, in the course of which he used this expression; "The farmers of Georgia will never enjoy general prosperity until they quit making the West their corncrib and smokehouse." It was in that same speech that Toombs said, referring to the soldiers of the South; "Liberty, in its last analysis, is but the sweat of the poor and the blood of the brave." Most of the great men in Georgia have been reared in the country. There seems to be something in the pure air, the broad fields, and even the solitude, conducive to vigor and self-reliance. Attrition and culture have finished the work laid up by the farmer boy, and that fertile section of middle Georgia, so rich in products of the earth, has given greatness to the State.

In August, 1872, General Toombs was invited by the alumni of the University of Georgia to deliver the annual address during commencement week. A large crowd was in attendance and the veteran orator received an ovation. He departed from his usual custom and attempted to read a written speech. His eyesight had begun to fail him, the formation of a cataract having been felt with great inconvenience. The pages of the manuscript became separated and General Toombs, for the first time in his life, is said to have been embarrassed. He had not read more than one quarter of his speech when this complication was discovered, and he was unable to find the missing sheets. Governor Jenkins, who was sitting on the stage, whispered to him; "Toombs, throw away your manuscript and go it on general principles." The general took off his glasses, stuffed the mixed essay into his pocket, and advanced to the front of the stage. He was received with a storm of applause from the crowd, who had relished his discomfiture and were delighted with the thought of an old-time talk from Toombs. For half an hour he made one of his eloquent and electric speeches, and when he sat down the audience screamed for more. No one but Toombs could have emerged so brilliantly from this awkward dilemma.

General Toombs opposed the nomination of Horace Greeley for President by the National Democratic convention in 1872. Mr. Stephens edited the Atlanta *Sun*, and these two friends once more joined their great powers to prevent the consummation of what they regarded as a vast political mistake. Greeley carried the State by a very reduced majority.

In January, 1873, when Mr. Stephens was defeated for the United States Senate by General John B. Gordon, General Toombs called a meeting of the leaders of the eighth district in his room at the Kimball House in Atlanta, and nominated his friend Alexander Stephens for Congress. He needed no other indorsement. He was elected and reëlected, and remained in Congress until he resigned in 1882, to become Governor of Georgia. Toombs and Stephens never lost their lead as dictators in Georgia politics.

The man in Georgia who suffered most frequently from the criticism of General Toombs during this eventful period was ex-Governor Joseph E. Brown. His position in taking his place in the Republican party, in accepting office, and separating himself from his old friends and allies, brought down upon him the opprobrium of most of the people. It was at a time when Charles J. Jenkins had carried away the great seal of Georgia and refused to surrender it to a hostile government. It was at a time when Linton Stephens, the most vigorous as the most popular public man during the reconstruction period, was endeavoring to arouse the people. Governor Brown's apostasy was unfortunate. No man was then more execrated by the people who had honored him. His name, for a while, was a byword and a reproach. Mr. Stephens defended his position as conscientious if not consistent, and gave Governor Brown the credit for the purity as well as the courage of his convictions. Governor Brown bore the contumely with patience. He contended that he could best serve the State by assuming functions that must otherwise be placed in hostile hands, and his friends declare to-day that in accepting the amendments to the Constitution he simply occupied in advance the ground to which the party and the people were forced to come. But his position did not compare favorably with that of the prominent Georgians of that day.

The relations of Governor Brown and General Toombs continued strained. The latter never lost an opportunity to upbraid him in public or in private, and some of his keenest thrusts were aimed at the plodding figure of his old friend and ally, as it passed on its lonely way through the shadows of its long probation.

On one occasion in Atlanta, in July, 1872, General Toombs among other things referred to a lobby at the legislature in connection with a claim for the Mitchel heirs. Governor Brown had remained quiet during his long political ostracism, but he turned upon his accuser now with unlooked-for severity. He answered the charge by declaring that if Toombs accused him of lobbying this claim, he was an "unscrupulous liar." The reply did not attract much attention until it became known that General Toombs had sent a friend to Governor Brown to know if the latter would accept a challenge. Colonel John C. Nicholls was the friend, and Governor Brown returned the answer that when he received the challenge he would let him know. General Toombs did not push the matter further. The affair took the form of a newspaper controversy, which was conducted with much acrimony on both sides. Colonel Nicholls stated in print his belief that Governor Brown would not have accepted a challenge but would have used it to Toombs' injury before the people. The prospect of a duel between these two old men created a sensation at the time. It would have been a shock to the public sense of propriety to have allowed such a meeting. It would never have been permitted; but Governor Brown seems to have been determined to put the issue to the touch. He had prepared his resignation as a deacon of the Baptist Church, and had placed his house in order. He seemed to realize that this was the turning-point of his career, and there is no doubt that General Toombs gave him the opportunity to appear in a better light than he had done for a long time; this incident was the beginning of his return to popularity and influence in Georgia. General Toombs was censured for provoking Governor Brown into the attitude of expecting a challenge and then declining to send it.

Both General Toombs and Mr. Stephens were believers in the code of honor. Mr. Stephens once challenged Governor Herschel V. Johnson, and at another time he called out Hon. Benjamin H. Hill. General Toombs peremptorily challenged General D. H. Hill after the battle of Malvern Hill. In 1859, when United States Senator Broderick was killed by Judge Terry in California, Mr. Toombs delivered a striking eulogy of Broderick in the United States Senate. He said; "The dead man fell in honorable contest under a code which he fully recognized. While I lament his sad fate, I have no censure for him or his adversary. I think that no man under any circumstances can have a more enviable death than to fall in vindication of his honor. He has gone beyond censure or praise. He has passed away from man's judgment to the bar of the Judge of all the Earth."

CHAPTER XXVIII.

HIS LAST PUBLIC SERVICE.

ONE of the reforms advocated by General Toombs upon the return of the white people to the control of the State Government was the adoption of a new State Constitution. He never tired of declaring that the organic law of 1868 was the product of "aliens and usurpers," and that he would have none of it; Georgia must be represented by her own sons in council and live under a constitution of her own making. In May, 1877, an election was held to determine the question, and in spite of considerable opposition, even in the Democratic party, the people decided, by nine thousand majority, to have a constitutional convention.

On July 10, 1877, that body, consisting of 194 delegates, assembled in Atlanta to revise the organic law. Charles J. Jenkins was elected president of the convention. He had been deposed from the office of Governor of Georgia at the point of the bayonet in 1866. He had carried the case of the State of Georgia before the national Supreme Court and contested the validity of the

Reconstruction measures. He had carried with him, when expelled from the State Capitol, the great seal of the State, which he restored when the government was again remitted to his own people, and in public session of the two houses of the General Assembly, Governor Jenkins had been presented with a facsimile of the great seal, with the fitting words cut into its face, " In Arduis Fidelis." These words are graven on his monument to-day. He was more than seventy years of age, but bore himself with vigor and ability. There was a strong representation of the older men who had served the State before the war, and the younger members were in full sympathy with them. It was an unusual body of men—possibly the ablest that had assembled since the secession convention of 1861. General Toombs, of course, was the most prominent. He had been elected a delegate from his senatorial district—the only office he had occupied since the war. His activity in securing its call, his striking presence, as he walked to his seat, clad in his long summer duster, carrying his brown straw hat and his unlighted cigar, as well as his tireless labors in that body, made him the center of interest. General Toombs was chairman of the committee on legislation and chairman of the final committee on revision. This body was made up of twenty-six of the most prominent members of the convention, and to it were submitted the reports of the other thirteen committees. It was the duty of this committee to harmonize and digest the various matters coming before it, and to prepare the final report, which was discussed in open convention. General Toombs was practically in charge of the whole business of this body. He closely attended all the sessions of the convention, which lasted each day from 8.30 in the morning to 1 o'clock P. M. The entire afternoons were taken up with the important and exacting work of his committee of final revision. Frequently it was far into the night before he and his clerk had prepared their reports. General Toombs was in his sixty-eighth year, but stood the ordeal well. His facility, his endurance, his genius, his eloquence and pertinacity were revelations to the younger men, who knew him mainly by tradition. General Toombs proposed the only safe and proper course for the convention when he arose in his place on the floor and declared; " All this convention has to do is to establish a few fundamental principles and leave the other matters to the legislature and the people, in order to meet the ever varying affairs of human life." There was a persistent tendency to legislate upon details, a tendency which could not be entirely kept down. There was an element elected to this convention bent upon retrenchment and reform, and these delegates forced a long debate upon lowering the salaries of public officers, a policy which finally prevailed. During the progress of this debate General Toombs arose impatiently in his place and declared that, " The whole finances of the State are not included when we are speaking of the Governor's salary, and you spend more in talking about it than your children will have to pay in forty years."

Occasionally he was betrayed into one of his erratic positions, as when he moved to strike out the section against dueling, and also to expunge from the bill of rights all restrictions upon bearing arms. He said: "Let the people bear arms for their own protection, whether in their boots or wherever they may choose."

But his treatment of public questions was full of sound sense and discretion. He warned the convention that those members who, from hostility to the State administration, wished to wipe out the terms of the office-holders and make a new deal upon the adoption of the new constitution, were making a rash mistake. They would array a new class of enemies and imperil the passage of the new law. He advocated the submission of all doubtful questions, like the homestead laws and the location of the new Capitol, to the people in separate ordinances. He urged in eloquent terms the enlargement of the Supreme Court from three justices to five. Having been a champion of the law calling that Court into being forty years before, he knew its needs and proposed a reform which, if adopted, would have cut off much trouble in Georgia to-day.

General Toombs was an advocate of the ordinance which took the selection of the judges and solicitors from the hands of the Governor and made them elective by the General Assembly. A strong element in the convention wanted the judiciary elected by the people. A member of the convention turned to General Toombs during the debate and said; " You dare not refuse the people this right to select their own judges." " I dare do anything that is right," replied Toombs. " It is not a reproach to the people to say that they are not able to do all the work of a complex government. Government is the act of the people after all." He reminded the convention that a new and ignorant element had been thrown in among the people as voters. " We must not only protect ourselves against them, but in behalf of the poor African," said he, " I would save him from himself. These people are kind, and affectionate, but their previous condition, whether by your fault or not, was such as to disqualify them from exercising the right of self-government. They were put upon us by people to make good government impossible in the South for all time, and before God, I believe they have done it."

In answer to the argument that those States which had given the selection of judges to the people liked it, General Toombs replied that this did not prove that it was right or best. "It is easy to take the road to hell, but few people ever return from it." General Toombs prevailed in this point. He was also the author of the resolution authorizing the legislature to levy a lax to furnish good substantial artificial limbs to those who had lost them during the war.

General Toombs declared frequently during the debate that one of his main objects in going to the convention, and for urging the people to vote for the call, was to place a clause in the new law prohibiting the policy of State aid to railroads and public enterprises. He had seen monstrous abuses grow up under this system. He had noticed that the railroads built by private enterprise had proven good investments; that no railroad aided by the State had paid a dividend. He declared that Georgia had never loaned her credit from the time when Oglethorpe landed at Yamacraw up to 1866, and she should never do it again. He wanted this license buried and buried forever. His policy prevailed. State aid to railroads was prohibited; corporate credit cannot now be loaned to public enterprises, and municipal taxation was wisely restricted. General Toombs declared with satisfaction that he had locked the door of the treasury, and put the key into the pocket of the people.

During the proceedings of this convention an effort was made to open the courts to review the cases of certain outlawed bonds, which the legislature had refused to pay, and which the people had repudiated by constitutional amendment. Impressed by the conviction that certain classes of these bonds should be paid, the venerable president of the convention surrendered the chair and pled from his place on the floor for a judicial review of this question.

No sooner was this solemn and urgent appeal concluded than General Toombs bounded to the floor. He declared with energy that no power of heaven or hell could bind him to pay these bonds. The contract was one of bayonet usurpation. Within a few days the legislature had loaded the State down with from ten to fifteen millions of the " bogus bonds."

The term " repudiation " was distasteful to many. The bondholders did not relish it; but he thought it was a good honest word. No one was bound by these contracts, because they were not the acts of the people. " I have examined all the facts pertaining to these claims," said Toombs, " and looking to nothing but the State's integrity, I affirm that the matter shall go no further without my strenuous opposition. The legislature has

again and again declared the claims fraudulent.
The people have spoken. Let the bonds die."
The convention agreed with Toombs.

On the 16th of August the convention, then in
the midst of its labors, confronted a crisis. The
appropriation of $25,000 made by the legislature
to meet the expenses of the convention had been
exhausted, and the State Treasurer notified the
president that he could not honor his warrants
any further. This was a practical problem. The
work mapped out had not been half done. Many
of the delegates were poor men from the rural
districts and were especially dependent upon their
per diem during the dull summer season. To proceed required about $1000 per day. To have
crippled this body in its labors would have been a
public calamity. To check upon the public treasury beyond the limit fixed by law involved a risk
which the State Government, not too friendly toward the convention at best, declined to assume.
To raise the money outside by a private loan presented this risk, that in the case of the rejection of
the constitution, then in embryo, the lender might
find himself the holder of an uncertain claim. The
convention, however, was not left long in doubt.
With a heroic and patriotic *abandon*, General
Toombs declared that if Georgia would not pay
her debts, he would pay them for her. Selling a
dozen or two United States bonds, he placed the

proceeds to the credit of the president of the convention, who was authorized in turn to issue notes of $1000 each and deposit them with General Toombs. The act was spontaneous, whole-souled, dramatic. It saved the convention and rehabilitated the State with a new constitution. By a rising and unanimous vote General Toombs was publicly thanked for his public-spirited act, and the old man, alone remaining in his seat in the convention hall, covered his face with his hands, and shed tears during this unusual demonstration.

When the convention had under review the bill of rights, General Toombs created a breeze in the proceedings by proposing a paragraph that the legislature should make no irrevocable grants of special privileges or immunities. The proposition received a rattling fire from all parts of the house. Governor Jenkins assailed it on the floor as dangerous to capital and fatal to public enterprise. It was argued that charters were contracts, and that when railroads or other interests were put upon notice that their franchise was likely to be disturbed, there would be an overthrow of confidence and development in Georgia. This was the first intimation of the master struggle which General Toombs was about to make, an advance against the corporations all along the line. It was the picket-firing before the engagement.

General Toombs had made a study of the

whole railroad question. He was a master of the law of corporations. He maintained a peculiar attitude toward them. He never invested a dollar in their stock, nor would he accept a place at their council boards. He rarely ever served them as attorney. When the General Assembly resolved to tax railroads in Georgia, the State selected General Toombs to prosecute the cases. In 1869 he had argued the Collins case against the Central Railroad and Banking Company, in which the court had sustained his position that the proposed action of the Central Road in buying up the stock of the Atlantic and Gulf Railroad, to control that road, was *ultra vires.* He had conducted the case of Arnold DuBose against the Georgia Railroad for extortion in freight charges.

The principles he had gleaned from this laborious record made him resolve to place restrictions upon corporate power in the new constitution. The time was ripe for this movement. The Granger legislation in the West had planted in the organic law of Illinois, Ohio, and Missouri the policy of government control over the railroads. The statutes of Pennsylvania also reflected the same principles, and the Supreme Court of the United States had decided this great case on the side of the people. General Toombs was master of the legislation on this subject in

England, and had studied the American reports on the right and duty of the state to regulate railroad companies. He declared, in proposing this new system, that these laws had been adopted by the most enlightened governments of the world. "From the days of the Roman Empire down to the present time," said Toombs, "it has never been denied that the state has power over the corporations."

At once the State was in an uproar. "Toombs is attempting a new revolution," was alleged. He was charged with leading an idolatrous majority into war upon the rights of property. Conservative men like Jenkins deprecated the agitation. Atlanta was filled with a powerful railroad lobby, and the press resounded with warning that development of the waste places of Georgia would be retarded by this unjust and nefarious warfare. Robert Toombs was not an agrarian. His movement against the corporations was reënforced by delegates from the small towns in Georgia, who had suffered from discrimination in favor of the larger cities. Railroad traffic had been diverted by rigid and ruthless exactions, and a coterie of delegates from southwest Georgia stood solidly by Toombs. These debates drew crowds of listeners. From the galleries hundreds of interested Georgians looked down upon the last public service of Robert Toombs. He never appeared to finer advantage.   His voice lacked its old-time ring, his beard was gray and his frame was bent, but he was fearless, aggressive, alert, eloquent. He was master of the whole subject.   Railways, he declared, were public highways.   Upon no other principle could they receive land from the State, under its right of eminent domain, than that this land was condemned for public and not for private use.   A public highway means that it must be used according to law.   In those States where people have been fighting the encroachments of public monopolies, it had been found necessary to use these terms, and Toombs prefaced his agitation with this announcement.

General Toombs did not mince matters.   He declared that the rapacious course of the railroads in Georgia had been spoliation.   Monopoly is extortion.   Corporations must either be governed by the law or they will override the law.   Competition is liberty.   Keep the hand of the law on corporations and you keep up competition; keep up competition and you preserve liberty.   It has been argued that the towns and counties in Georgia had grown rich.   That is the same argument that was made in the English Parliament.   They said; " Look at your little colonies, how they have grown under our care."   But the patriotic men of America said; " We have grown rich in spite of your oppressions."   Shall we not restrain this tax-gatherer who has no judge but himself, no limit but his avarice?

General Toombs wanted it placed in the constitution that the legislature shall pass these laws restricting railroads. He declared he had twice drawn bills for that purpose; they had passed the House, but crumbled as though touched with the hand of death when they came to the forty-four (the Senate). "What," said he, "do I see before me? The grave. What beyond that? Starving millions of our posterity, that I have robbed by my action here, in giving them over to the keeping of these corporations. The right to control these railroads belongs to the State, to the people, and as long as I represent the people, I will not consent to surrender it, so help me God!"

The spirit of Toombs dominated that convention. Men moved up the aisle to take their seats at his feet as he poured out his strong appeal. One-half of that body was filled with admiration, the other half with alarm. "It is a sacred thing to shake the pillars upon which the property of the country rests," said Mr. Hammond of Fulton. "Better shake the pillars of property than the pillars of liberty," answered this Georgia Sampson, with his thews girt for the fray. "The great question is, Shall Georgia govern the corporations or the corporations govern Georgia? Choose ye this day whom ye shall serve!"

The house rang with applause. Members clustered about the old man as about the form of a prophet. The majority was with him. The articles which he had advocated came from the committee without recommendation, but they were substantially adopted, and are now parts of the supreme law of the land. The victory was won, and Robert Toombs, grim and triumphant, closed his legislative career, and claimed this work as the crowning act of his public labors.

These principles are contained in Article IV. of the State constitution of Georgia. It declares the right of taxation to be sovereign, inviolable, and indestructible, and that it shall be irrevocable by the State; that the power to regulate freight and passenger tariffs and to prevent unjust discriminations shall be conferred upon the General Assembly, whose duty it shall be to pass laws for the same; that the right of eminent domain shall never be abridged; that any amendment to a charter shall bring the charter under the provisions of the Constitution; that the General Assembly shall have no authority to authorize any corporation to buy shares of stock in any other corporation, which shall have the effect to lessen competition or encourage monopoly. No railroad shall pay a rebate or bonus.

Under these provisions, the Railroad Commission of Georgia was organized in 1879. This

idea, as it finally worked out, was General Toombs'.
He did not favor fixing the rates in the law, but
the creation of such a commission to carry out
these provisions. The present law was framed by
Judge William M. Reese, Hon. Samuel Barnett,
Ex-Senator H. D. McDaniel, and Superintendent
Foreacre of the Richmond and Danville Railroad.
It has worked well in Georgia. Twice has the
legislature attempted to remodel it, but the people
have rallied to its support and have not permitted
it to be amended in so much as a single clause.
It has served as an example for imitation by other
States, and was cited as strong authority in Congress for the creation of the Inter-State Commerce
Law. The railroad men, after fighting it for ten
years, have come round to acknowledge its value.
It has stood as a breakwater between the corporations and the people. It has guaranteed justice
to the citizen, and has worked no injury to the
railroads. Under its wise provisions Georgia has
prospered, and leads the Union to-day in railroad
building. And when, during a recent session of
the legislature, an attempt was made to war upon
railroad consolidation, the saving, overmastering,
crowning argument of the railroads themselves
was that General Toombs had already secured
protection for the people, and that, under his
masterly handiwork, the rights of property and
the rights of the people were safe.

When the convention had concluded its labors, General Toombs went before the people and threw himself with enthusiasm into the canvass. He took the stump, and everywhere his voice was heard in favor of the adoption of the new organic law. Many of the officers whose term had been cut off, and whose salaries had been reduced, appeared against the constitution. General Toombs declared that those public men who did not approve of the lower salaries might "pour them back in the jug." This homely phrase became a by-word in the canvass. It had its origin in this way: In the Creek war, in which "Capt. Robert A. Toombs" commanded a company made up of volunteers from Wilkes, Elbert, and Lincoln counties, a negro named Kinch went along as whisky sutler. As he served out the liquor, some of the soldiers complained of the price he asked. His answer was, "Well, sir, if you don't like it, sir, pour it back in the jug."

In the State election of December, 1877, the new constitution was overwhelmingly adopted, and will remain for generations the organic law of the Empire State of the South.

CHAPTER XXIX.

DOMESTIC LIFE OF TOOMBS.

THERE never was a public man in America whose home life was more beautiful or more tender than that of Robert Toombs. As great as were his public virtues, his lofty character, and abilities, his domestic virtues were more striking still. He was a man who loved his family. In 1830 he was married to Julia A. Dubose, with whom he lived, a model and devoted husband, for more than fifty years. She was a lady of rare personal beauty, attractive manners, and common sense. She shared his early struggles, and watched the lawyer grow into the statesman and the leader with unflagging confidence and love. There was never a time that he would not leave his practice or his public life to devote himself to her. His heart yearned for her during his long separation in Washington, when, during the debate upon the great Compromise measures of 1850, he wrote that he would rather see her than "save the State." He considered her in a thousand ways. He never disappointed her in coming home, but, when traveling, always returned when it was possible, just at the

time he had promised. During the exciting scenes
attending his first election to the United States
Senate, he writes that he feels too little interest in
the result perhaps for his success, and longs to
be at home. Political honors did not draw him
away from his devotion to this good woman. He
never neglected her in the smallest way. His attentions were as pointed and courtly in her last
days as when they were bright-faced boy and girl,
lovers and cousins, in the twenties. During his
labors in the constitutional convention of 1877, he
one day wore upon his lapel a flower she had
placed there, and stopping in his speech, paid fitting tribute to the pure emblem of a woman's
love. A man of great deeds and great temptations, of great passions and of glaring faults, he
never swerved in loyalty to his wedded love, and
no influence ever divided his allegiance there.
Writing to her on May 15, 1853, while he was
United States Senator, he says:

My Dear Julia :
  This is your birthday, which you bid me remember, and
this letter will show you that I have not forgotten it. To-
day Gus Baldwin and Dr. Harbin dropped in to dinner, and
we drank your good health and many more returns in
health and happiness of the 15th of May. I did not tell
them that you were forty, for it might be that some time
or other you would not care to have them know it, and I
am sure they would never suspect it unless told. In truth
I can scarcely realize it myself, as you are the same lovely

and loving, true-hearted woman to me, that you were when I made you my bride, nearly twenty-three years ago. There is no other change except the superior loveliness of the full blown over the budding rose. I have thrown my mind this quiet Sunday evening over that large segment of human life (twenty-three years) since we were married, and whatever of happiness memory has treasured up clusters around you. In life's struggle I have been what men call fortunate. I have won its wealth and its honors, but I have won them by labor, and toil, and strife, whose memory saddens even success; but the pure joys of wedded love leave none but pleasant recollections which one can dwell upon with delight. These thoughts are dearer to me than to most men, because I know for whatever success in life I may have had, whatever evil I may have avoided, or whatever good I may have done, I am mainly indebted to the beautiful, pure, true-hearted little black-eyed girl, who on the 18th of November, 1830, came trustingly to my arms, the sweetest and dearest of wives. You need not fear, therefore, that I shall forget your birthday. That and our bridal-day are the brightest in my calendar. and memory will not easily part with them.

Yours,

Toombs.

So well known was this domestic trait of Mr. Toombs that Bishop Beckwith of Georgia, in delivering his funeral sermon, declared that " no knight, watching his sword before the altar, ever made a holier, truer, or purer vow than when Robert Toombs stood at the marriage altar more than fifty years ago. The fire that burned upon the altar of his home remained as pure and unfailing as the perpetual offering of Jerusalem."

Mrs. Toombs was a woman of warm heart and strong convictions. She was noted for her benevolence and piety, and these she carried through life. Her Christian example was a steadying influence often in the stormy and impetuous career of her husband, and finally, when she had closed her eyes in peace, brought him to the altar where she had worshiped. Her household and her neighbors loved to be under her influence. No one who ever saw her fine face, or her lustrous dark eyes, forgot her. Her face was, in some respects, not unlike that of her husband. It is the best tribute that can be paid to her to say that for more than fifty years her influence over so strong a character as that of Robert Toombs was most potent. In June, 1856, while driving in Augusta, the horses attached to the carriage ran away, and Mrs. Toombs was thrown from the vehicle and sustained a fracture of the hip. General Toombs hastened to Georgia from Congress, and remained incessantly at her bedside for several weeks. In November, 1880, General and Mrs. Toombs celebrated their golden wedding, surrounded by their grandchildren and friends. It was a beautiful sight to see the bride of half a century with a new wedding ring upon her finger, playing the piano, while the old man of seventy essayed, like Washington, to dance the minuet. The old couple survived their three children, and lived to bless the lives of grandchildren and great-grandchildren. They were fond and affectionate parents.

A friend, who had known them in their own home, describes "the great fire in the open fireplace; on one side the venerable statesman, with that head which always seemed to me of such rare beauty; on the other side, the quiet wife busy with home affairs, her eyes lighting, now and then, the wonderful conversation that fell from his eloquent lips."

General Toombs was a liberal provider for his family, and his grandchildren and connections were constant objects of his bounty. Large sums were spent in charity. No church or benevolent institution appealed to him in vain. His house was open, and his hospitality was princely and proverbial. No one was more genial at home. Few prominent persons ever visited Washington without being entertained by Toombs. His regular dinners to the bar of the circuit, as, twice a year, the lawyers came to Washington to court, are remembered by scores of Georgians to-day. On one occasion when the townspeople were discussing the need of a hotel, General Toombs indignantly replied that there was no need for any such place. "If a respectable man comes to town," said he,

" he can stay at my house. If he isn't respectable,
we don't want him here at all." •

No religious conference could meet in Washington that the Toombs house was not full of
guests. Many Northern people visited the place
to hear the statesman talk. Newspaper correspondents sought him out to listen to his fine conversation. These people were always sure of the
most courteous treatment, and were prepared for
the most candid expression. General Toombs was
not solely a *raconteur*. He did not draw upon his
memory for his wit. The cream of his conversation was his bold and original comment. His wit
flashed all along the line. His speech at times
was droll and full of quaint provincialisms. He
treated subjects spontaneously, in a style all his
own. Strangers, who sat near him in a railroad
car, have been enchanted by his sage and spirited
conversation, as his leonine features lighted up, and
his irresistible smile and kindly eye forced good-
humor, even where his sentiments might have
challenged dissent. He was the finest talker of
his day. A close friend, who used to visit him
frequently at his home, declares that Toombs'
powers did not wait upon the occasion. He did
not require an emergency to bring him out. All
his faculties were alert, and in a morning's chat he
would pour out the riches of memory, humor,
eloquence, and logic until the listener would be

enthralled by his brilliancy and power. He delighted to talk with intellectual men and women. He was impatient with triflers or dolts. He criticised unsparingly, and arraigned men and measures summarily, but he was a seeker after truth, and even when severe, was free from malice or envy.

General Toombs was a man of tender sympathies. Distress of his friends moved him to prompt relief. In 1855 a friend and kinsman, Mr. Pope, died in Alabama. He had been a railroad contractor and his affairs were much involved. General Toombs promptly went to his place, bought in his property for the family, and left the place for the wife and children, just as it stood. From Mobile he writes a grief-stricken letter to his wife, December 28, 1855:

I feel that I must pour out my sorrows to someone, and whom else can I look to but to one who, ever faithful and true, has had my whole heart from my youth till now? This has been one of the dark and sad days of my life. The remains of my lost friend Mr. Pope came down on the cars this morning. I met them alone at the depot, except Gus. Baldwin and the hired hands. This evening I accompanied the remains to the boat. Oh, it was so sad to see one whom so many people professed to love, in a strange place, conveyed by hirelings and deposited like merchandise among the freight of a steamboat on the way to his long home. I can scarcely write now, at the thought, through the blindness of my own tears. As I saw him placed in the appointed spot among the strangers and bustle of a departing boat, careless of who or what he was,

I stole away to the most retired part of the boat, to conceal the weakness of friendship and relieve my overburdened heart with a flood of tears. I felt it would be a profanation of friendship even to be seen to feel in such a crowd. But for my overwhelming duty to the living I would have taken the boat and gone on with his remains. This is the end of the just in this world. He was a good and an upright man; never gave offense to a human being. His family are ruined, but his only fault was want of judgment, and too great confidence in his kind. He could not make money, and it really seemed that his every effort to do so plunged him deeper into debt. His great fault was a concealment of his own difficulties and trials. I would have done anything to have relieved them upon a full disclosure. He was idolized at home, and I have wept at the sorrows of the poor people in his employment, upon the very mention of his death. I know I cannot control my grief and am sensitive of my own weakness. I could not find relief without pouring out my sorrows to you. There let them rest.　　　　Yours,

　　　　　　　　　　　TOOMBS.

General Toombs resided in a three-story frame house in Washington, built after the manner of the olden time, with the spacious piazza, heavy columns, the wide door, and the large rooms. He lived in ease and comfort. He was an early riser, and after breakfast devoted himself to business or correspondence. At midday he was accessible to visitors, and rarely dined alone. In the afternoon he walked or drove. At night he sat in his armchair at his fireside, and in his lips invariably carried an unlit cigar. Smoking did not agree

with him. While in Europe he delighted to test
the tobacco of the different countries, but the
practice always gave him pain above the eyes. His
last attempt was in the army of Virginia. Convinced that smoking injured him, he never resumed it. Fond of his dry smoke, he had a peculiar cigar made to order, very closely wrapped,
with fine tobacco.

General Toombs made frequent trips away from
home, even during the latter part of his life. The
State retained his services in important cases.
One of his last public acts was the prosecution of
certain railway companies for back taxes. He
recovered thousands of dollars to the State. He
was summoned to Atlanta in 1880 to prosecute a
defaulting State treasurer. He appeared very
feeble, but his speech was a model of clearness
and logic. During the latter part of his life there
was a return of his early fault of quick, nervous,
compressed speech. He grasped only the great
hillocks of thought and left the intervening ground
to be filled by the listener. His terse, rapid style
was difficult to follow. As a presiding judge said,
"His leaps are like a kangaroo's, and his speech
gave me the headache." But his argument in the
Jack Jones case was a model of eloquence and convincing law. A large number of friends attended
the court, convinced that General Toombs was
nearing the end of his great career, and were as-

tounded at the manner in which he delivered his
argument. As he concluded his address he turned
in his place and caught the eye of Rev. Father J.
M. O'Brien, an old friend of his. "Why, Father
O'Brien," he said, wringing his hand, "I am glad
to see you taking an interest in this case. These
people are trying to usurp your functions. They
want to grant the defendant absolution." "But,
General," replied the quick-witted priest, "even I
could not grant absolution until he had made res-
titution." "That's the doctrine," said the delighted
lawyer, pleased to find that the point of his speech
had taken so well. His face was all aglow with
the *gaudia certaminis* of the forum. This was his
last appearance in court, and he won his case.

His mother Georgia claimed his allegiance always, and he gave her his last and best powers.
He worked for the commonwealth, and gave the
people more than he ever received in return.

In Augusta, in 1871, when he appeared before
the Georgia Railroad Commission and arraigned
the lease of the State road as illegal and un-
hallowed, he declared in a burst of indignation;
"I would rather be buried at the public expense
than to leave a dirty shilling." It was the acme
of his desire to live and die like a gentleman.

He had always been a safe financier. Scorning
wealth, he had early found himself wealthy. It is
estimated that he made more than a million dol-

lars by his law practice after the war. He spent his money freely, careful always to avoid debt. Further than this, he kept no account of his means. Like Astor, he invested much of his holdings in land, and owned a large number of fine plantations in middle Georgia. When he died his estate probably reached two hundred thousand dollars.

CHAPTER XXX.

No just biography of Robert Toombs can be written that does not take into notice the blemishes as well as the brightness of his character. He was a man on a grand scale. His virtues were heroic, his faults were conspicuous. No man despised hypocrisy more than he did, and no one would have asked any sooner to be painted as he was, without concealment. During the latter part of his life, many people knew him principally by his faults. Few knew what the wayward Prince Hal of the evening had been to King Henry in the morning hour. Like Webster and Clay, he was made up of human frailty. As his intimate friend, Samuel Barnett, said of him : " In spite of splendid physique, a man of blood and passion, he was not only a model of domestic virtue, but he avoided the lewd talk to which many prominent men are addicted. A fine sportsman and rider, a splendid shot, he was nothing of the racer or gamester. After all, he was more of a model than a warning." Among his faults, the one which exaggerated all the others, was his use of ardent liquors. This habit grew upon him, especially after the failure of the war. A proud, imperious nature, accustomed to great labors and great responsibilities, was left without its main resource and supplied with the stimulus of wine. No man needed that stimulus less than he did. His was a manhood vibrant in age with the warm blood of youth, and always at its best when his spirits and intellect alone were at play. He was easily affected by the smallest indulgence. When he measured himself with others, glass for glass, the result was distressing, disastrous. The immediate effect of excess was short. The next morning his splendid vitality asserted itself, and he was bright and clear as ever. The habit, however, grew upon him. The want of a physical check was bad. This was the worst of all his faults, and was exaggerated by special circumstances. It was less indulged in at home and greatly circulated abroad. Frequently the press reporters would surround him and expose in the papers a mere caricature of him. His talk, when under the influence of wine, was racy, extravagant, and fine, and his sayings too often found their way into print. In this way great injustice was done to the life and character of Robert Toombs, and Northern men who read these quaint sayings and redolent vaporings formed a distorted idea of the man.

To a Northern correspondent who approached

him during one of these periods, General Toombs said: "Yes, a gentleman whose intelligence revolts at usurpations must abstain from discussing the principles and policies of your Federal government, or receive the kicks of crossroad sputterers and press reporters; must either lie or be silent. They know only how to brawl and scrawl 'hot-head' and 'impolitic maniac.' Why, my free negroes know more than all your bosses. Now, damn it, put that in your paper."

Robert Toombs was built to live ninety years, and to have been, at Gladstone's age, a Gladstone in power. He took little pains to explain his real nature. He seemed to take pains to conceal or mislead. He appeared at times to hide his better and expose his worse side. If he had been Byron, he would have put forward his deformed foot. He was utterly indifferent to posthumous fame. Time and again he was asked to have his letters and speeches compiled for print, but he would never hear of it. He waived these suggestions away with the sententious remark, "that his life was written on the pages of his country's history." With all his faults, his were strong principles and generous impulses. "We know something of what he yielded, but we know nothing of what he resisted." Include his strength and his weakness and measure him by other men, and we have a man of giant mold.

One who was very near to Toombs in his last days said of him when he was dead: "It was a thing of sorrow to see this majestic old man pausing to measure his poor strength with a confirmed habit, rising, struggling, falling, and praying as he drifted on."

General Toombs used to say that Webster was the greatest man he ever knew, that Clay managed men better, and Calhoun was the finest logician of the century. "The two most eloquent men I ever heard were Northern men," said he; "Choate and Prentiss." "Pierce," he used to say, "was the most complete gentleman I ever saw in the White House. He was clever and correct. Zachary Taylor was the most ignorant. It was amazing how little he knew. Van Buren was shrewd rather than sagacious. Tyler was a beautiful speaker, but Webster declared that a man who made a pretty speech was fit for nothing else."

Toombs met Abraham Lincoln while he was in Congress. He related that Mr. Lincoln once objected to sitting down at table because he was the thirteenth man. Toombs told him that it was better to die than to be a victim to superstition. At the Hampton Roads Conference, President Lincoln expressed to Judge Campbell his confidence in the honesty and ability of Robert Toombs. He was a great reader. General Toombs often said that if the whole English literature

were lost, and the Bible and Shakespeare remained,
letters would not be much the poorer. Shakespeare was his standard. He was fond of Swe-
denborg, and in his early youth relished Tom
Paine.

General Toombs had a great affinity for young
men, upon whom he exerted a great influence. He
once said to a party of friends that gambling was
the worst of evils because it impoverished the
pocket while it corrupted the mind. " How about
drinking, General?" he was asked. " Well, if a
man is old and rich he may drink, for he will have
the sympathy of his sober friends and the support of his drinking ones."

CHAPTER XXXI.

In 1880 General Toombs appeared in Atlanta, and addressed the Georgia Legislature in behalf of the candidacy of General A. R. Lawton for the United States Senate. His appearance, as he walked up the aisle, grim, venerable, and determined, awoke wild applause. He preserved his power of stirring the people whenever he spoke, but his speech was not as racy and clear as it had been. " This was one of the occasions," to quote from a distinguished critic of Toombs, " when the almost extinct volcano glowed again with its wonted fires—when the ivy-mantled keep of the crumbling castle resumed its pristine defiance with deep-toned culverin and ponderous mace; when, amid the colossal fragments of the tottering temple, men recognized the unsubdued spirit of Samson Agonistes."

His last public speech was in September, 1884, when the people of Washington carried him the news of Cleveland's election to the Presidency. He came to his porch and responded briefly, almost inaudibly, to the serenade, but he was full of the gratification which Southern people felt over that event. He declared that he did not know that there was enough manhood in the country as to break loose from party ties and elect a President. The fact had revived his hope for the whole country. He had, before this, taken a gloomy view of the nation. He had, on one occasion, declared that the injection into the body politic of three million savages had made good government forever impossible. He had afterward said that the American Constitution rested solely upon the good faith of the people, and that would hardly bind together a great people of diverse interests. "Since 1850," he once said, " I have never believed this Union to be perpetual. The experience of the last war will deter any faction from soon making an effort at secession. Had it not been for this, there would have been a collision in 1876." But the election of Cleveland he regarded as a national, rather than a sectional victory—a non-partisan triumph in fact; and it was at this time, the first occasion since the war, that he expressed regret that he had not regained his citizenship and gone back into public life.

But his great power had begun to wane. His tottering gait and hesitating speech pointed unmistakably to speedy dissolution. The new-born hope for his country came just as his steps neared "the silent, solemn shore of that vast ocean he must sail so soon."

In March, 1883, General Toombs was summoned to Atlanta to attend the funeral of his lifelong friend Mr. Stephens. The latter had been an invalid for forty years, but was kept in active life by the sheer force of his indomitable will. Emerging from the war a prisoner, he had finally secured his release and had been elected United States Senator. Being prevented from taking his seat, he had returned home and finished his constitutional review of the "War Between the States." In 1873 he had been reëlected to Congress, where he had remained for ten years, resigning this position to accept the nomination for Governor of Georgia, which his party had offered him at a critical moment. It had been the desire of the "Great Commoner" to "die in harness," and there is no doubt that his close attention to the arduous duties of Governor hastened his death. Thousands of Georgians repaired to the State Capitol to honor his memory, but he who attracted most attention was the gray and grief-stricken companion who stood by the coffin of the man he had honored for fifty years. Mr. Stephens, in his diary, recalls the fact that his first meeting with Mr. Toombs was in court, when the latter generously offered to lend him money and look after his practice so that Stephens could take a trip for his health.

Like Damon and Pythias, these two men were bound by the strongest ties. They entered public

life together in the General Assembly of Georgia.
Together they rode the circuits as young attorneys,
and each was rewarded about the same time with
a seat in the national councils. Both were conspicuous in the *ante-bellum* agitation, and both were
prominent in the Civil War. As age advanced
their relations were closer still.

General Toombs at the funeral of his friend pronounced a eulogium on the dead. His words
were tremulous, and the trooping, tender memories
of half a century crowded into the anguish of that
moment. Toombs and Stephens, so long united
in life, were not long parted in death.

In September, 1883, Mrs. Toombs died at her
summer residence in Clarkesville, Ga. Their devoted friend, Dr. Steiner, was with them at the
time, and rendered the double offices of family
physician and sympathetic friend. Between these
two men there had been a warm and long friendship. Dr. Steiner talked with General Toombs
about his spiritual condition. A godly man himself, the doctor thought that he might remove any
doubts that might linger in the mind of the
stricken husband. He was gratified to hear that
the way was clear. "Why, doctor," said General
Toombs, "I am a prayerful man. I read the Bible
and the Prayer Book every day." "Then why not
be baptized, General?" "Baptize me, doctor,"
was his prompt reply. Dr. Steiner answered that

there was no immediate need of that. The general was in good health. Dr. Steiner had baptized patients, he said, but it was in times of emergency. It was the desire of General Toombs to be baptized at the bedside of his wife. In a short time Robert Toombs was in communion with the Southern Methodist Church. It was his wife's beautiful example, "moving beside that soaring, stormy spirit, praying to God for blessings on it," which brought him to a confession of his faith, and left him in full fellowship with God's people.

General Toombs' health commenced visibly to fail after his wife's death, and the loss of Mr. Stephens made life lonely. His younger brother Gabriel, himself in the shadow of a great affliction, was with him constantly. They were devotedly attached to each other. Mr. Gabriel Toombs is, in personal appearance, very much like his brother. The long, iron-gray hair, brushed straight out from his head, reminds one of Robert Toombs. He is smaller in stature, and is a man of strong abilities, even temperament, and well-balanced mind. His brother had great regard for his business judgment and political sagacity, and often consulted him on public matters. These men lived near each other in Washington, their families grew up together, and General Toombs regarded his brother's children almost as he did his own.

On the 30th of September, 1885, Robert Toombs was confined to his house by illness. It was a general breaking down of his whole system. It was evident that he was nearing his end. During his last illness his mind would wander, and then his faculties would return with singular clearness. He suffered little pain. As Henry Grady said of him, it seemed that this kingly power and great vitality, which had subdued everything else, would finally conquer death. His ruling instinct was strong in dissolution. He still preserved to the last his faculty of grasping with ease public situations, and "framing terse epigrams, which he threw out like proverbs."

During one of his lucid intervals he asked for the news. He was told; "General, the Georgia Legislature has not yet adjourned."

"Lord, send for Cromwell," he answered, as he turned on his pillow.

Another time he was told that the Prohibitionists were holding an election in the town. "Prohibitionists," said he, "are men of small pints."

His mind at this period dwelt mainly on serious thoughts. The Bible was read to him daily. He was perfectly aware of his condition. He said to Dr. Steiner: "Looking over my broad field of life, I have not a resentment. I would not pang a heart."

He talked in his delirium of Mr. Stephens and

Dr. Steiner. The latter recalled him and said: " General, I am here by your side; Mr. Stephens, you know, has crossed over the river." Coming to himself, he said: " Yes, I know I am fast passing away. Life's fitful fever will soon be over. I would not blot out a single act of my life."

Dr. Steiner declared that he never before realized so fully the appropriateness of Mr. Stephens' tribute to Toombs; " His was the greatest mind I ever came in contact with. Its operations, even in its errors, remind me of a mighty waste of waters."

When the time came for Dr. Steiner to return to his home in Augusta, General Toombs bade him good-by. I am sorry," said he, " the hour is come. I hope we shall meet in a better place."

After Thursday, December 10, General Toombs did not regain consciousness. On Monday, December 15, 1885, at 6 o'clock P. M., he breathed his last. Just as the darkness of a winter evening stole over the land the great spirit of the statesman walked into eternal light.

He was buried on Thursday, December 18, at twelve o'clock. The funeral exercises were held in the little brick Methodist church where his wife and daughter had worshiped.

The funeral was simple, according to his wishes. A large number of public men in Georgia attended the services. Dr. Hillyer, a prominent Baptist divine and classmate of General Toombs, assisted in the services. Rt. Rev. John W. Beckwith, Episcopal Bishop of Georgia, who had been his closest religious adviser after the death of the Methodist Bishop George F. Pierce, delivered a beautiful eulogium.

The remains were interred in the Washington cemetery, by the side of the body of his wife. A handsome marble shaft, bearing the simple and speaking inscription " Robert Toombs," marks the spot which is sacred to all Georgians.

THE END.

INDEX.

B 79

Printed in the United States
111973LV00002B/101/A